BETTER RÉSUMÉS FOR SALES AND MARKETING PERSONNEL

Second Edition

by
ADELE LEWIS
Former President and Founder
Career Blazers Agency, Inc.
New York City

and

GENE CORWIN
Director
Career Blazers Résumé Service
Boca Raton, Florida

BARRON'S

All inquiries should be addressed to:
Barron's Educational Series, Inc.
250 Wireless Boulevard
Hauppauge, New York 11788

Library of Congress Catalog Card No. 95-37704

International Standard Book No. 0-8120-9597-9

Library of Congress Cataloging-in-Publication Data
Corwin, Gene.
    Better résumés for sales and marketing personnel. — 2nd ed. / by Gene
Corwin and Adele Lewis.
        p.   cm.
    Rev. ed. of: Better résumés for sales and marketing personnel / by Adele
Lewis. c1985.
    Includes bibliographical references.
    ISBN 0-8120-9597-9
    1. Résumés (Employment)   2. Selling—Vocational guidance.
3. Marketing—Vocational guidance.   I. Lewis, Adele Beatrice, 1927–.
II. Lewis, Adele Beatrice, 1927–   Better résumés for sales and market-
ing personnel.   III. Title.
HF5383.L475 1996
650.14'024381—dc20   95-37704
                                                      CIP

PRINTED IN THE UNITED STATES OF AMERICA

9876543

Contents

Introduction

If you are reading these words in a bookstore or library, trying to decide whether this book is worth your time and money, let us help you decide. We assume that, having turned to this page, you are interested in improving or changing your position. We also assume you know that a powerful, effective resume is one essential tool toward accomplishing that goal.

Probably you want to continue working in your current career area; or you are changing career fields but know precisely in what new area you want to apply past career interests, skills, and achievements. From these assumptions we frame our entire universe of prospective readers, and we welcome you among them. This book will show you how to apply your skills to finding the job that satisfies you most.

In looking for a job, you should always aim for the very best and try to avoid settling for less. Be sure, however, that you maintain an open and realistic attitude, evaluating each opportunity with a flexible, far-sighted view. It is also our belief that you should take the job where you'll be happiest. Every job has psychological fringe benefits, and these, in the long run, can more than counter what might be viewed as a slight initial salary deficiency. If you are happy in your job, you'll do better work (and conversely, if you do better work, you'll be happy). Soon you will receive tangible recognition of that work. The contentment in your work will spill out into other areas of your life and is, therefore, an important and vital job asset. May this book ultimately bring you happiness.

Acknowledgments

I gratefully acknowledge the research assistance provided by John Ratcliff, President, Sales Search, Ltd., and Jeffrey Gitomer, author of *The Sales Bible*.

I also wish to thank my lovely wife, Bobbi, for her help, support, and patience during the many hours required to revise and update this edition.

—Gene Corwin

1

The Art of Job Hunting

Whether you're unemployed, just starting out, or simply looking for greener pastures, your job hunt can be either a triumphant experience or a complete catastrophe. From our long experience with dealing with a variety of job seekers, we've come to realize there is a definite skill to the looking for and getting of jobs. We call this skill *self-marketing*, the ability to sell one's self. For those lucky few who intuitively possess self-marketing skills, job hunting is an exhilarating, rewarding experience. Conversely, for those not possessing this skill, job hunting can be a depressing, traumatic task. Fortunately, learning to sell one's self can be mastered. It is rarely innate, never offered as part of an educational curriculum, and hardly ever recognized as an independent skill. It requires lots of thought, a dedication to assume new, *positive* attitudes, self-discipline, and lots of perseverance before it can be mastered. Once acquired, self-marketing skills will stay with you for the rest of your life and serve as a tremendous source of security in a variety of situations. You are always selling something, a thought, an idea, and in a job search, you are selling the benefits of hiring you over the competition. Self-selling skills are even important after you get a job, to help keep it.

Part of being a good salesperson means you must always maintain a cheerful, optimistic, and positive attitude. Keep in mind, always, that you will get a job, and it really doesn't matter if it's this week or next month. When you consider that you spend more than seventy thousand hours of your life on the job, doesn't it make sense to be generous with the time allotted to secure one?

Give up all *negative* attitudes such as "I can't; it's impossible," as well as those negative presuppositions about the job market: "It's not what you know; it's who you know," "No one over 40 stands a chance of getting a good job," "You have to have the exact experience they're looking for," "They never hire anyone who's been fired," "Large employment gaps are the kiss of death," "It's impossible to change careers."

Anyone involved in recruiting will tell you that there is no validity to these beliefs. At our companies, we are constantly placing people over age 40 in excellent positions in prestigious companies. We continually have job listings for persons interested in changing fields or careers. If it were true—"It's not what you know but who you know" there would be no employment agencies, executive search firms, and no ads in the paper. Our placement files prove that "exact" experience is rarely a requirement. Employers are flexible, and although initially they might ask for certain qualifications, they tend to lose their rigidity and hire the person who best convinces them that he or she is right for the job.

People involved in hiring are relatively sophisticated; they don't automatically prejudge anyone who has been fired. They are aware that a person fired from a particular position at a different company might be extremely valuable to their company. They realize that since changing jobs is such a stressful experience, many people are willing to stay in intolerable situations rather than face the great unknown. Company A's loss may very likely be Company B's gain.

It is true that large gaps in employment history may require additional effort in job hunting. However, those people who remain confident and true to themselves as well as others will ultimately meet with success.

People are constantly changing careers. A person with a scientific background has excellent prospects for a career in technical sales. We've seen engineers become salespersons, teachers metamorphosed into publishers' reps, copywriters filling slots in marketing areas.

Dwelling on the negative has no validity. Every negative thought or disadvantage can be overcome. A positive attitude yields positive results. Being negative gets you nowhere. To be successful, you must focus on the positive aspects of your work history and accentuate the positive skills you have acquired. Most importantly you must believe you can, and you will.

Looking for a job requires a great deal of effort, much insight, the necessity of developing a high frustration tolerance, and a strong determination not to become discouraged and negative. Our vast experience in helping people find jobs tells us that a negative attitude is a luxury no job seeker can afford. This has become one of our favorite mottoes, and we believe every job seeker should incorporate it into his or her personal philosophy.

The Skill or Art of Job Hunting—a 4-Step Career Strategy
❖❖❖

Step I is to first start your job hunt with a little research. Make sure your salary requirements are in line with those currently offered. The classified section of your local newspaper offers a wealth of such information. A few calls to appropriate search firms is another simple method of learning a great deal about market conditions.

You know exactly the kind of job you're looking for. You are qualified (both education and work history). And your salary expectations are realistic. You are well on your way.

Step II is your résumé. You know there are jobs available. You must now let the world know you are ready, willing, and available. You want to put your credentials on display and broadcast the fact that you are up for hire. Your résumé is the best possible vehicle for this information. It must look good, be easy to read and—most important—it must create interest in its product: You. After all, you are the greatest product you will ever sell. To be successful, your résumé must totally and instantly convince the reader that you are, indeed, a person of substance and should be interviewed. Chapter 2 will show you in a logical, step-by-step approach just how this can be accomplished.

Step III follows with how to most effectively circulate your résumé. Chapter 5 gives you a crash course in cover letters that gets the reader's attention and maximizes the impact of your résumé so as to prompt interviews. Chapter 6 discusses networking and job sources for effective career strategy.

Step IV is changing an interview into an offer. Chapter 7 discusses the skills of self-marketing at an interview. It presents the necessary ingredients of effective self-selling, tells you how to handle multiple interviews, and gives you proper techniques for salary negotiations. You'll learn how to control the interview and, finally how to convert that interview into a solid job offer. We are convinced that once these basic skills have been mastered, you will find job hunting to be a positive, uplifting experience.

Go for it!

Sales Approach to Résumé Writing
◇◇◇

You are a salesperson—and selling is your game. You are in the unique position to utilize your own occupational skills and experience to aid in your job search.

You are, above all others, the best equipped to develop a résumé, the sole purpose of which is to make an effective and compelling sales presentation of yourself. You must now apply all of your experience, selling skills, and techniques to fashion this résumé. The sales savvy and know-how that you use to sell any product, such as a car, refrigerator, or intangible service, are the same when it comes to selling yourself.

Your task is to convince a potential employer to grant you an interview. The résumé is designed to do just that. Rarely does it get a job directly. It is unusual for an employer to hire an applicant without a face-to-face interview.

A resume is thus more like an advertisement, whereas the interview is the actual selling. In a face-to-face situation you have the benefits of undivided attention when making your presentation, immediate reaction, and feedback. However, a good advertisement overcomes the absence of these elements by capturing the reader's attention and keeping his or her interest alive until the entire presentation is read.

In this sense, the approach to résumé writing follows the classic selling techniques used with any product: You must talk about "Features—Benefits—Advantages."

FEATURES   In the case of a résumé, features may be considered a person's background and the specific knowledge that has been acquired. It would indicate whether an applicant has the know-how to handle a particular job. Features discusses the field you are in, such as the automotive, insurance, electronics, and so on; your job title or level of attainment within a company; and your areas of responsibility.

However, people don't buy features. They buy benefits.

BENEFITS

Benefits are what the buyer gains from the features. It is important to know that a can opener has an automatic turn-off feature, but buyers want to know how that feature will benefit them.

So, although the employer wants to know what job you performed, knowing how well that job was performed is more important. Your achievements and successes are the perceived benefits for which an employer is looking. Therefore, your achievements and successes must be presented in the very beginning of the résumé.

You must strive to promise a benefit that is uniquely better. That can be difficult sometimes, because there are so many similar products. That which distinguishes you from any other salesperson is not that you sold cars, but how many you sold and how that number compares to the average performance.

Every time a feature (in this case, work experience) is mentioned it should be immediately translated to a corresponding customer (employer) benefit (success or achievement).

SPECIFICITY

Further, in writing a résumé, specificity is important. It takes your achievements out of the realm of "blue sky." Saying you increased sales and market penetration in 1996 is not as convincing as the far stronger and more compelling: "Increased sales by 25% in 1996, personally generating sales in excess of $750,000." Strong presentation of benefits leads to more attention, interest, desire, and ultimately action.

The final phase is the "suggestion of value" or the "promise of value to be received" by hiring you.

The use of gimmicks, gadgets, or clever techniques in a résumé is distinctly subordinate to a presentation of strong benefits. The most important element in producing sales results is the benefit to the customer described in the advertisement (résumé).

KEYS

The key to good résumé writing is the following:
1. Capture attention.

2. Describe immediate benefits.

3. Give an illustration: Cite specific achievement.

4. Promise value to be received.

Organized logically, these are the elements of an advertisement. They should build sufficient interest so that the reader wants to dig deeper into the message.

Take a walk in your customer's shoes. That should give you a feeling of what he or she is looking for and what is best to stress and emphasize.

2

Contents and Style of a Résumé

There was a time when job seekers could simply visit a potential employer and be interviewed, but that time has long since passed. In this complex world where distance, time, and sheer numbers mitigate against personal involvement, the résumé has become the most essential ingredient in both the job search and hiring process. As such, your résumé must represent you in the clearest, most forceful manner possible. It must represent you when you are not there to speak for yourself. In essence, your résumé becomes an embodiment of you, and will serve as your representative. The success of your job campaign is completely dependent on the effectiveness of your résumé. A good résumé results in interviews; an inferior one is simply discarded.

Employers tell us it is not unusual for them to receive hundreds of résumés each day. Under these circumstances, they spend no more than 10 or 20 seconds scanning each résumé before allowing time for a thorough read through. If a résumé is more than 2 pages long, it will be immediately rejected, as will those that appear cluttered and don't invite easy reading. Spelling or grammatical mistakes are never tolerated. In order to warrant a thorough read through, your résumé must *show immediately* that you have the ability to organize information and present it in a clear, concise manner. You must instantly communicate to the reader that you know where you are going with your career, and that you have just the right background to make you a valuable staff addition.

But let's begin with the basics. Every résumé must identify and describe the writer. It must include:

- ❏ Your name, address, and telephone number
- ❏ A description of your educational history
- ❏ A description of your work history
- ❏ Work-related honors or citations
- ❏ Publications you may have been featured in

It may also include:

- ❏ A summary of qualifications
- ❏ Your job objective or career goal
- ❏ A capsule description of your work history
- ❏ Memberships in any professional organizations
- ❏ Foreign languages you may know
- ❏ Information on hobbies only if they relate in some way or show personal success, such as an award or outstanding achievement
- ❏ Military service, if any

❑ Security clearance, if any (technical sales)
❑ Willingness to travel or relocate

It should **not** include the following information:

❑ Reasons for leaving past jobs
❑ Past salaries or present salary requirements
❑ Personal data—age, height, weight, marital status, number of children
❑ Health status
❑ Names of spouse or children
❑ A photograph of yourself
❑ Names and addresses of references

Résumé Styles

Although every résumé should contain a brief, concise summary of your work history and educational background, the style or approach differs in the arrangement of this data. Though there are several résumé styles, we believe the chronological is the most effective, and we strongly recommend that you choose this approach in writing your résumé. We will, however, discuss others as well and evaluate each style.

Despite minor variations, there are basically three different résumé styles or approaches.

❑ Chronological (Historical)
❑ Functional
❑ Imaginative, Creative, or Informal

We'll discuss each, with consideration of their usefulness.

The Chronological (Historical) Résumé

As the name applies, this style presents the information in chronological sequence. The succession of facts must be presented in **reverse** chronological order, starting with the present or most recent experience and moving backward in time.

As with any résumé, start with your name, address, and phone number. It is traditional in some industries to list your education before your work experience. There are no hard and fast rules about this, and certainly if you have a good, solid background of experience but have not completed your degree, then it makes sense to place the education at the end of the résumé instead. Usually, however, your most advanced degree is shown first, followed in reverse order by all other degrees. Again dates should always be used. State the name of the university, city, state, degree earned, and the dates attended. Academic honors would be included in this grouping.

If you have opted to use a career objective or résumé capsule, place it near the top of the first page. Keep it brief and realistic.

Your work history should list each job (in reverse chronological order), specifying your job title, the name of your employer, the address (city and state; number and name of street are not necessary), and giving a summary of your achievements and responsibilities. These summaries should be brief but specific. Always include dates; they can be in vertical columns to the left of the other information, on a line before the description of each job held, or included as a integral part of the paragraph. Generally, placing the dates in a vertical column is preferable, as employers like to be able to determine at a glance the times involved.

The chronological résumé should be brief and take no more than 2 pages. This type of résumé offers a clear, concise picture of you, and it is probably the easiest to assimilate in a quick reading. Without exception, the chronological format was preferred by the corporate executives we've talked to; they felt it does the best job of indicating an individual's direction, background, accomplishments, and general qualifications.

The Functional Résumé

As its name implies, the functional résumé emphasizes the writer's qualifications and abilities. This approach rejects a chronological sequence of employment and educational history, and instead provides analyses of particular professional strengths. The employment strengths or skills are the important facts in this style of résumé.

Your work history, volunteer experience, and educational record are fragmented into significant talents, and each skill is listed separately. Because these functions or responsibilities usually cross over a number of jobs, the sequence of job history has been sacrificed to emphasize ability. Names of employers and dates are omitted from this section of the résumé, since the expertise has been gained from more than one position.

The functional résumé should be brief, concise, and well structured. It should start with your name, address, and phone number, your job objective, and a résumé summary (if needed). The body of the résumé should consist of 4 or 5 paragraphs, each one with a heading that names a particular area of expertise or involvement.

The skills paragraphs should be listed in order of importance. We define the most important skill as the function that is most similar to your present career goal or job objective.

Typical headings might be Marketing, Legal Secretarial, Research, Sales Management, and so on. A brief summary of your accomplishments in each category would follow.

Though this type of résumé has gained in popularity over the past few years, very few employers, personnel directors, or managers approve of this approach. Our employment experts tell us that they become very suspicious of the functional résumé. They feel it is often used to cover up a spotty work record (for example, 7 jobs in 4 years or a long period of unemployment), to exaggerate certain abilities, or to disguise some "whole truth." One corporate executive put it succinctly when he said, "It raises more questions than it answers."

The only situation that lends itself to the functional résumé is one in which you are attempting a career change. In that case, this style résumé may be advantageous because it shows at a glance the kinds of jobs within your capacity. Because most résumé readers feel that résumés lose their effectiveness if dates or names of employers are not shown, you should overcome this by adding a very concise historical (always in reverse chronological order) listing of employers, job titles, and job descriptions with the appropriate dates. This history should follow your description by function.

The Imaginative-Creative Résumé
◇◇◇◇

You may feel that an imaginative, highly unusual approach is the ideal thing to shake loose your résumé from the pack. Using artwork, illustrations, cartoons, or a unique format may very well create an impression, but not necessarily a good one.

We have received résumés that were over 2 feet long, wound up like a scroll; very, very small ones put together to resemble a passport (the print so reduced you would have to use a magnifying glass, if you wanted to read it); résumés in the format of menus, playbills, calendars, stock certificates, and even a summons. True, these résumés caught the eye. They amused and charmed us, but they did not sustain enough interest to become effective. Such résumés are usually difficult to read, unprofessional, and impossible to file. Corporate employers share our opinion that a résumé is a business matter and, accordingly, should be presented in a businesslike, professional manner.

Putting Yourself on Paper

When preparing your résumé, always keep in mind the purpose of that résumé—to serve as a personal advertisement, generating enough interest in you to secure an interview. As an effective advertisement, it should be attractive, easy to read, concise, and informative. Because the chronological résumé is the most preferred style, we will use this approach in showing you how to write your résumé.

The information contained in the résumé should be presented in the following order.

- ❏ Identifying information
- ❏ Summary or résumé capsule (optional)
- ❏ Employment history
- ❏ Educational history
- ❏ Honors or citations, if any
- ❏ Publications you may have been featured in
- ❏ Membership in professional organizations (optional)
- ❏ Military service

Mention of hobbies, knowledge of foreign languages, a willingness to travel or relocate, and other personal information is included only if they are relevant to the position you are applying for. When used, this information should appear near the end of the résumé.

Identifying Information

Always start with your identifying material in a conspicuous position, either flush left (leaving room for the margin) or on the top center (again leave about ¾ to 1½ inches for the margin). Give your complete name, street address, city, state, zip code, and phone number, complete with area code. If you can be reached at an office, that number should also be listed.

The use of the summary, also called résumé capsule, is optional. It is used mainly by candidates with at least 5 years of experience. To be effective, it must include information indicating that you are indeed qualified for the position sought. Although the summary is optional, we have been told by more than one personnel director of an important company that it is the first piece of information they scan. If the summary, essentially a digest of the résumé, sustains their interest, they will continue to read the résumé in its entirety. Similarly, if it is poorly worded, too long or too vague, the candidate will be immediately rejected. The beauty of the summary is that it gives you the power of the functional résumé and, at the same time, excludes all of its disadvantages. Here is your opportunity to combine and build on similar aspects of your background that may have been acquired over a period of many years in a number of different positions.

Suppose one of your accomplishments occurred in an early job. If you were using a straight reverse-chronological style presentation, this important information might not be noticed by the reader. It probably would appear near the bottom of the page or possibly on the second page, and would very likely be missed. The summary allows you to emphasize it at the beginning. It is the space where you can list the highlights or whatever else you might consider your biggest career accomplishment, regardless of when it occurred.

The summary should consist of one strong sentence, 3 or 4 at the most. Those sentences should be enough to highlight the aspects of your background that will most appeal to a potential employer.

Here are some samples of summary paragraphs:

Seventeen years' of sales growth achievement in the medical field, having established strong rapport with professional practitioners.

More than 12 years' involvement in the C language, UNIX area of programming both in Systems and Applications. Thoroughly experienced in designing, implementing, and debugging.

Fifteen years' experience in Nuclear Power Plant Engineering, including start-up, modifications, construction, installation, and testing of ASME Code Class I, II, and III Systems.

We suggest that you write down every skill, responsibility, job duty, and accomplishment that will qualify you for your next position. Think of every problem you had some part in solving, any new idea you contributed that was ultimately used by your employer, any achievements or capabilities you have that would demonstrate or suggest that you can do the job better than anyone else.

Study your list and pare it down to 5 or 6 points. Combine those that are similar in function so that you can write a brief narrative that has a convincing tone to it. Be brief. Choose your words carefully.

You may have to write several drafts—shortening sentences, changing a word here and there, deleting unnecessary adjectives or phrases that might be repetitive. Work on it until you have it perfect.

The summary or capsule résumé is the best way of emphasizing solid work background and highlighting specific qualifications to a targeted employer. Although it often involves retyping the résumé for each potential employer, the capsule résumé can be the only part of your résumé that does have to be adjusted to suit different employers' needs.

Employment History

✧✧✧

The heart of your résumé is the section that describes your experience or employment history. It is important to remember that your résumé must be honest as well as logical. Never put anything in your résumé that is not 100 percent true. Stay with the truth, even if you feel a small exaggeration or distortion might make you more marketable. Any information that is not true can become an insurmountable liability. Employers usually expect that a new employee will require some training, and they are quite willing to provide it. If, however, you claimed certain strengths and are unable to demonstrate those abilities, you can be sure your credibility on all other matters will be questioned.

Begin your employment history with your present or most recent experience. Work backwards, treating each position as an independent entry. Each job mentioned should include the name and address (city and state; no streets or numbers) of the employer, the dates involved (month and year), and a concise description of your responsibilities. If you are presently employed, use the present tense in describing your current position and, obviously, the past tense for former jobs. Use only implied pronouns in crisp, simple language. Writing in the third person (he/she) is stylistically objectionable, as well as suggesting a certain detachment. Using the first person (I) is redundant; plainly the person reading the résumé is aware that you are the subject of your own résumé. For example, compare the following "bits" of information:

She/he was responsible for creation of marketing concepts

I was responsible for creation of marketing concepts

Responsible for creation of marketing concepts

Always give the name of each company you have worked for, including your present employer, even though you may wish this to be considered confidential. You will weaken your résumé by not including specific names. Once we received a résumé without any company identifying information, and decided we were not interested in that candidate. Luckily, he followed up with a phone call. It was only when he told us the name of the company, which happened to be a direct competitor of our client company, that we realized his experience was exactly what we were looking for. It is understandable that you might be circumspect about the fact that you are looking for a job. However, all agencies and employers treat this information as confidential.

Your goal in this section of the résumé is to make as much as you can of each position you have had, while keeping the descriptions as brief as possible. Describe your major responsibilities while concentrating heavily on the accomplishments you legitimately claim as your own or share.

Always be as specific as possible and avoid generalities or long descriptions of the company you worked for. Describe exactly what you did and what your responsibilities were. Think of as many problems as you can that you faced and were able to solve. Our questionnaire on page 18 will help you to organize these thoughts. Mention any improvements you were responsible for, any ideas adopted by your employer. Describe actions you took to solve problems and the positive conditions that were the consequences of your efforts. Don't be shy; never be humble. But never be arrogant, either. Be proud of your achievements.

The job descriptions should be just that and, although it is important to list accomplishments, they also have to paint an accurate picture of what your daily routine included.

You may assume that an interviewer's interest will be piqued by each of your employment history entries, and you will be asked to elaborate on them in the interview. View each bit of information you provide as the basis of a future leading question. It's a good idea to mentally rehearse your responses as you write your job description.

Use active verbs; they give a certain power to your résumé. And choose your words carefully; make each word count. Avoid being flowery; too many adjectives, especially an overabundance of superlatives, lessens the impact of your résumé.

Keep in mind, always, that you're aiming for a single-page (2-page maximum) résumé. Be brief, concise. Keep narratives describing each position succinct—no more than 5 to 10 lines. Each accomplishment should be broken up into bite-sized entities for the reader to spot and digest quickly. Information concerning past positions should **not** be as extensive as current or recent ones. Avoid repetition—if your job responsibilities were similar in more than one job, describe in detail only the most recent position. Also, it is not necessary to use complete sentences. Indent and use "banner" statements to emphasize accomplishments. Start such entries with an asterisk (*) or bullet (•) so they appear to "pop" out.

Rewrite your first draft. It may be necessary to rewrite it several times, striking out unnecessary words and phrases and tightening sentences until they say exactly what you mean. Reread it several times, checking for spelling and grammatical errors. After several rereadings, have a friend or colleague scan it. Another person may pick up errors that you have missed and possibly suggest some additional qualifications.

Educational History
❖❖❖

Start with your most advanced degree and include the name and location of the college or university you attended, the degrees you earned, and the year you graduated. Mention your major field of study and all career-oriented scholarships and academic awards. Thereafter, list—in reverse chronological order—all other degrees until you reach your B.A. or B.S. Include the same information for each as described for the advanced degree. Though abbreviations generally should not be used in résumés, it is acceptable and correct in listing your degrees; for example, Ph.D., M.S., B.A., B.S. If you have attended college, it is not necessary to include information concerning high school.

Recent graduates should mention their grade point average if it is 3.5 or higher. Obviously, there is no point in calling attention to a C average. If you were Phi Beta Kappa, Summa or Magna Cum Laude, or if you received other high academic honors, no matter what level of experience you have, by all means mention it.

Professional Societies and Publications

List all professional associations and organizations that are career related. Your membership in such groups implies dedication to your field and an ability to get along with others. If you are or have ever been an officer in any organization, be sure to mention that fact. Also mention any publications in which you have been featured.

Personal Information

Remember a very simple rule: *Personal information should never be included in your résumé.* Never put in writing or discuss at an interview such personal matters as your height, weight, marital status, number of children, and so on.

Your résumé should include only information describing your qualifications; any other information is considered inappropriate and unprofessional.

Because the passage of employment laws have made it illegal for an employer to question individuals as to their age, sex, race, or religious preference, such information does not belong on a résumé.

Your state of health (it's always "excellent" anyway) is superfluous. If, however, you have a disability and feel you want the potential employer to know about it before the interview, mention it in your covering letter, *not* in the résumé. Bear in mind that your résumé should emphasize your *abilities*, not your disabilities.

Should you include your hobbies and leisure-time activities? Again, the answer is usually no. The only time these should be put into a résumé is in the case of an award for outstanding achievement. Take for instance a track star or swimmer who wins a major award in that sport. This is noteworthy on a résumé. It indicates to an employer you have the personal drive and potential to be successful at anything you do. Otherwise, they simply are not necessary. Keep in mind that every word in your résumé should be there for a reason and there is no purpose to a description of your nonprofessional or non-work-related interests.

References

Never, never supply the names of your references on your résumé. Not only is it unprofessional, but it can cause a lot of bother to those individuals listed. Simply state, as the last entry on your résumé, "References on Request" or "References will be furnished upon request."

Always get permission from those individuals you wish to use as references. Don't put yourself or them in the position in which any calls about you will come as a surprise to them. Try, if possible, to get references that can be reached quickly. For that reason, it is preferable to list persons who can be reached by phone rather than by mail. Make certain you have all of their current addresses and phone numbers. If you are giving a person's business phone number, check to see if he or she is still employed by the same company.

If your name has been changed through marriage or for any other reason during your work or educational history, be sure that your references know you by your new name. It is wise for women who have married and adopted their husband's name to indicate their maiden name as well. Lastly, you should give permission to call your references only when an employer has indicated that you are under serious consideration.

Photographs

Never, never send photographs unless you are looking for a job such as a model or salesperson. Not only are photographs on résumés unprofessional, but their legality is questionable. If an employer kept résumés containing photographs on file, that action could be considered a covert form of racial, sex, or age screening and, as such, could be considered illegal. But more important to you, don't risk prejudicing your chances by sending a photo.

Reasons for Leaving Past Jobs

Should you mention why you left earlier positions? An emphatic NO! Your résumé should be a businesslike summary of your talents, qualifications, goals, work history, and education. Since the reasons you left previous employers do not add to that summary, they should not be included in your résumé.

Salaries, Past and Present

Salaries—neither your present minimum nor your past earnings—should be discussed or listed in your résumé. A potential employer will probably arrange a series of interviews, and the subject of salary will most often be discussed close to or at the final meeting.

Every employer we've had contact with considers salary a most confidential matter. It is considered extremely unprofessional as well as indiscreet for employees to discuss salaries among themselves. Your résumé will be seen by many individuals in the company who normally would not and **should not** know your salary range, so no indication of it should appear in your résumé.

Should you at least include your salary requirements? No. Including your salary requirements might eliminate you from certain positions in which the remuneration has not yet been decided; or it might preclude you from obtaining a certain position with an already established higher salary. As we've indicated before, reserve your discussion of salary for the final interview.

Résumé Appearance

Visualize an employer who, after placing an ad, receives more than 200 résumés. He or she is also developing new systems, planning programs, and has a desk filled with other projects demanding attention. He or she is now faced with selecting the résumé to read more closely. Obviously, the first step is to scan. This is why we recommend a 1-page résumé. They are read more often than multi-page résumés. As we've mentioned earlier, our inquiries have, shown that an average recruiter rarely gives more than 10 seconds attention to a résumé in deciding whether it merits a complete reading.

Put yourself in the reader's position. Do you actually read every word in every newspaper or magazine you look at? We're sure your answer is in the negative. In this fast-paced world, who has the time or even the interest? Rather, you automatically scan the material to decide which articles, advertisements, or stories are worth your time for a thorough read through. The print media has proved that "eye appeal" is as important as content; people simply discard that which is difficult to read. And we are aware that many staff managers and employers discard résumés containing excellent material because they were poorly presented. Remember—your résumé, to do its job, must pass the "quick scan test."

To pass this test, your résumé must be visually inviting. Start by selecting a format. You will find some samples that have been successful beginning on page 24. Whether you choose one of these samples or create your own, be sure that the total effect is pleasing to the eye. Be equally sure that it is easy to read, and that the different sections are clearly separated from one another.

Separate thoughts into paragraphs with pleasing white space between them. There is nothing more difficult to scan than a long, solid block of text, with no breaks or indentations. Even better, itemize and highlight thoughts with dashes or asterisks. At the very least, separate each job by white space, providing different sections to the résumé.

Use good-quality paper, a computer, word processing software, and a high-quality laser printer. That is the state-of-the-art today for producing clean, crisp professional-looking copy. If you decide to use a paper color other than white, be sure it is pastel. Avoid vibrant, bizarre, or otherwise loud, offbeat paper colors. They are unprofessional looking and do not fax well.

The best paper color for faxing material is white. The more color that is used, the grayer the copy becomes. Also, colored paper does not scan as well on an optical scanning device.

Use standard 8½ by 11-inch bond paper. It is a professional size, is easily handled, and is convenient to file. Avoid legal size paper, plastic sheet covers, or report folders—again, all too difficult to file. Keep away from unprofessional visual effects: photographs, illustrations, wild formats, or too many mixed-type styles.

Aim for 1, maximum 2 pages of typewritten material. Use only one side of the paper, and if the résumé is more than 1 page, staple the pages together, being sure that your name appears on each page.

Giving Your Résumé "Eye Appeal"
❖❖❖❖

A professional layout should be subtle and unobtrusive, but at the same time it should direct the reader's eye to the most important information. You can accomplish this by using proper width margins, combining upper and lower case, and underlining special items.

Use the ground—the white space on your paper—effectively. Use your margins imaginatively; use wide margins to lend importance to the information on the page and, at the same time, to provide a restful, easy-on-the-eye appearance. Create white space by double or triple spacing between blocks of information.

Be selective in your use of upper case; perhaps reserve it for job titles or names of employers. You might underline major accomplishments, but this, too, should be done sparingly. Avoid allowing your résumé to look too "busy," which is what often results when you use too many type faces and a plethora of underlines.

The Use of Computers
❖❖❖❖

Computers have become the new standard in résumé and cover letter writing. Recently, we helped the personnel department of an international airline review hundreds of résumés for a new position coming available. It was apparent that 90% of the résumés were generated by a computer. Most were perfectly typeset, had instant eye appeal, and emphasized key personal achievements and headlines with bold, attractive fonts.

It's no wonder computers are widely used, when you consider the many advantages they bring to the job search process. There are many reasons why you should consider owning, renting, borrowing, or hiring a keyboarder with a computer to help you with your job search.

Utilizing word processing software programs, such as WordPerfect or Microsoft Word, or the résumé-specific Résumé Maker or Résumé Creator programs, facilitates your ability to create and edit a basic résumé very quickly. You'll need a few hours to become practiced at using these programs if you aren't familiar with them, but it's time well spent. Unlike using a conventional typewriter, with these programs you can edit and revise quickly without having to retype the entire résumé. Also you can store your résumé in the computer and retrieve it for additional revisions or printing more copies any time you wish.

You can select various printshop-quality fonts to enhance the appearance of your résumé and cover letter, all with a few quick key strokes.

If you already have a computer with word processing programs but don't wish to invest in a high-quality laser printer (which gives the best-looking results), you may have access to "copy shops" that offer "desk top publishing." At these locations, available in most cities, you can print out your résumé from your own computer disk on the copy shop's high-tech printers and achieve the graphic excellence you want.

Either way—at home or in a copier services store—you can produce dozens of résumés tailored for each position you are applying for. Targeting your résumé and fulfilling a specific need for a particular company can only increase your chances for an interview.

As you probably have realized, an effective job search is a numbers game. A computer helps you to play the numbers game faster, smarter, and quicker than the noncomputerized job seeker.

One final note while we are on this subject. Facsimile machines have also made their debut into the high-tech job search campaign. It is in good taste to fax your résumé only if a manager or recruiter has requested that you do so. When you speak with one of these individuals by phone, it is appropriate to ask if it is okay to fax them your résumé. If they say "yes," you are also expected to send the original copy of the résumé and cover letter in the same day's mail. Mailing the originals work in your favor, in that you benefit from more contact with the key recruiter, and in a sense "double advertise" yourself. You have achieved more name recognition.

Organizing Your Thoughts

Before you sit down to actually write your résumé, it is imperative that you organize all your information in terms of dates, education and courses, employers, job responsibilities, and all the other data that will be included. We've found that the most difficult part of writing a résumé is putting your thoughts and data into a meaningful form. To help you accomplish this, we have provided a series of workspaces: forms and worksheets that will force you to analyze your data and organize it to correspond with the standard résumé formats. Using these worksheets will force you to examine the natures of your previous jobs and your particular skills and strengths, and will pay off tremendously later on when you begin writing your résumé and when you have your job interviews. This chapter actually becomes a skeleton version of the first draft of your résumé.

Résumé Workspace

IDENTIFYING INFORMATION

Use the space that follows to provide the information indicated. Complete the following information.

Name: _____
        (If married woman include married and maiden names.)

Address: _____
         (Street and number, city, state, and zip code)

Home Phone: _____
             (Be sure to give area code.)

Business Phone: _____
               (Be sure to give area code.)

Note: If your business phone is confidential, state that; for example:

Business phone: (212) 555-1280 (confidential)

RÉSUMÉ CAPSULE

The résumé capsule, as with the job objective, is an optional feature. However, one or the other must be used if you are trying to change careers. Use this space to write a résumé capsule, whether you decide to use it on your final résumé or not.

_____

_____

_____

_____

_____

_____

EMPLOYMENT HISTORY

Your employment history should be listed in **reverse chronological order.**

Name of Company: _____

Address of Company: _____

_____

Job Title: _____

Dates:		Description of Responsibilities: _____
From	To	
(Month/Year)	(Month/Year)	_____
_____	_____	_____
		_____
		_____
		_____
		_____

Name of Company: _____

Address of Company: _____

_____

Job Title: _____

Dates:		Description of Responsibilities: _____
From	To	
(Month/Year)	(Month/Year)	_____
_____	_____	_____
		_____
		_____
		_____
		_____

Name of Company: _____

Address of Company: _____

_____

Job Title: _____

Dates: Description of Responsibilities: _____

From   To
(Month/Year)   (Month/Year)   _____

_____   _____   _____

_____

_____

_____

_____

EDUCATIONAL HISTORY

List your education as you did your employment history, in **reverse chronological order;** your most advanced degree or your most recent education is first. Be sure to list all pertinent details-dates, degrees earned, educational institutions attended, and so on.

Advanced Degree

Dates:

From   To
(year)   (year)   _____
(Name of university)

_____   _____   _____
(Address of university)

Undergraduate Degree

Dates: _____
(Degrees or credits earned)

From   To
(year)   (year)   _____
(Name of university)

_____   _____   _____
(Address of university)

_____
(Degree or credits earned)

_____   _____
(Major)   (Minor)

PERSONAL INFORMATION

Publications and Major Achievements: _____

_____

_____

Foreign Languages or any other special skills: _____

_____

ASSOCIATIONS

_____

_____

_____

_____

_____

_____

REFERENCES Though the names of your references should **never** be included on your résumé, it is a good idea to assemble your data at the time you are preparing your résumé. Have a minimum of 3 people as references. It is advisable to include a statement that references will be furnished upon request.

Note: List the complete address—street and number, city, state, and zip code. Give area code with telephone number.

Name of Reference: _____

Position: _____

Company Affiliation: _____

Company Address: _____

_____

Business Phone and Extension:_____

Name of Reference: _____

Position: _____

Company Affiliation: _____

Company Address: _____

_____

Business Phone and Extension:_____

Name of Reference: _____

Position: _____

Company Affiliation: _____

Company Address: _____

_____

Business Phone and Extension:_____

Name of Reference: _____

Position: _____

Company Affiliation: _____

Company Address: _____

_____

Business Phone and Extension:_____

Action Words

◇◇◇

Linked up with identifying your responsibilities and portraying your previous jobs is the matter of using strong, descriptive words to describe those activities. Look over the list of words below to help you identify ones that reflect or describe your job responsibilities and/or accomplishments. Use these words as needed to complete the Employment History Worksheets.

A
accomplish	appraise
account	approve
accumulate	arrange
acquire	assign
activate	assist
adhere	assume
administer	assure
advertise	audit
advise	augment
allocate	authorize
analyze	automate

B
brought	built
budget	

C
catalog	consider
change	construct
code	consult
collect	continue
communicate	contract
compare	contribute
compile	control
complete	cooperate
compose	coordinate
compute	correct
conceive	correlate
concentrate	create
conduct	credit
configure	

D
debug	develop
decrease	direct
define	disperse
delegate	display
delete	distribute
design	document
determine	

E
edit	establish
educate	examine
emphasize	execute
employ	exercise
engage	expand
engineer	expedite
enhance	extend
enlarge	evaluate
ensure	

F
fix	function as
flowchart	furnish
forecast	

G
generate	graph
grant	guarantee

H
head	hire
help	

I implement   instruct
improve   integrate
include   interfere
increase   interpret
inform   interview
initialize   invent
initiate   investigate
inspect   involve
install   issue

J join   justify
judge

L lease   load
lessen

M maintain   meet
manage   modify
market   monitor
master   motivate
measure

N negotiate   normalize
neutralize   notify

O open   order
operate   organize
orchestrate

P participate   produce
perform   program
persuade   project
plan   promote
post   propose
prepare   protect
present   provide
process   publicize
procure   purchase

Q qualify   quench
quantify

R reclaim   requisition
recommend   research
reconstruct   reshape
recruit   responsible for
release   retain
report   retrieve
represent   review
request   revise
require

S schedule   stimulate
screen   strengthen
secure   structure
select   subcontract
sell   submit
serve   succeed
set objectives   summarize
set up   supervise
solve   supply
sort   support
specify   synthesize
staff   systematize
standardize

T teach   train
test   transfer
trace   translate
track

U update   underscore
upgrade   utilize

V validate   visualize
verify

W weigh   write
word process

Name
Street Address
City, State, Zip Code
Home Phone
Business Phone

Employment History

<u>Job Title</u>
From (date)   Name of Company
To present   Address of Company

Write out duties and responsibilities of job in question.

<u>Job Title</u>
From (date)   Name of Company
To (date)   Address of Company

Write out duties and responsibilities of job in question.

<u>Job Title</u>
From (date)   Name of Company
To (date)   Address of Company

Write out duties and responsibilities of job in question.

Educational History

From (date)   Name of College
To (date)   Address of College
                     Degree Earned

References: On Request

Name
Street Address
City, State, Zip Code
Home Phone #
Business Phone

Employment History

Job Title

From (date)   Name of Company
To present   Address of Company

Duties and responsibilities of job written out.

Job Title

From (date)   Name of Company
To (date)   Address of Company
                   Duties and responsibilities of job written out.

Educational History

From (date)   Name of College
To (date)   Address of College
                   Graduate Degree

From (date)   Name of College
To (date)   Address of College
                   Undergraduate Degree

References: Available on Request

Name
Street Address
City, State, Zip Code
Home Phone #
Business Phone #

Career Objective

To use the experience gained in ...

Educational History

Name of College	From (date)
Address of College	To (date)
Advanced Degree	

Name of College	From (date)
Address of College	To (date)
Bachelor's Degree	

Employment History

Job Title
Name of Company	From (date)
Address of Company	To present

Description of duties and responsibilities in the above company.

Job Title
Name of Company	From (date)
Address of Company	To (date)

Description of duties and responsibilities in the above company.

Job Title
Name of Company	From (date)
Address of Company	To (date)

Description of duties and responsibilities in the above company.

References: Available on Request

Name

Street Address
City, State, Zip Code
Home Phone #
Business Phone

Employment History

Job Title

Name and Address of Company

Description of job, giving duties and responsibilities.

From (date) to present

Job Title
Name and Address of Company

Description of job, giving duties and responsibilities.

From (date) to (date)

Educational History

Name and Address of College
Degree Received

From (date) to (date)

<u>References</u> Available on Request

Name

Street Address   Home Phone
City, State, Zip Code   Business Phone

Career Objective   To work as a ...

Employment History

From (date)   Job Title – Name of Company
to Present   Address of Company

                                    Description of duties and responsibilities in this position.

From (date)   Job Title – Name of Company
To (date)   Address of Company

                                    Description of duties and responsibilities in this position.

From (date)   Job Title – Name of Company
To (date)   Address of Company

                                    Description of duties and responsibilities in this position.

Educational History   Degree – Name of College
                                             Address of College

References   Furnished on Request

Developing a Successful Marketing Plan

Y ou have followed the rules, and have a superior, hard-hitting résumé. Now, how are you to make the best possible use of it?

Moving Up

The most usual, and simplest, plan is to move up the ladder in a relatively straight line, assuming more and broader responsibilities as part of your job while staying in the same industry. Chances are you are looking for a position similar to the one now held by your boss.

The "how" to get the job you want is relatively straightforward. You must be in the right place at the right time. True, a certain amount of luck is involved, but most successful people make their own luck. It's **more** than luck when an individual sends a well-written résumé to an appropriate employer, obtains an interview, interviews successfully, and then is offered a job. That "lucky" person set the wheels in motion to get those positive results. In essence, that's the whole secret of job hunting: getting your résumé to the right place and then converting the interview into a job offer.

Though it is common knowledge that American industry is bursting with job opportunities, how do you find the one job that is perfect for you? Knowing what's out there obviously maximizes your chance of getting the job you want. To become more familiar with the opportunities that are open for you, consult the following sources:

- ❏ Employment agencies/Executive recruiters
- ❏ Newspaper ads
- ❏ "Networking"—among friends and colleagues
- ❏ Industry journals and newsletters
- ❏ Direct mail campaign or "cold calling"

Let's take them in turn.

Employment Agencies

An important source of job openings is the appropriate private employment agency. Since their only source of income is the fees paid by employers for successful job placements, it is in the agent's best interest to pursue this function in a diligent, aggressive manner. Private employ-ment agencies recruit and screen applicants for many different compa-nies and, therefore, are in a position to introduce you to a number of prospective employers.

Finding the appropriate agency is a very important consideration in the job hunt.

Read the classified section of your newspaper to find out if there are employment agencies in your area that either service or specialize in sales or marketing personnel. The best way of finding a really good agency is to call a few companies in which you would like to be employed and ask someone in the personnel department to recom-mend employment agencies used by that organization.

Executive Recruiters
◆◆◆

If you are at a high management level, you may want to check out exec-utive recruiters, who are likely to have positions available in your field and at your level. They differ from employment agencies in that they usually only handle positions for mid-management levels and up. You can purchase a reference book entitled Directory of Executive Recruiters in the business section of most bookstores. (Fitzwilliam, NH: Kennedy Publications, current price $39.95). It contains a list of execu-tive recruiters (some with offices all over the world), including their addresses, phone numbers, fields covered, minimum salaries of posi-tions handled, and an indication as to whether each accepts résumés or is willing to set up an interview regarding opportunities in general.

INTERVIEWS

Once you have a list of the agencies you feel can be helpful to you, make an appointment, either by phone or with a letter, for a personal interview at the agency. It is more important to establish a rapport with a few agents than to make a career of interviewing with many agencies.

The interview with the counselor at the agency is almost as important as the job interview itself. This is the point at which you can be completely frank in describing exactly what your job requirements are in terms of salary, location, benefits, type of work, growth opportunities, and so on.

The agency will describe every opening they have currently listed that would be relevant to a person with your background. They will leave you the choice of which ones you want to investigate further. Effectively, the agency does your legwork for you and will keep you informed of new job openings as they arise. Most agencies expect and need résumés, and you should be prepared to give them several copies.

RÉSUMÉS

Almost every agency will, at a minimum, recopy your résumé onto their own letterhead. Many will make helpful suggestions about the content or style of your résumé, and frequently they will change the format to one that is standard for their agency. There are pluses and minuses when this happens. Since the agency uses its own paper and format, there will be nothing to distinguish your résumé from any other sent out by this agent. So forget about that special paper you may have picked out or the particular type font you may have planned to use. In some cases, agents have actually hurt a candidate's chances by changes they made on the résumé. In one extreme case, the candidate's last name was omitted! In another case, the contents of the résumé were changed so radically that it no longer described the candidate. During the interview, one employer asked about something mentioned in the résumé and received the reply, "Oh, does it say I did *that*?"

On the other hand, a good agent can play a critical role in improving your résumé and getting that résumé in front of a prospective employer. The most important rule to follow when you work with an agent is to make sure that you see and approve the résumé that will actually be sent to the prospective employer.

LEADS

Once the agent presents you with some leads for job openings, it's a good idea to be flexible in terms of which opportunities you are willing to investigate. For example, even though your background may be entirely research-oriented and your intention is to continue in this direction, you may find an opportunity in the commercial world much more interesting than you imagined. In fact, frequently if the employer likes the applicant, the job might be redefined in terms of qualifications or salary. Of course, if you don't go on the interview that can never happen.

POST INTERVIEW

It is very important to check back with your counselor after every job interview. This will help the agent have more insight into your unique needs and requirements.

The agent can also play a large role in the salary negotiations once a job offer is to be made. It is always easier to have a third party represent you in negotiations for a higher salary or better conditions.

FEES

As mentioned earlier, the agency fees in specialty fields are generally paid by the employer. However, don't hesitate to ask the agency interviewer to clarify any questions about your obligations. As with any other business arrangement, it is best to have a complete understanding of the terms at the very beginning of your relationship.

Newspaper Ads
✧✧✧

Though it has been said that the odds of getting a job by responding to a newspaper ad are about equal to breaking the bank at Vegas, we disagree. We've known many people who get jobs—extremely good jobs—by this route. By all means, include responding to classified ads as part of your job campaign. You may be surprised to find that many of the ads that appear to be placed by employers actually come from employment agencies. You should respond to these just as you would to any other ad.

In general, most employment ads and services are listed in the classified sections of the local Sunday newspapers. However, it is important to study your daily newspapers to find their unique pattern for listing job opportunities. For instance, *The Wall Street Journal* features specialty ads every Tuesday, while *The New York Times* lists job opportunities in both their Sunday and Wednesday business sections, as well as in the daily classified columns. Because *The New York Times* business section is circulated nationwide, while the classified is distributed locally, the higher-level positions are more often placed in the business section. Study both the classified and business sections of your newspapers.

Another good source, not to be overlooked, is the *National Business Employment Weekly*, a newspaper published and distributed nationally by *The Wall Street Journal*.

Start by responding to ads whose requirements are closest to your qualifications. Send an individually typed cover letter and a copy of your résumé. We suggest you answer every ad that you feel you are capable of handling, regardless of whether you have all the stated requirements, since employers are usually more flexible than their advertisements would imply. Ads usually describe the ideal candidate, just as applicants look for the ideal job. But in reality, both will compromise.

Keep a record of the date you answered each ad and continue on your job search (see page 36). You should call the personnel department about a week after you respond to the ad, and try to arrange an interview. Naturally, if you are responding to an ad that gave only a box number this will not be possible.

Networking

Networking is a word for a process that job seekers have used since we evolved from feudal times and individuals sought employment. It's simply letting people know you're looking for a job and asking them for any leads they might know about. Of all the various job sources, the most convenient—and at times, the best—are your friends, relatives, and colleagues. If you are still employed, naturally you should be discreet with your current employer and immediate colleagues. However, an integral part of your campaign is to let as many people as possible know that you are job hunting.

Don't be embarrassed by asking for suggestions. Everyone you know has been in your position and realizes that any help is appreciated. Were the positions reversed and a friend asked for help, wouldn't you be willing to assist in any way you could?

Colleagues, alumni groups, fraternity brothers, sorority sisters, golf or tennis partners are important contacts. Consider the individuals you meet during leisure-time activities as possible sources. Professional organizations such as the American Marketing Association, Direct Marketing Association, or Association of National Advertisers International are fertile territories for making contacts.

Most female executives and professionals are great "networkers." Because of previous and ongoing sexual discrimination, women have learned to cope and scramble in an alien world, a bit like a new immigrant trying to assimilate into a new culture. As a result, they are not reluctant to ask the right questions of anyone who might help them break down barriers.

Often people working in a particular company hear of job openings before the jobs are advertised or listed with employment agencies and recruiters, and they are actually given a bonus if a candidate they recommend is hired. The typical employer feels more secure about an applicant referred by someone he or she knows than an individual recruited from a newspaper ad or from commercial recruiters.

If you hear about a job opening in a particular company or believe one is about to occur, use your contacts to find out who knows somebody in power. Don't hesitate to ask a friend to introduce you to the proper person.

Though job hunters have always elicited the help of friends, the technique of networking is now an accepted strategy for getting contacts and getting the word out that you are looking for a specific type of work. Networking need not be face-to-face. Joining one of several online computer services like America Online, Compuserve, or Prodigy will permit you to network through bulletin boards and forums to exchange information about jobs and job availability.

TRADE PUBLICATIONS

Allocate several hours a week for time at your public library to read trade journals and business magazines. You'll want to assemble a system effective enough for you to anticipate trends that are likely to trigger job openings. Read magazines and newspapers such as *Advertising Age*, *Sales Manager's Handbook*, and *Marketing Practices and Principles* on a regular basis to make yourself an expert on current business information. Check the back-of-the-magazine classified ads for openings you might want to follow up.

A Direct Mail Campaign
✧✧✧

The method of planning a job search campaign is not unlike preparing a sales/marketing campaign for any product. There are several paths to take to maximize the return on the time you invest in the job search. In addition to all the above methods, there is also prospecting or, in the task of job hunting, launching a direct mail campaign and the subsequent follow-up calls. If we do not make cold calls (that is, prospecting) we will have done little, if anything, to further our job search.

In all probability you've read ads of the many career service organizations offering you access to the hundreds of job opportunities that are never advertised. These services offer, for a fee of several thousand dollars, to give you a method of contacting this vast market. Their ads are convincing. But is it worth the money?

There are, in fact, a tremendous number of opportunities in the hidden job market. It has been estimated that 90% of the job openings filled each year have never been advertised nor have they been listed with either an employment agency or an executive recruiter. They were filled by individuals who either tapped into the network or made contact with the particular employer by sending an unsolicited résumé.

The major contribution of these high-priced career services is the assistance they offer in conducting a direct mail campaign. By initiating your own campaign you can get the same results and save yourself a bundle of money. There are several new ways to start your campaign.

RÉSUMÉ BANKS

There is a growing trend today in the use of computerized data base services known as "résumé banks." Various business associations and educational institutions are employing them for use in their specialized areas. However, as widespread as their use has become, they are still largely confined to technical areas, such as engineering and computers. There are, however, independent résumé banks that do include sales personnel and on which, for a fee, you can list your résumé in the appropriate occupational category. Job seekers store their résumés in these data banks; employers, including many *Fortune* 500 corporations, call when they have an opening and ask for suitable applicants.

Given the growing enthusiasm with which companies are using the independent data banks, anyone who is launching a job hunt should probably consider signing on with one. The cost is fairly low—typically $20 to $50 for 6- to 12-month listing. Some of the more active and largest résumé banks are Job Bank USA (800-296-1872), Skill Search (800-258-6641), and National Résumé Bank (813-896-3694).

INTERNET

If you have access to a computer and a modem, you are ready to cruise the information highway. This is hi tech networking, where you can get online and mingle with people globally to talk about job leads and job search strategies. There are specific "newsgroups" you can browse through, such as misc.jobs.misc., dealing with jobs and careers. You can use them to pick up valuable information and even job listings. Then you can surf the WWW (World Wide Web) pages and find job listings and career opportunities. If you are unfamiliar with the Internet, you might start with a book entitled *Internet for Dummies* and get online.

Because so many industries are enjoying such rapid expansion, this is the ideal time to get positive results from a properly executed direct mail campaign. If an individual with specific industry experience sends a résumé to 25 companies, it is probable that 20 of them will have a job opening at the present time. Like any sales campaign it is a numbers game. The more résumés you send, the higher the degree of probability of success. It is almost predictable.

Using the direct mail method of job hunting has another advantage. You take the active role. You choose the companies that interest you rather than passively answering ads as they appear.

POTENTIAL EMPLOYERS

Obviously, your résumé will be an integral part of this campaign. Since you have already prepared the best possible résumé, you are ready to start. Your next step is to compile a list of potential employers. Possible sources for your list of companies could be the Yellow Pages of the telephone book, newspaper ads (even though they may not be advertising jobs for which you qualify), organizational membership lists, business directories, financial directories, trade journals, and magazines.

Learn as much as possible about the companies you have chosen. Research them thoroughly. Find out the names and titles of their officers, the number and location of branch offices, the nature of their products or service, and any information regarding acquisitions, mergers, or expansions. Such information is readily available in a variety of business directories that can be found in your local library. Directories exist for every field. An excellent reference directory is Dun & Bradstreet's *Million Dollar Directory*.

Read current and back issues of trade journals and gather more information on exciting companies. This research will help you decide which companies interest you enough to be on your list.

The list of prospective companies should not be too long. Though you're looking for a minimum of facts, you don't want to feel that you have involved yourself in an interminable project. Bear in mind that every company on your list must receive your résumé accompanied by an individually typed cover letter addressed to the appropriate person. You should, if at all possible, determine the name and title of the person you plan to be your addressee. Reference books such as *Standard & Poors* can give you this information.

The remainder of your direct mail campaign involves the actual mailing of the résumés and cover letters and the follow-up with phone calls.

There are several compelling reasons to make follow-up calls. First, you are never sure if the right person received your résumé. Second, you initiate the action. Don't wait for them to call. Don't neglect it, because it may be the thing that will prod the employer to set up an interview with you. Your making the call prevents your letter from remaining unanswered, and at the same time gives a more professional, aggressive impression.

Don't be timid in prospecting. Persistence is one of the key elements in successful job hunting.

Employ all of your sales techniques and skills when cold calling to overcome the most common objections or excuses and to ascertain that you are indeed speaking to the right decision-making person.

VOICE MAIL

In today's world of hi tech apparatus you must develop stratagems to deal not only with protective secretaries and administrative assistants but also with voice mail. Never leave a message on voice mail stating that you are looking for a job. Just say your name and number and that you are looking forward to speaking with the individual. Be a little mysterious, but pleasant. Once he or she calls you back, have a brief speech ready. Planning what you will say in advance is essential...make the most of your sales pitch!

Keeping a Record

Keep a record of each résumé sent and note the dates of your calls and interviews. Also indicate the results of each call and interview, and remember your follow-up letters. Don't leave anything to your memory; maintain a written record.

The simplest way of maintaining a record of your direct mail campaign is to make a photocopy of each cover letter as you finish it. On the bottom of the copy, you can note date and result of your phone call, date of interview, result of interview and follow-up note. These can be kept in a file folder with a separate sheet—or calendar page—with dates and times of interviews noted. It would be disastrous to set up 2 interviews for the same time.

A second system is to set up a large sheet of paper with column headings across the top of the sheet. The information, of course, would be the same as that maintained by using photocopies. Below is the suggested heading for each column. The headings would be separated by lines drawn vertically down the full length of the sheet, and horizontal lines would be drawn, each about 2 inches below the other, to separate the entries for each company written.

Résumé Mailing	Follow-Up Phone Call	Interview	Thank-you Letter
			Date_____
Name_____	Date_____	Date_____ Time_____	**Job Offer**
Title_____	Results_____	Interviewer_____	☐ Yes ☐ No
Company_____	_____	Results_____	**Confirmation or "No Thank You, But" Letter**
Address_____	_____	_____	Date_____
_____	_____	_____	☐ Confirmed
Date Sent_____	_____	_____	☐ No Thank You

Note that record-keeping sheets of this type have been provided on pages 41 through 44 for your convenience.

The third system involves the use of 4" × 6" index cards. Again the information would be the same as the other systems. A sample layout for the card follows.

Mr. Richard Rowe   Mailed 3/22/96
Chief Draftsman
Systems, Inc.
424 Park Place
Buford, PA 21370

Phone Call: _____
                                           (indicate date)

(Note results) _____

Interview:_____
                               (indicate date, time, and interviewer)

(Note results) _____

Thank-You Letter_____
                                           (indicate date)

Job Offer _____

Confirmation or "No Thank You, But" Letter _____
                                               (indicate date and letter type)

This system is the best for a very large mailing. I suggest that you have the index cards printed up cheaply rather than trying to type them yourself

A direct mail campaign is not an inexpensive way of looking for work, but no way really is. Direct mail involves an expenditure of money—for reproduction of résumés, envelopes, postage, and phone calls—and time. But any other method involves as much time. The difference is that the direct mail time is spent in the comfort of your home instead of on buses, on the pavement, and in waiting rooms. If you are pounding the pavements looking for work, you also have expenses for car fare, lunches, and the continual cups of coffee. We point this out mainly to remind you that the job hunt is going to cost you regardless of how you do it. You've got to spend in order to earn.

On the following pages you will find sample follow-up notes. Use them as a guide in creating your own personal responses.

413 W. Church Street
Ithaca, New York 14851

May 7, 1996

Mr. Richard Trump
Director of Social Work
Rockland Hospital
Rockland, Connecticut 06013

Dear Mr. Trump:

I regret that your job offer came a day too late. Just yesterday, I accepted a job as a social worker for another hospital. I am really sorry because I was impressed with your institution and probably would have fit in very well.

As I am not at all sure how my new job is going to work out, would you please be kind enough to keep my application on file, and contact me if there is another opening in the next few months?

Thank you for your offer, and again, I am sorry I have to refuse it.

Sincerely,

Anne Paulson

Anne Paulson

79 Coastal Highway
Miami Beach, Florida 33110

September 7, 1996

Mr. Marc Thomas
Leisure Realty Corporation
Miami, Florida 33133

Dear Mr. Thomas,

I just wanted to write to tell you how pleased I was to meet with you last Wednesday.

I was particularly impressed with the quality of homes you are constructing in Glen Garry and Boca Raton, and the total-market concept your organization has used to shape these developments.

Thank you for considering me for the position of Sales Agent at Leisure Realty.

I look forward to hearing from you.

Sincerely,

John Villiers

John Villiers

25 Harbor Hill Road
Gorham, Maine 04038

September 22, 1996

Ms. Joanna Crosley
Marketing Director
The Johnson Crumpf Company
1435 Commonwealth Avenue
Boston, Massachusetts 02117

Dear Ms. Crosley:

I am delighted to confirm my acceptance of the job as Senior Marketing Analyst. As you already know, I am not going to report for another two weeks. But I have just given my present firm two weeks' notice, and will report to you on October 4th.

Let me reiterate how pleased I am at getting this job. I was hoping that I would, as I feel that it is the perfect job for me and I know that I will fit into your company well.

Sincerely,

Barton Rockwood

Barton Rockwood

Résumé Mailing	Follow-Up Phone Call	Interview	Thank-you Letter
Name _____	Date _____	Date _____ Time _____	Date_____
Title _____	Results _____	Interviewer _____	**Job Offer**
Company _____	_____	Results _____	❏ Yes ❏ No
Address _____	_____	_____	**Confirmation or "No Thank You, But" Letter**
_____	_____	_____	Date_____
Date Sent _____	_____	_____	❏ Confirmed ❏ No Thank You

Résumé Mailing	Follow-Up Phone Call	Interview	Thank-you Letter
Name _____	Date _____	Date _____ Time _____	Date_____
Title _____	Results _____	Interviewer _____	**Job Offer**
Company _____	_____	Results _____	❏ Yes ❏ No
Address _____	_____	_____	**Confirmation or "No Thank You, But" Letter**
_____	_____	_____	Date_____
Date Sent _____	_____	_____	❏ Confirmed ❏ No Thank You

Résumé Mailing	Follow-Up Phone Call	Interview	Thank-you Letter
Name _____	Date _____	Date _____ Time _____	Date_____
Title _____	Results _____	Interviewer _____	**Job Offer**
Company _____	_____	Results _____	❏ Yes ❏ No
Address _____	_____	_____	**Confirmation or "No Thank You, But" Letter**
_____	_____	_____	Date_____
Date Sent _____	_____	_____	❏ Confirmed ❏ No Thank You

Résumé Mailing	Follow-Up Phone Call	Interview	Thank-you Letter
Name	Date	Date Time	Date_____
Title	Results	Interviewer	**Job Offer**
Company		Results	❏ Yes ❏ No
Address			**Confirmation or "No Thank You, But" Letter**
			Date_____
Date Sent			❏ Confirmed ❏ No Thank You

Résumé Mailing	Follow-Up Phone Call	Interview	Thank-you Letter
Name	Date	Date Time	Date_____
Title	Results	Interviewer	**Job Offer**
Company		Results	❏ Yes ❏ No
Address			**Confirmation or "No Thank You, But" Letter**
			Date_____
Date Sent			❏ Confirmed ❏ No Thank You

Résumé Mailing	Follow-Up Phone Call	Interview	Thank-you Letter
Name	Date	Date Time	Date_____
Title	Results	Interviewer	**Job Offer**
Company		Results	❏ Yes ❏ No
Address			**Confirmation or "No Thank You, But" Letter**
			Date_____
Date Sent			❏ Confirmed ❏ No Thank You

Résumé Mailing	Follow-Up Phone Call	Interview	Thank-you Letter
			Date_____
Name	Date	Date Time	**Job Offer**
Title	Results	Interviewer	❏ Yes ❏ No
Company		Results	**Confirmation or "No Thank You, But" Letter**
Address			
			Date_____
Date Sent			❏ Confirmed
			❏ No Thank You

Résumé Mailing	Follow-Up Phone Call	Interview	Thank-you Letter
			Date_____
Name	Date	Date Time	**Job Offer**
Title	Results	Interviewer	❏ Yes ❏ No
Company		Results	**Confirmation or "No Thank You, But" Letter**
Address			
			Date_____
Date Sent			❏ Confirmed
			❏ No Thank You

Résumé Mailing	Follow-Up Phone Call	Interview	Thank-you Letter
			Date_____
Name	Date	Date Time	**Job Offer**
Title	Results	Interviewer	❏ Yes ❏ No
Company		Results	**Confirmation or "No Thank You, But" Letter**
Address			
			Date_____
Date Sent			❏ Confirmed
			❏ No Thank You

Résumé Mailing	Follow-Up Phone Call	Interview	Thank-you Letter
Name	Date	Date Time	Date_____
Title	Results	Interviewer	**Job Offer**
Company		Results	❏ Yes ❏ No
Address			**Confirmation or "No Thank You, But" Letter**
			Date_____
Date Sent			❏ Confirmed
			❏ No Thank You

Résumé Mailing	Follow-Up Phone Call	Interview	Thank-you Letter
Name	Date	Date Time	Date_____
Title	Results	Interviewer	**Job Offer**
Company		Results	❏ Yes ❏ No
Address			**Confirmation or "No Thank You, But" Letter**
			Date_____
Date Sent			❏ Confirmed
			❏ No Thank You

Résumé Mailing	Follow-Up Phone Call	Interview	Thank-you Letter
Name	Date	Date Time	Date_____
Title	Results	Interviewer	**Job Offer**
Company		Results	❏ Yes ❏ No
Address			**Confirmation or "No Thank You, But" Letter**
			Date_____
Date Sent			❏ Confirmed
			❏ No Thank You

The Cover Letter

A cover letter should be enclosed every time you send out or fax your résumé. Its enclosure is not only an act of courtesy but a means of adding a personal touch. It gives each individual you approach an indication of your personal attention to his or her situation—which would not be the case if the résumé arrived unaccompanied. The cover letter also neutralizes the tone of the impersonal, reproduced résumé.

A resume is fact. It is a recapitulation of your work experience. It says, in effect, this is what I have done. It is objective. A cover letter, on the other hand, says, "This is what I would like to do," or "This is what I am good at." It focuses in more closely on a particular job or occupational area in which you are interested. It states your objective.

Now you can blow your own horn. The cover letter is your chance to let your individual style, personality, and unique strengths stand out from the crowd. Don't be afraid to "sell" yourself here by describing some unique incident or experience. If you wish to do something flamboyant, the cover letter, rather than the résumé, is the place to do it.

Our corporate experts tell us they are much more likely to read a résumé accompanied by a cover letter than one received without a letter. The letter removes the look of a mass mailing.

It doesn't matter whether you are sending your résumé in answer to an ad, to an employment agency, or as part of your personal mailing campaign. The cover letter will always follow the same, simple rules. It should be brief—limited to 1 page and no more than 4 paragraphs. Needless to say, it should be neatly typed and conform to the standards of business correspondence.

Whenever possible, address your cover letter to a particular individual in the company, preferably by name and title. If it is impossible to ascertain the name, address the letter to "Personnel Director" or, by title, to the head of the department in which you are hoping to work. In answering an ad, however, address your letter as the ad indicates. If there is no more than a box number, simply address it to that box number.

An effective cover letter is a very calculated self-marketing tool that follows key guidelines. A cover letter has 3 distinct paragraphs:

1. An opening that will get the reader's attention
2. A statement of facts about yourself that would benefit the company
3. A closing that will prompt the reader to take action and call you

The purpose of the first paragraph is to get the reader's attention. This is where you interject a few outstanding facts or features about yourself. There is a gentleman who applied this advice after one of our college seminars. He had cleaned pools all through school. He felt there was nothing about cleaning pools that would get anyone's attention in his cover letter. In actuality, he increased his customer base from 35 to 50 over the years. That should get anyone's attention. He also remained a faithful and loyal employee all through college. He put these "attention getters" in the first paragraph of his cover letter. It wasn't too long after that he began to get interviews and landed a job with a major telecommunications company making $26,000 a year! As you can see, it's not always what you did, but it's how you perceive yourself and how you say it.

The first paragraph of your letter determines whether or not the reader continues to read. just as in a newspaper article, the first sentence or "lead" should be original and informative, and it should set the tone for the rest of the letter. It should tell why you are writing to that particular person or company. If it is an answer to an ad, say so, and give the name and date of the publication where the ad appeared. If the letter is part of your direct mail campaign, explain in 2 or 3 lines either why you would like to work for that particular company or why you feel their hiring you would be in their company's best interest. A frequent mistake in cover letters is to describe why the job is in the candidate's best interest, rather than to stress what the candidate can do for the employer. For example, to say "I believe your firm can offer me the dynamic challenges and responsibilities I seek" does not convince a recruiter of what you have to offer that company.

If a friend who is an employee has suggested you make contact with this particular company, you should give the name, title or job category, and the department where the friend is employed.

Some typical opening lines are:

Dorothy Johnson, a programmer in the systems programming department, suggested that I write to you.

I am replying to your ad which appeared in The New York Times *on Sunday, May 12.*

Your recent acquisition of Zebulon Textiles Company led me to believe that you might be interested in my 9 years' experience as a marketing manager with extensive industry experience.

The second paragraph of a cover letter should tell the manager or recruiter the benefits of hiring you. Don't just give them the facts. Give them benefits about these facts and how the facts relate to their company. It is not sufficient to say you have received extensive training. Give the benefit, too. Explain that because of this training there will be minimal learning time and immediate results. Now they can visualize what your training will mean once you are employed. Don't always assume the reader or listener will make this correlation. You have to do it for them. Without stating a benefit, the person you're writing to or speaking with has no clue as to how it will profit them. This same technique can be used effectively at an interview.

Be absolutely positive that you understand how to utilize this technique. It is extremely valuable. Complete the statements on the following worksheet. It will be good practice. The first two are done for you.

PERSONAL STATEMENTS AND BENEFITS WORKSHEET

Statement	Benefit
1. I have extensive computer and word processing experience.	1. You will save both time and money as I will need little or no training.
2. My organizational skills are exceptional.	2. Because I am so organized, I am usually able to provide my boss information quickly, saving time and minimizing problems.
3. I get along with others very well.	
4. At my previous place of employment I had perfect attendance.	
5. Working long hours and sticking with a task until completion is how I get things done when necessary.	
6. It is my belief to always deliver more than what is expected.	
7. In my free time I like to play sports and volunteer at the local Rescue Mission.	
8. I am always eager to learn and try new things.	
9. My friends and co-workers always comment as to how reliable and punctual I am.	
10. I am career oriented and take my work seriously.	

The second paragraph should also point out the salient features of your résumé that could be of interest to your correspondent. These paragraphs are the very guts of your cover letter. In a sentence or two, tell why you would be an asset to the company receiving your letter. Succinctly lay out your credentials and refer to your accomplishments, skills, or areas of expertise. In certain circumstances, you might elaborate on one or two entries on your résumé.

Use the cover letter to describe special projects in which you played a key role, or the features of a program you worked on that were unusual. Another frequent use of the cover letter is to summarize your achievements in a somewhat more readable form than the optional summary portion of the résumé.

Because different aspects of your résumé are highlighted in each cover letter, the same résumé can be used to pursue different job opportunities. The cover letter stresses your most appropriate skills and talents and can be geared uniquely to each particular company on your mailing list.

The third paragraph is very easy to construct and is the most important in many ways. However, many individuals just seem to have a hard time doing it. Close for action! Get the reader to call you. The companies that send you marketing mail know the value of closing for action. They want you to call them and order. You want the reader to take action by picking up the phone and calling you. Write, "When can we arrange an interview? I can be reached at [and give them your telephone number]."

Do not make statements such as: "Hope to hear from you soon." or "Thank you for your consideration, I'll be calling you next week." The first phrase sounds weak. The second phrase sets you up for a secretary who is going to make sure that you don't get through. You are in a better position to interview and negotiate if they call you.

When an employer calls you it means that they have a sincere interest in you. This places you in a much better position to negotiate and sell yourself at the interview. If you must call them don't announce it in your letter. Just call them a week to 10 days after your letter was sent.

Do not try to get a job with your résumé and cover letter! The résumé and cover letter are to get you an interview. Companies do not hire someone because a résumé and cover letter looked good. Companies do set up interviews for people with good résumés and cover letters. The interview is where you actually sell yourself and get a job offer.

TYPES OF COVER LETTERS

There are several situations that require you to mail your résumé and cover letter. These are:

❏ A response to an ad.
❏ An unsolicited inquiry to a targeted employer as part of your direct mail campaign.
❏ A letter to an employment agency.
❏ A letter to a friend or colleague who might offer assistance in a job search.

RESPONSE TO AN AD

Read the ads carefully, marking or clipping those of interest to you. Examine the requirements thoroughly. Employers advertise for the "ideal" candidate and, more often than not, actually hire an individual not possessing every qualification listed in the original ad. For that reason, it is a good idea to reply not only to those ads that fit you perfectly, but also to those for which you meet just some of the requirements.

Now reread each ad you intend to answer. Study each separately. Assume that the requirements are rank ordered, and deal with each as sequenced in the ad. List on a piece of scratch paper every qualification, skill, strength, or accomplishment you possess relevant to the particular advertisement. If you don't have all the requirements, make a note of any experience in either your education or work history that demonstrates other capabilities that would make you an asset to that particular company. Write and rewrite this information until you have eliminated all excess words. Communicate your strengths clearly and succinctly. Work on your letter until each idea flows effortlessly to the next. Let's look at a typical ad and consider how to respond to it.

SALES MANAGER/TRAVEL

Famous-brand "Last Ever" sporting goods offers excellent opportunity. Territory includes N.Y., Mass., Vt., N.H., Me. Must have previous sales and travel experience. Salary, commission, bonus. Car & travel expenses plus complete benefits. Write Box 6214.

An appropriate reply can be found on page 39. Address your letter to the company and person listed in the ad, or simply to the personnel director if no individual's name is listed.

It's a good idea to research each company whose ad you intend to answer, and then include in your letter any new information you have become aware of: an expansion, recent or imminent merger, acquisition, or new product developments or services. Mention how you would be able to help the organization implement or maximize its current goals. (Obviously, if the ad lists only a box number, this will not be possible.)

Don't be discouraged if you don't get an immediate response. We've found it is not unusual for a recruiter to hold résumés for more than 6 weeks before setting up interviews.

DIRECT MAIL LETTER

A successful technique in a job campaign is to select a number of employers of your choice and simply send each a copy of your résumé with an individually written cover letter. Compile a list of prospective employers using professional journals, business directories, and other references. Learn as much as possible about the companies you have chosen. Address the letter to a specific person. Call the company and ask for the name of the personnel manager. Be sure to have the name spelled correctly.

Don't let this research overwhelm you; you're looking for a minimum of facts. If you are planning to send out 50 or more letters, research the 10 or 12 companies in which you have the most interest. For the remaining organizations, it is enough to simply address the letter to the appropriate person and then mention the company name once or twice in the body of your letter. In essence, you are trying to make the letter appear as personal as possible, bearing in mind that most people don't read form letters.

In each letter point out the particular strengths and accomplishments that would be of interest to the reader and indicate where they are described in your résumé. The tone of the letter should generate interest in you. Refer to a particular qualification that will demonstrate why it would be particularly advantageous to the potential employer to add you to its staff. Always discuss how you can be of value to them rather than how they can help you.

LETTERS TO EMPLOYMENT AGENCIES

Start by calling each target employment agency and executive search firm in your area, and talking with—or get the name of—the highest ranking individual. In some cases, you might set up a meeting; in other instances, you'll get "permission" to send your résumé. For the out-of-town agencies or to those whose names are unavailable, simply address your cover letter to the president.

The purpose of your letter is to set up a conversation with the appropriate recruiter in each agency—best done in person; second best by phone. Request your résumé be kept on file so that you can be notified of any suitable job openings. Though we recommend that you discuss your feelings concerning relocation, the cover letter is not the place to mention salary requirements. You should keep your cover letter brief, but at the same time make reference to certain of your strengths.

On frequent occasions, executive recruiters rewrite résumés, (not always to the candidate's advantage). **You must ask them to show you your "rewritten" résumé before it is sent to a potential employer.** We cannot emphasize this too strongly!

The last paragraph, similar to the other types of cover letters, should include an indication that you will phone in a week or so to set up either a phone or a personal interview.

LETTER TO COLLEAGUE OR FRIEND

Colleagues, friends, or relatives can often be an excellent source of leads. For that reason, you should give them a copy of your résumé. When sending your résumé, include a short informal note instead of a businesslike cover letter. The note should simply say that you're in the process of seeking employment or attempting to change jobs and would appreciate any suggestions he or she can offer. You might mention how you feel about relocation. Mention if your job search is confidential. Don't discuss your salary requirements, but you might ask if it would be useful to send additional résumés.

Sample Cover Letters
✧✧✧

On the following pages are sample cover letters. You may wish to use one as an example to follow, or parts from different letters. Never copy them exactly. Use these samples as guides to create your own letter that will reflect your own style and personality. Then use your cover letter to point out your unique strengths and why the company would benefit from hiring you.

16 4th Street
Ft. Lauderdale, Florida 33311
(305) 162-4690

April 19, 1996

Mr. James Arter
Personnel Director
Sun & Tan, Inc.
1200 Biscayne Blvd.
Miami, Florida 33125

Dear Mr. Arter:

Please find the enclosed résumé in response to your advertisement for Sales, which appeared in the *Miami Herald* on Sunday, April 14, 1996.

Please note that I have had eight years' experience selling cosmetics and hair products for Jackson and Andrews. In this position I was responsible for the Florida, Alabama, and Georgia territory.

Realizing that this summary, as well as my résumé, cannot adequately communicate my qualifications in-depth, I would appreciate having the opportunity to discuss with you in person how I might become an asset to your company. When can we set up an appointment for an interview? I look forward to meeting you.

Sincerely,

Amy Lawson

Amy Lawson

Encl.

200 Erie Avenue
Rochester, N.Y. 14610
(716) 681-1144

May 12, 1996

Box 6214
Rochester Times
10 Broad Street
Rochester, N.Y. 14610

To Whom It May Concern:

I enclose my résumé in response to your sales advertisement in the *Rochester Times* on Sunday, May 1.

My sales/marketing background includes an eight-year association with Gordon's Sporting Goods, Inc., where I was in charge of developing the New England territory. This involved recruiting, training, and working with the sales force. It was also my responsibility to develop and implement sales/marketing plans and strategies in support of the field sales effort.

I am presently employed as Sales Manager of Woodrow and Martin, Inc., a men's clothing manufacturer. I am very eager to return to the sporting goods industry.

In my present position, I call on, sell, and service mass merchandisers, retail chains, department stores, and military exchanges. I achieved success in these and other related activities, and enjoy the fine rapport and reputation developed through my ability to communicate and work with people on all levels.

I am a results-oriented manager who enjoys traveling and working with people, motivating them, and developing their skills to maximum potential. It would be difficult to indicate every area of expertise in my résumé, therefore I would appreciate meeting with you to discuss my qualifications for this position in greater detail.

I may be reached at the above phone number to set up an appointment for an interview.

Sincerely,

Harry Ellis

Harry Ellis

29 Ridge Road
Elmira, New York 10623
Phone (607) 439-2343

April 14, 1996

Box X3349
New York Guardian
749 East 56th Street
New York, New York 10022

Dear Sir:

I am replying to your advertisement of this date offering a position as copy editor on a sports car publication.

As my résumé demonstrates, I have my B.S. in journalism and have been working as copy writer and assistant copy editor on magazines for the past six years.

Your ad specified an interest in and knowledge of sports cars. I did not feel it appropriate to mention it in my résumé, but I am the owner of one of the few surviving Type 57 Bugattis in this country, and have rebuilt and maintain the car myself. The car is registered with the Bugatti Club of America to which I also belong. As you can see, I have established credentials as a sports car enthusiast.

Please contact me at your convenience to explore my background further.

I appreciate your consideration.

Yours truly,

Anthony Lo Bello

Anthony Lo Bello

Encl.

16 Chilton Street
Cleveland, Ohio 40612
Phone: (216) 223-3344

April 9, 1996

Mr. George Teasdale
Personnel Manager
United Chemical Corporation
452 Sorrent Drive
Teeterboro, New Jersey 11402

Dear Mr. Teasdale:

I am replying to your advertisement in the April issue of *Cosmetic Chemistry*.

While having no specific background in cosmetic chemistry, I would like to point out that my work with Basic Pharmaceutical's Anesthetic and Analgesic division consisted primarily of developing and testing non-oleaginous bases for topical anesthetics. The basis, of course, had to be broadly anti-allergic if they were to be of commercial value and were tested for same. Our procedures, in both development and testing, were similar to those used in the cosmetic industry, and our tests were at least as rigorous.

My résumé also shows, as your ad requested, heavy Quantitative Analysis and Quality Control experience.

We should speak further. I will be in New York for the Pharmaceutical Chemists' Society meeting next month. When can we arrange an interview for that time?

Thank you for your consideration.

Yours truly,

John Villiers

John Villiers

Enclosure

320 Garrity Drive
Chicago, Illinois 11625
Phone: (312) 996-6421

May 24, 1996

Mr. Henry Wilford
President
Seafarer's Museum
Xenobia, Maine 10874

Dear Mr. Wilford:

I am applying for a position with your museum as I feel my experience in developing a museum Sales Department will be of interest to you.

As my résumé indicates, I held the position as Sales Manager of Woodbury Reconstruction Company for six years. In this capacity, I developed a mail order sales department and created a successful bookshop specializing in native crafts.

I expect to be in the vicinity of Xenobia in the first week of July. When could we arrange an interview for that time? As I am currently employed, I would appreciate this being kept in confidence.

Your consideration is greatly appreciated.

Sincerely yours,

Richard Shelton

Richard Shelton

Enclosure

14 Seagate Avenue
Grand Rapids, Michigan 49505

September 3, 1996

Mr. Ernest Chapman
Vice-President for Marketing
Cargon & Fuller, Inc.
280 Wall Street
Grand Rapids, Michigan 49505

Dear Mr. Chapman:

I believe my 10 years of solid marketing background would be an asset to Cargon & Fuller, Inc.

In my association with General Dynamics, Inc., I was responsible for increasing sales of a $40 million product line between 15% and 34% in twenty markets after years of consistent decline. I also reversed continual losses of what once was $150 million profit center and restored profitability to several smaller operations scheduled for write-offs. I have also been successful in opening market areas previously unknown to the company.

As you will see from the enclosed résumé I am also experienced in new product development, acquisitions, licensing, and export. When can we set up an appointment to discuss a sales or marketing position with your firm? I may be reached at 616/757-7775.

Sincerely,

Samuel Davis

Samuel Davis

2121 Toronto Street
Buffalo, N.Y. 14229

May 19, 1996

Mr. Arthur Bigelow
Personnel Director
Niagara Industries, Inc.
10 Chambers Street
Buffalo, N.Y. 14281

Dear Mr. Bigelow:

In September 1996, I will receive my Bachelor of Arts Degree in Marketing from the University of Buffalo, and I am interested in obtaining an entry-level position with your company. Friends have told me about Niagara, Inc., and I understand you have a superior marketing department.

My undergraduate studies covered a wide range with concentrations in statistics, economics, and law as well as in marketing. As such, I believe I have a strong business background and would work well in your organization.

I have enclosed my résumé showing my work experience during summers and part-time employment while in college. From this information, you will see that I am an active, motivated person and will continue this aggressiveness with your organization.

I look forward to meeting you. When can we set up an appointment for an interview? I may be reached at 716/225-4422.

Sincerely,

Caroline Houston

Caroline Houston

26 James Street
Chicago, Illinois 60602
Phone: (313) 656-4399

April 6, 1996

Mr. John Anderson
Personnel Director
Digital Corporation
Detroit, Michigan 51073

Dear Mr. Anderson:

I am a graduate student in Computer Science at Yale University, and I will be awarded an M.S. degree in June 1996. 1 am currently looking for a position related to Database/Graphics Package Design in the research and development department of a major company.

Before coming to Yale, I designed, supervised, and completed a CAD system. The function covers vector, character and curve generation, windowing, shading, and transformations.

At Yale, my research work involves Compilation of Relational Queries into Network DML. To enhance my background, I have taken some courses in Computer Graphics and Database, and I have experience in and understanding of the design of Database. With this strong background, I certainly believe that I am competent to meet challenging tasks and can make a good contribution to your company.

Enclosed please find my résumé, which indicates in some detail my training and experience. I sincerely hope that my qualifications are of interest to you and that an interview might be arranged at your convenience.

Thank you for your consideration and I am looking forward to hearing from you soon.

Sincerely yours,

Martha Levine

Martha Levine

Encl.

19 Bayside Lane
Bethesda, MD 21058

July 21, 1996

Mr. Robert Nash
Vice-President of Sales
Nelson & Murphy Inc.
2100 Broad Street
Baltimore, MD 21245

Dear Mr. Nash:

I am applying for a position as Sales Manager with your company, as I feel my background in developing a sales department will be of interest to you.

As my résumé indicates, I joined Kobin, Inc., in the capacity of a trainee and moved up the ladder to my current position of Sales Manager. In each year of my employment I was successful in opening new accounts, penetrating existing ones, and reopening closed businesses. As a result, I was responsible for sales increases of 20% to 25%.

As sales manager I was involved in recruiting, training, and supervising a staff of 120 salespeople and was responsible for sales worldwide.

I am looking forward to meeting you. When can we set up an appointment for an interview? I may be reached at 301/665-6728.

Sincerely,

James Wilson

James Wilson

1900 Hillside Terrace
Boston, Mass. 02126
Phone: 617/778-9086

April 15, 1996

Mr. Donald Reed
Personnel Director
Chase & Morris, Inc.
615 Main Street
Boston, Mass. 02120

Dear Mr. Reed:

I am writing to you today in hope you will read my résumé and consider me for a marketing position with your company.

I was very interested in the article about your company which appeared in *The New York Times* on April 1, 1996. Your paternalistic policy which involves a "no turnover" company, complies with both my short-term and long-range goals, as I am really interested in a stable opportunity.

As my résumé indicates, I offer 12 years of solid marketing experience. In my association with Stanley, Inc., my present employer, gross sales have increased by $15 million due to a concentrated Product Marketing Plan introduced by me.

I was also responsible for the development of strategies and implementation of a direct mail strategy for 7 new packages and 5 offers, which resulted in a package that beat the control by 250%.

Please call at your convenience to set up an interview. Your consideration is greatly appreciated.

Sincerely yours,

Adam Stane

Adam Stane

Encl.

1800 Harrison Road
Los Angeles, CA 90063

April 30, 1996

Martha Livingston
Personnel Manager
Vogue Patterns, Inc.
100 Pace Street
Los Angeles, CA 90002

Dear Miss Livingston:

I believe my ten years of accounting experience might be an asset to Vogue Patterns and therefore I have enclosed my résumé for your consideration.

I was very impressed with the articles about your company, which appeared in the *Los Angeles Times* on Sunday, April 28, 1996. Your commitment to low turnover and a secure work force fits my short-term and long-range employment goals, as I am really interested in a stable opportunity.

In my 10-year association with Helen Curtis, I was fully responsible for the preparation of monthly consolidated financial statements for management and public reporting— Forms 10K, 10 2 and the Annual Report to Shareholders, and shared responsibility with the Corporate Controller in maintaining operating units compliance with the FASB and SEC pronouncements.

When can we set up an interview? I may be reached at 310/223-2260. Your consideration is greatly appreciated.

Sincerely,

Anita Parsons

Anita Parsons

Encl.

110 Tenth Ave.
New York, NY 10011
May 10, 1996

Miss Anne Tully
Personnel Director
Deeth & Johnson, Inc.
165 Madison Avenue
New York, NY 10016

Dear Miss Tully:

In June, 1996, 1 will receive my Bachelor of Arts degree from Columbia University and I am interested in obtaining an entry level accounting position with your company.

As you will see from the enclosed résumé, I majored in accounting, minored in economics, and maintained a 3.2 grade average from my freshman through senior years. For the past three summers I have been employed as a temporary accounting clerk by Career Blazers Temporary Personnel, Inc. and my assignments have included such agencies as Benton & Baroles, Cunningham & Walsh, B.B.D. & Gray. These assignments convince me that my ultimate career goal lies in the advertising industry.

Not noted in my résumé is my intention of returning to Columbia University's evening sessions to pursue an MBA in accounting and business.

I will call early next week to set up an appointment for an interview. I am confident that I have the qualifications to become an asset to Deeth & Johnson.

Sincerely,

Karen Reed

Karen Reed

106 East End Ave.
New York, NY 10028
(212) 874-3614

January 16, 1996

Walker Associates
517 Fifth Ave.
New York, NY 10017

Gentlemen:

I would appreciate it if you would place my enclosed résumé in your files.

I graduated from Ohio State University in 1986 and my 10 years of financial experience consist of 4 years as controller of a ladies ready-to-wear manufacturer, 3 years as assistant controller in a sportswear firm, and 3 years as an accountant with a book publisher.

My "hands-on" operations experience has included developing professional accounting, reporting, and data processing functions. My strengths include problem-solving, producing order out of confusion, and getting things done.

I would like to discuss my salary requirements when we meet at a personal interview. Because my time is flexible, I am available to meet you at your convenience. I shall call early next week to set up an appointment.

Sincerely,

Kenneth Newman

Kenneth Newman

18 Dogwood Lane
Hastings, NY 10706

June 16,1996

Mrs. Dorothy Mitchell
Career Blazers Agency, Inc.
590 Fifth Ave.
New York, NY 10036

Dear Mrs. Mitchell:

Thank you for taking the time to discuss opportunities available to me through Career Blazers. As I mentioned in our conversation, I have nearly as much paralegal as legal secretarial experience. However, my interest at this time lies in the area of paralegal.

I am enclosing 10 copies of my résumé as you suggested. You will notice that I have emphasized my paralegal expertise. I am particularly interested in a position in the metropolitan area and would consider a temporary assignment if it had potential to become permanent.

I expect to be in New York City in early July. Let's get in touch before then to set up another meeting. I may be reached at 914/536-2909.

Sincerely,

Allen Oxman

Allen Oxman

Enclosure

14 Sommers St.
Newburgh, NY 12550

May 10, 1996

Miss Lynn Brown
Career Blazers Agency, Inc.
590 Fifth Ave.
New York, NY 10036

Dear Miss Brown:

I've been told by several personnel directors in the publishing field that Career Blazers specializes in placing recent college graduates. I will receive my Bachelor of Arts degree in English from Skidmore College in September, 1996, and am interested in obtaining an editorial position with a book or magazine publisher.

As my résumé indicates, I maintained a 3.5 average for my 4 years in college and worked as an Administrative Assistant for the Skidmore Office of University Systems for 3 years (1993–96), part-time during school and full-time through the summers and other vacations. I am an excellent typist, and though I am not looking for a secretarial position, I would be willing to exchange my typing skill and secretarial expertise for an entry level position with potential.

I am looking forward to meeting you in the near future and will call you early next month to set up an interview.

Yours truly,

Nancy Hanks

Nancy Hanks

1900 Driftwood Drive
No. Miami Beach, Florida 33160

August 25,1996

Ms. Nola Chestor
Management Recruiters, Inc.
180 Collins Avenue
Miami, Florida 33139

Dear Ms. Chestor:

I am enclosing a copy of my résumé in hopes that your firm may assist me in locating a position as Corporate Controller with a Fortune 500 company.

As my résumé indicates, I have 10 years' experience in Financial Management and Control, having served in the past as Treasurer, Controller, Corporate Accountant, Consolidation Manager and Director of Financial Planning. In my present position at Thompson Chemical Corp., I initiate, develop, and supervise all internal audits.

As I have not yet given notice, I would appreciate your discretion in this matter.

I am looking forward to meeting you in person, at which time I can explain in depth both my qualifications and aspirations. I will call early next week to set up a personal meeting.

Yours truly,

Warren Barth

Warren Barth

16 South Street
Darien, Connecticut 06490
February 8, 1996

Ms. Patricia Schwartz
Taft Computer Company
1800 Broad Street
Philadelphia, Pennsylvania 20171

Dear Patricia:

It was a very pleasant surprise running into you at the Philadelphia Computer Show this morning. I have enclosed my résumé, so that it may be circulated to the appropriate department heads, when you contact them.

As we discussed today, I am interested in working for Taft in the Philadelphia area and in dealing with customers. An experienced software specialist, I have proposed, planned, designed, managed, developed, and delivered major software systems to users. Project management of a multi-person effort has been the primary responsibility of my latest job. In addition to having management and technical skills, I enjoy people, giving presentations, and consulting. Taft appears to offer opportunities in marketing, customer support, and development that would use my computing expertise, along with my verbal abilities.

Having recently delivered a significant software application, I would like to begin a new challenge as soon as possible.

Talking with you was a pleasure and has given me a very positive impression of Taft as a company.

When can we meet again to further explore the next step in our discussion? I may be reached at 203/561-3426.

Yours truly,

Carl Ferguson

Carl Ferguson

encl.

474 Hardscrabble Road
Millville, New York 10901
April 4, 1996

Ms. Bernice Luddington
Art Director
Abington's Department Store
1502 Mamaroneck Avenue
White Plains, New York 10603

Dear Ms. Luddington:

The controller of your Paramus branch, William Scott, who is a neighbor of mine, has told me that you have an opening for a display designer in your White Plains store.

As you can see from my résumé, I had extensive experience in the field prior to the birth of my first child. While I have been unable to seek employment in the field for several years, I have kept my hand in, as it were, by designing displays of art and handicrafts as a volunteer at our local library.

My youngest child is now in high school and able to take care of himself. In addition, my sister lives nearby and has agreed to take care of any emergency that might arise; so, I will be able to devote myself wholeheartedly to my job.

I would welcome an opportunity to speak with you. When can we meet? Please call 914/989-3214 at your convenience.

Thank you for your consideration.

Yours sincerely,

Helen Fries

Helen Fries

Enclosure

95 Valentine Lane
Melville, NY 11747
Phone: (516) 894-3241

June 8, 1996

Ms. Jane Raymond
Personnel Director
North Bank of America
White Plains, NY 10603

Dear Ms. Raymond:

Mr. John Smith, an executive in your Manhattan office, who is a friend of my father, suggested I write to you about the possibility of an opening in your international department.

As you can see from my résumé, I am a French major and Spanish minor and am very interested in a position where I can use my knowledge of languages. I have worked as an office temporary for the past three summers and some of my assignments were in the banking field. I am a good typist (70 wpm) and would be quite willing to start in a clerical capacity.

I would like very much to meet you and am available for an interview any time convenient to you.

Sincerely yours,

John Osterio

John Osterio

3200 Bayview Drive
Scarsdale, NY 10583
April 11, 1996

Ms. Claire Lunt
Beacon Press, Inc.
16 W. 49th St.
New York, NY 10020

Dear Ms. Lunt:

Rita Marks, an editorial assistant with your company, told me of your plans to expand your accounting department. For that reason, plus my avocational interest in books, I am enclosing a copy of my résumé in hopes that my background will be of interest to you.

I am a graduate of Columbia University (June 1995) with a degree in accounting and economics, which emphasized taxation and managerial accounting. I will receive a Master of Business Administration from Columbia University in June 1997. For the past three summers I worked as an accounting clerk with Shiller & Rogers and, because some of their clients are involved in publishing, I have gained some actual experience in accounting for the book industry.

I feel sure that I have the education, experience, potential, and enthusiasm to be successful with your firm and would appreciate an opportunity for a personal interview. When can we set up a time to meet? At your convenience, I may be reached at 914/998-7456.

Thanking you in advance for any courtesies, I remain

Sincerely,

Lillian Robbins

Lillian Robbins

119 Grattan Ave.
Oyster Bay, NY 11771
Phone: (516) 295-3344

December 19, 1995

Roger Smaridge, Controller
General Rent-A-Car, Inc.
118 W Second Avenue
Dayton, OH 45424

Dear Mr. Smaridge:

Nadine Foster, an attorney with your company and a long time friend, recently told me about an opening for a tax accountant at General Rent-A-Car, Inc. I feel that I am extremely qualified for that position and I have enclosed a résumé for your consideration.

As you can see from my résumé, I have over 10 years' experience in the area of tax accountancy. In my present position with the Whitney Bowes Credit Corporation, I am heavily involved in property and sales tax research, which includes finding solutions to problems unique to the leasing industry. I am also responsible for any property tax appeals and audits that might affect Whitney Bowes. I have also gained expertise in the preparation of income and franchise tax in selected states.

I would appreciate an opportunity for a personal meeting, at which time I hope I can explain why I would be a very important asset to General Rent-ACar.

When can we set up an interview? I may be reached, at your convenience, at the above phone number.

Yours truly,

Patrick Johnson

Patrick Johnson

41 Cumberland Drive
Scarsdale, New York 10583

September 18, 1995

Mr. Bob Brody, President
Walker Brody Personnel, Inc.
509 Fifth Avenue
New York, New York 10017

Dear Mr. Brody:

Bill Lewis of Career Blazers Personnel Services, Inc. suggested you might be of assistance to me in my desire to find new employment. I became acquainted with Bill while I was Assistant Controller at Parker Press.

As you can see from my enclosed résumé, all of my accounting experience has been in publishing. I started with R. R. Majors, Inc., then Parker Press, and am presently employed as Controller in Walker & Walker & Co. As you've probably heard, Walker & Walker is moving to Washington, DC and because it is now imperative that I remain in the metropolitan area, I am available for a new position. Bill spoke very highly of you and I am looking forward to getting together with you to discuss my background and qualifications in depth.

Let's get in touch at your convenience to arrange a meeting. I can be reached at 914/567-7255.

Yours truly,

Bob Miller

Bob Miller

1440 N.W. 56th Ave.
Tampa, FL 33610

July 17, 1995

Dear Mike,

I'm finally taking your advice and decided to pull up stakes and make the move to New York City.

Just last week I gave notice at Peat & Marvich and I think we actually found a buyer for our condo down here. We plan to move in with Jan's mother and then slowly look for either a co-op in the city or ultimately buy a house in Westchester County.

As you probably remember, all of my experience has been in public accounting, but I would consider any opportunity that offers both stability and potential.

I'd really appreciate any suggestions you might have that could be helpful in finding a job. If you know any employment agencies or executive recruiters that specialize in financial personnel, please let me know of them.

I'm enclosing a few copies of my résumé. Because I've already given notice, please feel free to circulate them.

We should be in New York in mid-September and will call as soon as we get settled. Jan and I are looking forward to seeing you and Louise again.

Yours truly,

Bill

19 Seneca Lake Avenue
Elmira, N.Y. 14901

November 19, 1995

Ms. Phyllis Grey
General Elevator, Inc.
1200 Meadow Drive
Elmira, N.Y. 14901

Dear Ms. Grey,

John Evans, a programmer with your company, suggested I send my résumé to you. John and I met while we attended Hobart College.

As my résumé indicates, I have solid background in sales and though I haven't had industrial experience, I minored in electrical engineering and feel I have an aptitude in any technical area. I understand you are expanding your sales staff and would greatly appreciate your consideration.

I am looking forward to meeting you in the near future and getting in touch early next week.

Yours truly,

George Clancy

George Clancy

140 Wenkover Road
Cleveland, Ohio 44112
March 30, 1996

Dear Yvette,

I ran into Dick Smith last week and he suggested I get in touch with you. Gene has been transferred to Dallas, so I decided to leave Pacific Records and try to get a job in that area.

Since I last saw you, I've been promoted to a marketing position but will consider any opportunity in either marketing or sales. I would prefer a job without a lot of travel but will consider any opportunity as long as it is based in the Dallas area.

I'd really appreciate any suggestions you might have that could be helpful in finding a job. If you know of any employment agencies that place sales and marketing people, please let me know about them.

I'm enclosing 6 copies of my résumé. Since I've already given notice, feel free to circulate them as you see fit.

We should be in Dallas by July. I'm looking forward to seeing you and Jim, and once again being neighbors.

Sincerely,

Margo

1400 State Street
Albany, New York 18246

May 15, 1996

Dear Ruth,

As you probably know, Paris Records has been sold to National Records and I've been merged out of a job. Though there are a few possibilities in this area, I think this might be the perfect time for me to relocate to Florida. It would be great to be near my old friends and, as you know, I've always loved the warm weather.

I'm hoping that one of your firms' clients has an opening that fits my qualifications. I'm enclosing several copies of my résumé for you to circulate at your discretion. Should you need more résumés, please let me know.

I'd really appreciate any suggestions you might have that could be helpful in my finding a job. Can you recommend any search firms/agencies that service the financial field?

I plan to be in Ft. Lauderdale in early July, but could fly down earlier if necessary.

I'm really looking forward to seeing you soon and am grateful for anything you might do.

Love,

Marge

7

Winning Interview Techniques

The interview has been set up. Finally the efforts of your job campaign have come to fruition—you have been granted an interview. You know the time, the place, and the importance of doing well. Suddenly you have an attack of nerves. You're both eager and anxious.

How will it go? Will you be able to convince the interviewer that not only can you do the job, but, indeed, you are absolutely the best person for it? You feel a little insecure. Will you be able to articulate your qualifications adequately?

What is happening to you happens to almost every job hunter: You're having a slight case of interview jitters. Don't worry; you're in good company. No matter how high up one is on the corporate ladder, being placed in the proverbial "hot seat" can be an unsettling experience. Our experience, as well as that of our colleagues all over the country, confirms that the great majority of job seekers find the interview the most stressful part of job hunting.

There are ways, however, of lessening that stress. The first step is to view the interview realistically. In most cases, job candidates tend to view the interview as an acid test of their abilities and self-worth. Such an attitude is extremely anxiety producing, and is guaranteed to elicit a negative response from the interviewer. But viewed realistically, the interview is simply a meeting between two equals—a buyer and a seller—to explore what each has to offer. Always keep in mind that feeling of equality between you and the interviewer.

The person conducting the interview is also under pressure. The interviewer must have the judgment to choose the most qualified candidate and must at the same time generate enough enthusiasm about the employer that when an offer is made, it will be accepted. Just as you are in competition with many other applicants, companies recruiting employees are similarly in competition with other employers trying to hire just the right person.

You were asked to be interviewed because some person in the company—an executive, an officer, the personnel director, or another representative of the employer—felt that the company's best interests would be served by knowing more about you. Your résumé generated interest in you. It indicated to them that you are qualified; now they are trying to determine if you are the best qualified.

With this in mind, you must now convince them that it is in their best interests to hire you. You must present yourself in such a manner that your assets and abilities are superior to any other candidate.

We are not surprised to find that the job does not always go to the most qualified person. It is possible to predict with a high degree of reliability which candidates will receive not one, but many job offers. We have analyzed the common denominator, the quality that these winners possess. It is that they give a first impression that projects honesty, sincerity, and enthusiasm. Given several candidates with virtually identical credentials, the job will almost invariably go to the individual projecting the most positive and enthusiastic attitude and image.

The interview, no matter how you describe it, is purely a selling situation and you are the product. Life in general is selling. We are all selling something—an idea to our children, a vacation plan to a spouse, or a special date to a friend.

Besides maintaining a positive attitude, another first goal is to get the interviewer to like you. This can be done by offering a sincere compliment or commenting about the beautiful art work in the lobby or the cordial and helpful receptionist. Do not offer personal compliments. Stay clear of commenting on personal photos on the desk or, if you are a gentleman, the jewelry a female interviewer may be wearing.

Another way to build an immediate friendship with this new person is to drop the names of anyone you both may know or have in common. Name dropping is always effective. It creates friendship and a sense of common ground. Name dropping can and should be used at anytime throughout the interview.

Positive Attitude
✧✧✧

A positive attitude is the single most important quality an individual could have to be successful at an interview. Simply stated, if you think you can't, you won't; and, if you think you can, you will. Your mind is very much like a computer. Are you programming your mind with positive or negative thoughts?

Often I hear individuals make negative comments before going on an interview. You have probably heard them or made similar statements yourself. They sound something like this: "I really don't know why I'm going, they're probably going to hire someone else. It's a waste of my time to even go," or "I'm really worried about this interview, there may be others more qualified than me." The list could go on and on.

Essentially, whatever statements you put in your mind before and during an interview will determine its outcome. There is a computer term that illustrates this point: "G.I.G.O." or garbage in, garbage out! What are you programming your mind with before you go on an interview?

Successful self-selling means you begin your interview at home, where you make positive statements to yourself as well as to family and friends. A winning, positive attitude will sound something like this: "I can do it. I just know I'm going to get this job." or "I'm going to work hard and get ready for this interview. They're going to like me." You can think of hundreds more statements to assure yourself that you have the right attitude to sell yourself with enthusiasm.

Dress Like a Winner
✧✧✧

To have a successful interview you must not only think like a winner but also dress like one. The day before your interview make sure your wardrobe is in order. Make sure your clothes are clean and pressed, and your hair and image are clean and simple.

It has been said many times, "You never get a second chance to make a first impression." Research has shown that people make judgments about others in less than sixty seconds of meeting them. A first impression is comprised of your mannerisms, hair, clothes, jewelry, and perfume or after shave, to mention a few. The best rule of thumb is to stay conservative in all of these areas. Save the trendy look for parties and weekends. In business, you want to draw attention to your skills, not your looks. When you leave an interview you want the interviewer to remember you, not something you were wearing.

Upon Arriving at the Interview
✧✧✧

A good candidate arrives at an interview at least 15 minutes early. When you arrive on time you are actually arriving late! When you arrive early you have arrived in plenty of time to fill out important pre-interview forms and applications.

Besides supplying pre-interview information there are many other benefits to arriving early. First, you arrive relaxed and not preoccupied with traffic and other commuter worries. You are in a better frame of mind to focus on completing a winning interview. Second, you provide yourself time to observe the company, gather valuable information, and rehearse in your mind your exact interview performance, much in the same fashion as an actor rehearses lines in his mind while waiting to go on stage.

Often an interviewer may ask a receptionist or employee who has observed you while you were waiting for their opinion of you. For this reason follow these guidelines when sitting in the waiting area:

Do sit professionally while waiting.

Do not read magazines or newspapers to pass the time.

Do review your prepared questions and interview notes.

Do rehearse your answers to questions you expect to be asked.

Interviewers may or may not offer to shake hands when they approach you in the reception area. Follow their cue and only shake hands if they offer.

Also, interviewers may offer you a cup of coffee or soda. This is a polite and cordial gesture on their part. It is best to refuse by simply stating: "No thank you, I just had a cup before I arrived." We are aware of stories from recruiters who have actually had applicants spill the beverage all over themselves and the desk. More than likely, you may have some stage-fright jitters, so don't add more fuel to the fire! However, it is perfectly acceptable to take coffee at the final interview after an offer has been made and you're more relaxed.

Listening Is Important
◇◇◇◇

Good listening skills are a crucial factor in interviewing successfully. With good listening skills you are able to gather a wealth of information that, when gathered, will give you power. Information always gives power in any situation. Listen for a while before you start blurting out what skills you have and how they will help the company.

Good listening is demonstrated in a number of ways. Maintain good eye contact at all times. It is not necessary to stare the person down, but don't look at the floor either. Take notes. Note taking helps you to remember key bits of information that you will use later in the interview to sell yourself. Note taking also creates a message about you. You appear both reliable and professional. Correct body language will help you to listen. Nodding your head, leaning forward occasionally, and other gestures demonstrate you are concentrating on what the interviewer is saying.

Asking Questions Is Important, Too
◇◇◇◇

Interviewers frequently pay as much attention to the questions candidates ask as to the answers they give. The questions you ask will serve as an indication of how much of the interviewer's information you have understood, and will show your level of competence and sophistication. Listen carefully and ask intelligent questions about the company. Research the company well before the interview. Prepare some good questions based on your research. Bring them to the interview. After all, you are also basing a decision about this job and this company on what you learn at the interview. Turn the interview into a true meeting of equals by politely, but firmly, asking the questions that are important to you.

Formulating good questions is not as easy as it sounds. Questions that gather information are called open-ended questions. An open-ended question is any question that can not be answered with yes or no. This type of question demands information. It is usually formed by beginning with who, what, where, when, how, or why. Some examples would be: "Why do you feel that way? What would be the best way to handle that? Where do we go from here?" etc.

The night before your interview prepare a list of questions you will ask at the interview. A person who asks good questions is perceived as more intelligent than one who has no questions. Here are some sample questions to get you started. Add to the list questions that obviously should be asked, based on the company that has arranged the interview.

SAMPLE QUESTIONS

1. What do you feel are the necessary skills needed to be successful at this position?

2. How have previous employees in this position demonstrated these skills?

3. Tell me more about the orientation and training program that I will initially be given.

4. Is there any formal recurrent or on-going training with this position?

5. Does your company offer tuition reimbursement for further training?

6. When may I see a copy of the job description?

7. What future plans are there for my department? Do you see any major changes coming soon? Will my responsibilities be growing or changing?

8. What are the next steps for advancement and growth from this position?

9. What can you tell me about the turnover ratio typical for this department?

10. What brochures do you have about your company and its compensation and benefits plan?

Add additional questions of your own here. These questions should target precisely the company, position, and situation that has requested the interview.

_____

_____

_____

Questions They Will Ask You

Though every interview is different, all will include questions requiring more than a "yes" or "no" answer. The interviewer will be listening not only for content, but for sincerity, poise, judgment, and the ability to think quickly.

Spend some time before the interview developing answers to the following questions that you think might give you trouble. The night prior to your interview is the time to role-play with a friend, spouse—or even a tape recorder—by going through each question. Going to an interview without some form of rehearsal is like an actor going on stage without practicing the script. Practiced simulation prepares you to demonstrate a confident and composed attitude at the interview. Prepare answers to give extemporaneously. There are no right or wrong answers. The purpose is to find out more about the subjective you. Aim for clarity, brevity, and, above all, honesty. Remember also that the actual wording and substance of these questions will vary to reflect the circumstances of each particular interview. Here is a list of questions frequently asked by interviewers.

1. What do you consider your strong points?
2. What do you consider to be your weak points?
3. What motivates you?
4. What is your definition of success?
5. Describe your previous sales experience.
6. Do you feel there is a difference selling a product versus selling a service?
7. Where would you like your career to be in 5 years?
8. What are your short-term career goals?
9. What kinds of rewards, financial or otherwise, are important to you?
10. How do you get along with your peers?
11. How good are you in motivating people?
12. To what magazines do you subscribe?
13. What newspapers do you read?
14. How do you deal with rejection?
15. What are your hobbies?
16. What is your strategy for keeping yourself motivated?
17. Are you active in community affairs? If so, describe.
18. Why do you want to change jobs?
19. Why are you unemployed?
20. Why do you think you would be an asset to the company?
21. How well do you work under pressure?
22. How do you feel about working overtime?
23. Would you be willing to relocate to one of our branch offices? Would you be willing to travel?
24. How do you feel about working for a woman/man or a younger person?
25. What did you learn in your last position?
26. How did you get along with your boss on your last job?
27. Do you see yourself as a disciplined person? If so, how? If not, why not?
28. Why do you want to work for this company?
29. What do you consider your outstanding achievements?
30. What kinds of problems do you enjoy solving?
31. How often have you been ill in the past 5 years?
32. What is your own personal sales style?
33. Are you willing to take a series of personality tests?
34. Have you ever been fired? If yes, why?

35. Do you have management ability? Describe.

36. How ambitious are you?

37. Have you ever had any formal sales training?

38. What was your last salary? What is your minimum salary at this time?

Salary Negotiation

Do not discuss salary at the first interview, in most circumstances. The interviewer will make it a point to ask you your salary requirements. If it is the first interview, always give an "open" response. Countless individuals have lost job opportunities by answering this question with an exact amount.

Odds are if you state a figure that is considered to be too high, you will appear demanding and over rated. Or conversely, if you state a figure that is too low, you will be perceived as a poor quality performer.

After you state that your salary requirements are open, explain to the interviewer that you have come to the interview with an open mind. Explain further that you believe that the right position with the right benefits would make your salary very negotiable.

Don't make the mistake of going to the first interview and making salary/compensation demands. It shouldn't even be discussed. It is assumed you would not have gone to the interview if you did not feel the position would at least be in the ballpark of your compensation requirements. Discussion of salary and compensation requirements come at the final interview, after a job offer has been made. At this point it has been determined that they want you. What a great feeling it is to be wanted! Now you are in a better position to negotiate.

Never begin salary negotiations until you are quite certain you have a job offer. In fact, always let the employer bring up the subject.

When asked about your present or last compensation package, answer concisely, including all bonuses and benefits. If you feel you were underpaid, mention that as one of the reasons for wanting to change jobs.

If you were referred to an employer by an employment agency or headhunter, it's a good idea to let them do the negotiating for you. Since they are very aware of market conditions and, in effect, will profit from your being hired, they will attack the question of compensation vigorously. Their fee is usually based on a percentage of your salary, so it is in their best interest, as well as yours, to get the highest possible salary. Besides, as mentioned before, it's always helpful to have a third party negotiate for you.

If you are forced to do your own negotiating, stay flexible. If you know what salary range is being offered, put your salary expectations at the high end of the range. Remember, the interview is a screening process; if your requested minimum salary is considerably higher than the employer intends to pay, this could knock you out of the running.

Don't get boxed into a specific figure before you have to. Always talk in $5,000 to $10,000 ranges. If the interview has gone well and you are really interested in the company, aim high and then negotiate. Be sure to get all the relevant information concerning benefits: medical and dental insurance, profit sharing plans, future salary increases, stock options, and so on. Consider all of the above as part of the total salary. If the subject of salary hasn't yet come up, and you are asked about your salary expectations, one approach is to answer the question with one of your own, "I'm glad you brought up the subject of compensation. What is the salary range for this job?" Give the employer a chance to give a figure, and then negotiate from there.

It's a good idea never to make a decision at the interview—whether it's the first, second or third interview. Ask for a few days to think it over.

Thank the employer for the offer and indicate that you will give it serious consideration. Let them know when you will call back with your answer—no longer than a few days or so. Bear in mind that the company will continue interviewing until the job has been filled, so don't delay too long. Give yourself just enough time to weigh any other offers and reflect more thoroughly on this one.

Sample Résumés

O n the following pages you'll see a great many sample résumés. One of them may appeal to you as an example to follow. Even though parts of the samples, especially the job descriptions, may resemble what you wish to express, never copy them verbatim. These samples are included only to give you ideas that you can use to write your own résumé.

Use your completed worksheets, along with the form of the résumé you decide to use, and start writing. You will probably have to rewrite several times before you are completely satisfied with the results. Don't get discouraged!

Be sure to include all the pertinent information, and adhere to basic rules governing presentation and content. Here are some of those rules, the do's of writing a job-getting résumé.

1. Do keep it brief; one, or at the most, two pages.

2. Do choose a chronological style format; list your last or present job first, continuing in reverse chronological order.

3. Do place your name, address, and phone number in a conspicuous position on your résumé.

4. Do make sure your career objective (should you decide to use one) gives your résumé focus and is relevant to your experience and background.

5. Do list all dates of both employment and education history, leaving no unexplained gaps.

6. Do avoid long paragraphs; keep job descriptions under eight lines.

7. Do strengthen your résumé by using implied pronouns and action verbs.

8. Do use 8½ × 11-inch paper, preferably white or light color (beige, cream, buff, gray).

9. Do use one side of the page *only*; if 2 pages are used, be sure the sheets of paper are stapled together and your name is on each page.

10. Do make your résumé visually attractive—use plenty of white space, wide even-spaced margins, and clean crisp type.

11. Do proofread your résumé more than once. Make sure there are no misspellings, grammatical errors, or typos.

Retail Sales and Services

MICHAEL B. COHEN
2234 Beaumont Circle
Boca Raton, Florida 33486
407-355-6543

QUALIFICATIONS SUMMARY:

Vice President of Store Operations for one of the leading retail jewelers in the Southeast United States, with more than fifteen years of broad-based sales/marketing and operations management experience. Responsible for the direction and profitability of 19 Florida stores, with a combined sales, technical and clerical force exceeding 270 employees, and gross annual sales of $100 million.

Expertise in planning and implementation if sales programs and the administration of store operations. Instrumental in formulating and developing the corperation's "University" to train sales force.

PROFESSIONAL EXPERIENCE:

SUISSE JEWELERS, INC., CORAL GABLES, FL   DECEMBER 1983 TO AUGUST 1995
Vice President of Store Operations

- Complete responsibility for all sales and in store marketing activities of 19 stores in Florida.
- Increased company's annual sales volume over 34% since promoted to current position in 1991. Increased net profitability 75% for the same period.
- Restructured management organizational chart, effectuating $200,000 annual payroll savings.
- Assisted in establishing Suisse's "University" sales training program, which successfully developed 14 new store managers and 3 Regional Vice Presidents since 1991 as well as educated all personnel in sales and "total quality customer service."
- Implemented unique, computerized store and individual sales tracking systems.
- Planned and developed innovative "We Care Program" to better anticipate and satisfy customer's needs and promote better customer relations.
- Substantially reduced area's chronic turnover problem by 60%.
- Developed and monitored all store budgets and oversaw training of store managers regarding P & L.
- Functioned as "Task Force" leader to analyze low producing stores and recommend programs to increase profitability.
- Planned and executed special in-store promotional events.
- Prospected new store locations, and planned, organized and directed new store openings.

RICHTERS JEWELERS, ORLANDO, FL   SEPTEMBER 1980 TO NOVEMBER 1983
Store Manager

- Directed all facts of retail store operations for major international jewelry chain.
- Initially employed as trainee and advanced to management after successful sales career.
- Increased store sales 150% in second month as manager, the highest percentage increase in Florida.
- Responsible for setting sales quotas and goals and motivating staff.
- Prepared budgets, payrolls and maintained inventory control.

EDUCATION:

BROOKLYN COLLEGE, BROOKLYN, NY   1976
Bachelor of Arts Degree

Major: History   Minor: Business Administration
Continuing Education:
- G.I.A. Diamond and Diamond Grading Course Graduate

REFERENCES:

Furnished upon request

JEFFREY R. BRENNER
4434 Encino Way
Boca Raton, Florida 33487
407-222-6565

EMPLOYMENT:

March 1993 to November 1994

GOODIE 2 SHOES, INC., Ridgewood, NJ
Sales Manager
- Established retail shoe store and increased annual sales to exceed $300,000 within the first year.
- Developed sales and marketing program and handled direct sales with customers.
- Trained and supervised staff.
- Complete responsibility for financial management and all accounting functions required in day-to-day operations.
- Conducted all merchandise buying and inventory control.

November 1990 to February 1993

JASPR SHOE CORPORATION, Bronx, NY
PAUL'S STRIDE RITE SHOES
Sales Manager
- Total responsibility for operation of a $750,000 footwear corporation.
- Developed strong working relationships with 25 district vendor and distribution operations.
- Purchased merchandise from international markets at trade shows and directly from vendors and suppliers.
- Planned and implemented sales and marketing strategies.

May 1990 to October 1990

DAPCO, INC., New York, NY
Administrative Assistant
- Handled telephone sales.
- Provided administrative support to traders.
- Confirmed trades with buyers.

January 1990

CIGNA, Bloomfield, CT
Internship Spring Semester
- Responsible for generating leads and new accounts.
- Assessed clients' needs for various financial services.
- Acquired training as financial planner.

EDUCATION:

May 1990

UNIVERSITY OF HARTFORD, West Hartford, CT
Bachelor of Science, Business Administration Degree
Major: Management
Activities: Treasurer, Intra-Fraternity Council

SKILLS:

IBM and Compatibles • Macintosh • Excel • WordPerfect

REFERENCES:

Furnished upon request.

MARGIE A. THOMPSON

89 WOODRIDGE ROAD
COLUMBUS, OHIO 43212
APARTMENT A 23
(614)443-7785

EXPERIENCE

August 1988–Present **CERO'S AND KLINES**
Canton, Ohio
Assistant to the Store Manager/Merchandising Hardlines

Redesigned departments including: redefining of classifications, merchandise and fixture presentations resulting in sales increases of 10–20%.

Coordinated the efforts of buyers and display department personnel to achieve aesthetically pleasing, cohesive vignettes representing market trends and store direction. Created more awareness of merchandise presentation and coordination throughout the home furnishings divisions.

June 1986–July 1988 **HOUSE FURNISHINGS, INC.**
Cleveland, Ohio
Buyer/Merchandiser/Coordinator: Accessories

Reduced the resource selection by 60% and increased volume by 15% while opening 50% fewer stores.

Raised the net profitability of department by 35%.

Raised the turnover rate of merchandise in stores from 1.5 to 2.5 times per year via tighter selections, controls and the implementation of an inventory control system.

Within capacity of merchandising consultant to over 250 stores in the area of gifts and accessories, have shopped all major national accessory markets and researched, coordinated and published 5 service manuals that are utilized for resources, merchandise and display techniques.

Directed dealers with designing, merchandising and displaying their in-store gift shops.

January 1983–June 1986 **SUNSHINE DEPARTMENT STORE**
Cleveland, Ohio
Department Manager: Men's Accessories, Candy, Smoke Shop

Reduced personnel budget by 30 hours per week through flexible staffing strategy.

Supervised 25 employees.

Reordered all merchandise sold in departments.

Responsible for all department areas including personnel, housekeeping, displays, merchandising.

EDUCATION

B.S. Business Management, 1983
Bowling Green University

References on Request

Scott Henderson

27 Hudson Street
Oneonta, New York 13820
(607) 226-7482

EXPERIENCE:

1993–Present

Eastern Iron & Steel, Binghamton, N.Y.
SALES REPRESENTATIVE, FIELD SUPERVISOR

Sell energy-related products to home owners, on the basis of good credit. The product line consists of insulation, U.S. Steel aluminum, vinyl siding, U.S. Steel thermopane windows, doors, kitchen remodeling, garages, additions and other energy related items. All sales are done by cold canvassing and the amount of leads received each day. Territory covered is all of Monroe County. Other responsibilities include teaching new employees how to canvass and set up productive appointments for the other salespeople, dropping off deposits at the bank, and picking up supplies for the contractors.

Accomplishments:

- Most productive appointments and leads that resulted in the most sales for the company, 1993 and 1994.
- Three mini-awards for the most productive number of leads and sales for a single week.

1990–1993

Mike's Pizzeria, Delhi, N.Y.
SUPERVISOR IN CHARGE OF DELIVERIES

Delivered food products to homes and businesses. The product consisted of pizza, subs, chicken wings, pasta, etc. Responsibilities included: making sure that the food got to the customer on time and assuring them that their food was hot, making sure that the customers were satisfied with their food, teaching new drivers the delivery route and making sure that they were doing their job.

Accomplishments:

- Broke the record for the most deliveries and the most tips received in one evening ($500 plus). The record still stands.

1987–1990

ABLE'S SANITARY PRODUCTS, INC., SYRACUSE, N.Y.
SALES REPRESENTATIVE

Sold janitorial products to businesses, factories, schools, restaurants, churches, banks, garages, hospitals, nursing homes, town halls, municipal buildings, food plants and more. The product line consisted of the following: floor cleaners, strippers, finishers, gym finish, degreasers, all-purpose cleaners, bowl cleaners, disinfectants, window cleaners, floor machines, and paper products. Territory covered was all of Monroe County, parts of Buffalo, Southern Tier as far south as Corning, west to Warsaw, north country as far north as Plattsburgh. Responsibilities included keeping in touch with every account each month and finding out if they need supplies, to make sure the service was satisfactory, to see if the customer was happy with the product and to answer any questions that they might have.

EDUCATION:

Delhi Regional High School, 1987.

REFERENCES:

Available upon request.

JOHN OATS

17 CLINTON ST. • YONKERS, N.Y. 17821 • (914) 681-4261

WORK EXPERIENCE:

*March 1995 to
January 1996*

Randolph Music, Inc.
Scarsdale, N.Y. 10510

Sales Representative

Sold computerized, remote control, whole-house audio sound systems and services directly to an affluent clientele, as well as the architect and design community by outside selling: phone soliciting, cold canvassing, direct-mail marketing and trade show selling; inside sales: phone-in leads, *New York Times Magazine* coupons, referrals and showroom sales. Directly participated in monthly advertisement meetings for development of *New York Times* and *Architectural Digest* magazine ads and brochure advertising. Average ticket sales: $12,000 to $14,000.

*September 1993 to
March 1995*

Schiller & Sons, Inc.
Ossining, N.Y. 10562

Retail Store Manager and Assistant Buyer

Managed and controlled all store operations, supervision and hiring of union store employees, inventory control, daily store reports and receipts, ordering and buying of store merchandise ranging from infant toys to children's furniture and clothing. Assisted Director of Stores in planning and developing of merchandise, projection of store budgets, expenses and sales, as well as working with company's Advertising and Promotion Division. Worked directly with City Education Department in developing and promoting local day care schools. Yearly sales upon leave—approximately $1 million in sales; $600.00 difference between actual and projected inventory upon leave.

*January 1991 to
September 1993*

Getty Square Liquors, Inc.
Yonkers, N.Y. 10710

Store Manager

Supervised two sales and stock clerks at night, placed orders of wine, responsible for stock and inventory, handled cash receipts at end of night and designed weekly advertisements in local papers, assumed purchasing of selected wines.

EDUCATION:

Graduated in January 1994 from the Fordham College of Business and Public Administration Night School with a B.B.A. degree in Marketing, Specialization in Retail/Sales Management.

COLLEGE ACTIVITIES: Member of American Marketing Association, Fordham College Chapter.

REFERENCES: Furnished upon request.

JOHN GADDARD

61 Dayton Street • Cambridge, Maine 01257 • (615)414-1122

May 1991 to present

SCHNAUZERS & SHEPHERDS INC., Cambridge, Maine
Successfully operating a canine business that specializes in exhibiting schnauzers and a variety of other canine breeds in national competitions throughout the Atlantic States under the auspices of the American Kennel Club. During this period developed an innovative showing methodology producing a winning National Champion within 18 months.

December 1987 to May 1991

MATTHEWS LABORATORIES, INC., Boston, Massachusetts
Full Line Representative. Duties included promotion of all prescription and OTC medications to physicians, hospitals, pharmacies, and wholesale houses. Territory consisted of the greater Boston area with district headquarters in Cambridge. Considered to have excellent rapport with all accounts and physicians. Highly specialized in hypertension and hyperalimentation. Led the Northern region (6 Districts) in selecting and conducting hospital hypertension workshops during 1989.

March 1984 to November 1987

LOFT CANDY CO., Miami, Florida
As Sales Representative for this nationally established confectionary firm, built record of outstanding effectiveness in working with distributors, supermarkets and specialty retailers. Worked vigorously with all accounts to achieve substantial increases in volume and profitability. Among company leaders in opening new accounts. Conceived innovative holiday promotion using demonstrators and increased sales 14%. Adroit presenter and negotiator in dealing with headquarter accounts. Expert in inventory control and stock rotation techniques. Supervised as many as 8 part-time inventory control specialists.

June 1983 to February 1984

NESCOTT DRUG PRODUCTS, INC., Orlando, Florida
As OTC Sales Representative, specialized in introducing and implementing special promotions. Trained dealer personnel in point-of-sale techniques. Coordinated advertising, promotion and displays for drug stores, pharmacies, and distributors from Vero Beach to Key West.

September 1982 to June 1983

U.S. CHAMBER OF COMMERCE, Orlando, Florida
Called on senior corporate executives of major firms as Public Relations and Sales Representative. Successfully presented benefits of Chamber membership and established sound working relationships with many top officers and managers throughout North Florida.

September 1980 to September 1982

WARNER & COMPANY, New York, N.Y.
As Professional Representative for this premier ethical drug firm, promoted a full line of prescription and OTC drugs to physicians, hospitals, and pharmacies. Strong medical/pharmacal orientation, coupled with superb product education and sales training, produced solid achievement record. Consistently excelled in competition with 12-person sales staff. Considered a persuasive communicator, able to win the confidence of physicians and other professional accounts. Effective in introducing new products and services.

EDUCATION   Florida State University. B.S. Marketing, 1973   Post-graduate courses in Marketing

MILITARY SERVICE   Lieutenant, United States Navy, 1973–1979

REFERENCES   References are available upon request.

HARVEY BLACK

4 Saw Mill Road
Jefferson, New York 10952
(914) 452-4178

EDUCATION:
State University of New York at Buffalo, Buffalo, NY
BS Business Administration...Graduated May 1995
➤ FINANCED 50% OF EDUCATION

Key Courses:
Corporate Finance...Business Strategies... Economic Statistics...
Micro Economics...Macro Economics...Securities...Principles of Marketing

Activities:
Intramural Baseball...1993–1995
Club Baseball...1993–1995

EXPERIENCE:

9/93 to 6/95
L.M.S. SALES COMPANY, Buffalo, NY
Owner

Initiated an entrepreneurial venture with two other associates, purchasing, designing graphics, and selling tee shirts to students.
➤ Negotiated with vendors and purchased tee shirts in bulk quantities.
➤ Developed screen-printed designs and logos for shirts.
➤ Generated sales among students, faculty and area residents.

Summers 1992 and 1993
SADDLE RIVER EXXON, Saddle River, NJ
Service Technician
➤ Assisted customers, pumped gasoline and assisted with minor repairs.
➤ Sold accessories and handled cash receipts.
➤ Managed the business in the owner's absence.

Summer 1991
GATE HILL DAY CAMP, Stony Point, NY
Counselor
➤ Worked with groups of children ages 6–8.
➤ Developed and implemented activities.
➤ Assured a positive learning environment.

SKILLS:
WordPerfect; Lotus 1-2-3

REFERENCES:
Excellent references provided upon request

PAULA REINERT

5 Biscayne Street • Smithtown, New York 11787 • (516) 444-3721

– EMPLOYMENT HISTORY–

Amoure, Thompson, and Flaunt Model Management Companies, New York, NY
Model/Actress   *1994/Present*

Work on a per diem basis in various media and fashion showroom settings.

The Donna Karan Company Store, Central Valley, NY
Sales Associate   *1994*

Worked closely with customers in the largest, highest grossing store at Woodbury Commons.

Identified customer needs and offered recommendations regarding styles, colors and outfit pieces.

Processed sales and monetary transactions. Utilized in-house computer program to research merchandise, track inventory and document sales data.

Accomplishments

- Developed solid rapport with customers resulting in repeat sales opportunities and referrals.
- Selected by senior managers to dress windows/mannequins to enhance customer awareness.

Viacom Inc., New York, NY
Administrative Clerk (long-term temporary position)   *Summer 1993*

Fulfilled various position responsibilities and gained a firm understanding of general business functions in a fast-paced corporate environment. Interfaced with individuals at all levels.

Structuretone, Inc., New York, NY
Receptionist   *Summers 1991 & 1992*

Answered and directed calls, scheduled appointments and processed mail for company representatives engaged in the development of interior construction contracts for domestic and international clients.

– EDUCATION, SKILLS AND TRAVEL EXPERIENCE –

- **Marist College,** Poughkeepsie, NY • *Bachelor of Business Administration* - May 1993
  Concentration: International Business
- **Fashion Inst. of Technology,** New York, NY • *Introduction to Business Fashion* - Fall 1994
  Gained in-depth understanding of fashion industry trades, buying, selling, designing, foreign trade/currency, textiles, consumer behavior and entrepreneurial operations.
- **Ealing College,** London, England • *Liberal Arts Courses* - Fall Semester 1990
- **Rockland Community College,** Suffern, NY • *Associates of Arts* - 1991
  Major: Liberal Arts
- **Skills:** *WordPerfect; Windows; MS Word; Lotus 1-2-3; Computer Literate*
- Traveled throughout Europe and the United States

REFERENCES WILL BE FURNISHED UPON REQUEST

HENRY O'CONNER

145-96 Smart Street
Chicago, Illinois 60698

(312) 598-9987 – Home　　　　　　　　　　　　　　　　　(312) 598-4217 – Work

PROFESSIONAL EXPERIENCE:

CHEMICAL BANK OF CHICAGO
Chicago, Illinois

6/95–1/96

MANAGER – TREASURY MARKETING UNIT

Handled corporate clients' Eurodollar investments and foreign exchange transactions. Promoted interest rate hedges and assisted in the development of new products. Coordinated the investigation and design of an automated information service.

8/93–5/95

NATIONAL EXPRESS, INC.
Chicago, Illinois

SALES EXECUTIVE – MEXICO, CENTRAL AMERICA AND CARIBBEAN

Sold computerized business information services to financial institutions, corporations and private investors in this region. Increased sales in my territory by 26% in less than one year. Carried out negotiations which prevented the loss of $200,000 worth of contracts. Planned and placed news releases and advertisements for distribution to specific target audiences. Instrumental in establishing price structures and forecasting sales. Created and implemented new products to serve special market needs.

6/91–7/93

AMERICAN OPTICAL CO.
Chicago, Illinois

MARKETING REPRESENTATIVE

Promoted software consulting and training services to data processing professionals. Developed a marketing program to penetrate a new region and tripled sales leads through a direct mail campaign and local advertising. Generated thousands of dollars of business in an 11-month period.

LANGUAGE:　　English/Spanish

EDUCATION:

University of Chicago, Chicago Illinois
B.S., Marketing – May 1991

Universidad de Seville, Spain
Overseas Academic Program – 1990

REFERENCES:　　On request.

JERRY FULTON

2106 The Birches   407-527-9919
Roslyn Estates, New York 11577

SALES • PRODUCTION • MANAGEMENT

Business Professional with more than fourteen years of diversified background, encompassing sales, production management and property management.

More than nine years of successful sales experience in new automobiles, with an additional five years as production manager for a large paper bag manufacturing company. Background also includes experience as Property Manager for commercial real estate holdings.

ACCOMPLISHMENTS:

Sales

- ◆ Consistently performed as one of the top producers in various auto dealerships, including Suburu, Chevrolet, Acura and Lexus.
- ◆ Promoted to Assistant Sales Manager of high-volume Acura agency, with responsibility for supervision, training and motivation of sales force.
- ◆ Proven skills and ability in the latest marketing techniques, including needs assessments, client profile evaluations, referral generations and commitment strategies.
- ◆ Strong aptitude in direct client contact and closing sales.
- ◆ Consistently achieved, or surpassed, established sales objectives and quotas.
- ◆ Fully knowledgeable about the auto sales business, including leasing.
- ◆ Responsible for inventory control and coordinating dealer trades.
- ◆ Complete familiarity with pricing, financing and negotiations.

Production Manager

- ◆ Complete responsibility for production operation of multimillion-dollar paper bag manufacturer, employing over 300 people.
- ◆ Scheduled production and coordinated materials, machinery and labor to assure availability of finished goods as required.
- ◆ Direct supervision and training of more than seventy employees, including two department heads and three foremen.
- ◆ Set production standards according to order volume and delivery dates.
- ◆ Purchased raw materials and maintained inventory.
- ◆ Overhauled manual production system to a new automated computerized program.
- ◆ Wrote procedural manual for operating new system.
- ◆ Successfully overcame employees' foreign language barrier by automatically translating all memos and instructions from English to Spanish.
- ◆ Created and set up all forms for production control.
- ◆ Substantial experience resolving both technical and nontechnical problems.
- ◆ Sent to Chicago to set up operations for branch facility purchased by company.

Property Manager

- ◆ Responsible for management of commercial property.
- ◆ Obtained tenants and negotiated leases.
- ◆ Oversaw maintenance and repairs.
- ◆ Performed all necessary financial functions for day-to-day business operations.
- ◆ Extensive contact with tenants to provide services and resolve problems.

WORK EXPERIENCE:

AUTOMOBILE SALES: 1986 to Present

Lexus Of Smithtown, St. James, NY
Sales and Leasing Consultant

Acura Of Roslyn, Roslyn, NY
Assistant Sales Manager

William Pape Chevrolet, Huntington Station, NY
Assistant Sales Manager

Majestic Chevrolet, Freeport, NY
Sales and Leasing Consultant
Estimator for bids on government sales

Bayview Nissan, West Babylon, NY
Sales and Leasing Consultant

Long Island City Subaru, Long Island City, NY
Trainee – Sales

PRODUCTION: 1981 to 1986

Canover Industries, Maspeth, NY
Production Manager

PROPERTY MANAGEMENT: 1984 to 1994

J.L. Properties, New York, NY
Manager

GOVERNMENT EMPLOYMENT: 1978 to 1981

Federal Aviation Administration
Air Traffic Control Specialist

RETAIL SALES: 1976 to 1978

Mays Department Stores, Brooklyn, NY
Assistant Manager – Department Manager – Management Trainee

MILITARY SERVICE:

U.S. AIR FORCE   1968 to 1972

Air Traffic Control Specialist   *Rank: Sergeant*
Service in Vietnam

EDUCATION:

C.W. Post College, Greenvale, NY   1976
Bachelor of Arts Degree
Major: Psychology/Management

REFERENCES:

Available upon request.

CAROL SMITH

41 Albany Street • Harrison, New York 10952
914-455-5521

WORK EXPERIENCE

1987–Present

PRUDENTIAL SERVICE CORP.
Paramus, New Jersey

Financial Consultant, Financial Center Division (December 1990–present)
- Managed clients through consultative selling and financial planning techniques to match investor needs with Dreyfus products.
- Performed all sales and servicing for shareholders interested in mutual funds, fixed and variable annuities, retirement plans and/or individual securities.
- Increased client base through referrals, seminars, appointments and telephone activity.
- Maintained Top Three status among Financial Consultants for four consecutive years out of approximately 100 nationwide.

Awards: Received Financial Consultant Sales Achievement award for the four years in the division.

Unit Sales Manager, Telemarketing Division (November 1989–November 1990)
- Responsible for overseeing group of ten representatives in Telemarketing Division by monitoring sales calls to ensure quality and improve sales results.
- Held meetings to motivate and educate staff on Dreyfus products and economic issues.

Evaluated performances and gave merit raises accordingly.

Sales Representative, Telemarketing Division (April 1987–November 1989)
- Generated sales of mutual funds through outbound telemarketing only.
- By using needs based selling, probing techniques and persistency became the Number One salesperson for two consecutive years (out of approximately forty representatives).

Awards: Received Sales Achievement awards for two years.

1985–1987

GARY GOLDBERG AND COMPANY
Suffern, New York

Executive Sales Assistant (September 1985–March 1987)
- Handled day-to-day transactions for Executive Vice President of financial planning company.

Responsibilities included qualifying sales leads, processing mutual fund business, taking security trades and servicing clients.

LICENSES

- NASD series 7 and 63
- Life Insurance License

EDUCATION

OSWEGO UNIVERSITY
Oswego, New York

Bachelor of Science in Business Management, May 1984
- Graduated Cum Laude

REFERENCES

Furnished upon request

CHARLES F. ALDRICH

421 N.W. Poinciana St.
Boca Raton, Florida 33432
407-333-9087

EXPERIENCE:

BDT FINANCIAL RESOURCES INC., Boca Raton, FL *September 1993–Present*
Vice President – Sales
- Organized, structured and managed the operations of this subsidiary owned by the Genett Group of Valhalla, NY, a holding company employing over 500 people.
- Successful in arranging financing for small to medium size businesses for all levels.
- Negotiated extensively with banks and other financial institutions.
- Obtained commercial mortgages.
- Conceived and implemented financial plans on a short or long term basis.
- Coordinated all accounting records and books.

BDT REALTY GROUP INC., Boca Raton, FL – Valhalla, NY *July 1991–August 1993*
Salesman
- Initiated and managed this division in conjunction with BDT Financial Resources.
- Reported directly to the President and CEO in Valhalla, NY.
- Provided consultant expertise in business management and financing.
- Developed packages and closed sales in commercial real estate.
- Full responsibility for all facets of operation.

SUPERIOR INVESTMENT PROPERTIES, INC., Boca Raton, FL *January 1991–June 1991*
Salesman
- Engaged in sale of memberships to effectuate resort and hotel acquisitions.
- Successfully pioneered leads, and followed up to close sales.

CENTURY 21, INTOWN HOME CENTER INC. *January 1990 to November 1990*
Salesman
- Organized, developed and managed commercial real estate department.
- Initiated and managed new business brokerage department.
- Strong client contact.
- Developed strong closing ability.

EDUCATION:

NOVA UNIVERSITY, Ft. Lauderdale, FL *1988*
Bachelor of Science Degree Candidate
   Major: Legal Studies
   Minor: Business Administration
   Activities: • Treasurer, Student Government for 2 years
            • Election Committee Chairman
            • Founder and 1st President of the Business Club

LICENSES:

Florida Real Estate Sales Associate.

REFERENCES:

Furnished upon request.

PETER CHEUNG

32 Burton School Avenue
Westport, CT 06880
(203) 226-7721
(203) 226-2124

AREAS OF MAJOR EXPERIENCE:

Sales/Marketing:

- Sell 403(b) Tax-Sheltered Annuities, Individual Retirement Accounts, as well as a portfolio of life insurance products to prospective clients. Prepare specific proposals and presentations, providing technical information. Review and advise on insurance and retirement objectives.
- Sold life and health insurance plans to the public; one of top 10 new agents in Northeast region.
- Develop brochures and promotional materials for sales campaigns.
- Determine new markets for increasing sales.

Management:

- Supervised staff to ensure smooth functioning of department serving 700 clients.
- Established liaison with outside agencies and represented organization to the public.

WORK HISTORY:

10/89 to Present	**SALES REPRESENTATIVE** **Academic Pension Fund** Darien, CT
12/88–10/89	**FIELD REPRESENTATIVE** **State Farm Insurance** Westport, CT
7/78–12/86	**CASEWORKER AND ACTING SUPERVISOR** **Connecticut Dept. of Social Services** **Special Services for Children** Westport, CT

EDUCATION:

Cornell University, MBA, major in Marketing, 1988
University of Connecticut, Bachelor of Science, 1978

REFERENCES:

Available upon request.

DOROTHY TURNER

415 Oak Street • Russell, Minnesota 55169 • (612)112-6540

SUMMARY: Extensive experience in Retail Sales, and understanding of retail operations; merchandising, co-op advertising, dating, end displays, off-shelf displays, end caps, arranging for newspaper ads, tear sheets, slicks, in-store promotions, and all aspects of Retail Sales Promotions— Store, and Chain wide, plus Professional Medical Sales, Hospitals, and Industrial experience.

- Extensive sales experience, working with all people in various retail sales situations, including clerk in-store promotions, point-of-purchase promotions, and special shelf-talker promotions.
- Extensive contact with Drug Wholesalers and Chain Drug Store Headquarters located throughout the thirteen Western States.
- Met Sales objectives set by Regional and Upper Management.

EXPERIENCE:

5/95–Present Burton Drug Co., Inc., St. Paul, Minnesota

Regional Marketing Sales Representative – Responsible for selling and marketing computers to pharmacy of Burton Drug Company and others. Following up on leads provided by Burton and mailers, to qualify customers for our Computer Systems. Calling for business by telecommunications.

7/94–10/94 Rosch Laboratories, Akron, Ohio

Western Region Sales Manager, Sales Marketing Division – Responsible for maintaining contact with Drug Wholesalers, Chain Drug Store Headquarters Accounts, and attending Drug Wholesale Sales Shows for Western Region and, where necessary, the Eastern U.S. upon request from Upper Management.

To develop sales materials for potential sales force for United Research Laboratories, Inc.

12/92–7/94 Bell Medical Laboratories, Akron, Ohio

Sales Representative, Marketing Division – Responsible for selling service and implementing Sales/Marketing Programs for all consumer items to major existing or potential accounts within the specified territorial boundaries.

To develop, maintain and expand good working professional relationships with Lay Diabetic Groups and Professional Association in the field of Diabetes.

1/84–5/92 Charles Laboratories, Lincoln, Nebraska

Sales Representative, Marketing Division – Responsible for preparing sales presentation to physicians, retail accounts, hospital clinics, and industrial accounts as directed by immediate supervisor.

Duties included generating sales gains on company ethical drugs, and retail products that were allocated for sales promotions.

EDUCATION:

1984–1987
1996

University of Minnesota – Associate of Arts Degree, Business Administration. In process of completing four-year Degree, Business Administration. Completion date approximately January 1997.

OUTSIDE INTERESTS:

Politics – Represented the City of Russell as Councilwoman from April 1991 to April 1995. Also Vice Mayor for two years. Other activities include camping, fishing and traveling.

REFERENCES: Available upon request.

HAROLD J. DONALDS

170 Seymore Street
Nashville, Tennessee 37204
(615) LO-3-5341

BUSINESS EXPERIENCE:

**September 1995
to present**

E.R. VICK COMPANY-PHARMACEUTICAL DIVISION
Nashville, Tennessee

Pharmaceutical Sales Representative

Responsibilities include pharmaceutical sales to physicians, hospitals, and retail pharmacies. Medical instrument sales to hospitals. Territory management includes work and travel scheduling, materials management, sales forecasting, and creation and analysis of various sales and market research reports. Lead and attend sales meetings and sales training seminars. Group presentations and public relations assignments.

Accomplishments:
➤ Exceeded quota for 3 consecutive years, increasing territory sales by 45%.
➤ Top Performers Award – 1994 and 1995.
➤ District Medical Instrument Sales Coordinator – October 1996 to present.

**March 1994
to September 1995**

CARNEGIE NURSING HOME
Nashville, Tennessee

Assistant Director of Pharmacy Services

Responsibilities included pharmacy purchases, inventory, and distribution for facility's 499 Beds (S.N.F. Beds). Created and implemented a new pharmacy ordering, stocking, storage, and distribution system. Aided in daily pharmacy operations, staff scheduling, and hiring.

**December 1992
to March 1994**

NEPRA DRUGS, INC.
Miami, Florida

Pharmacist

**August 1991
to December 1992**

Pharmacy Intern

**September 1990
to August 1991**

DAYTON PHARMACY, INC.
Miami, Florida

Pharmacy Intern

**May 1988
to September 1990**

FASHION IN PARTS INC.
New York, New York

Assistant to Director of Operations

EDUCATION:

15 Continuing Education Credits in Finance/Management
Bachelor of Science in Pharmacy—January 1993
Miami College of Pharmacy and Health Sciences, Miami University, Miami, Florida

Honors Diploma—June 1988
Brooklyn Technical High School

PROFESSIONAL LICENSE:

Registered Pharmacist—State of Florida—September 1993

REFERENCES:

Upon request

ANDREW WAXMAN

710 DEVOE STREET
NOVATO, CALIFORNIA 94917

HOME (415) 789-4414
WORK (415) 234-9000

EXPERIENCE:

Burke-Meadow, Inc., Novato, California   *June 1991 to Present*
AGENT/COMMERCIAL SALES

Develop sales/listings of multiple-unit investment properties valued at $300,000 to $2.3 million; utilize computer to generate cash flow/appreciation projections; consult with buyers/sellers on tax liability of real estate transactions; investigate financing options with loan brokers to meet needs of clients; manage investment properties.

Futtermas & Sons, Inc., Novato, California   *April 1987 to June 1991*
AGENT/RESIDENTIAL SALES

Organized/managed seven syndications involving multiple partners and properties valued at $3 million to $5 million; marketed partnership shares; coordinated all legal requirements; created viable solutions for buyers/sellers in depressed market of 1988–1990.

Ures Brothers, Inc., Albany, New York   *October 1985 to April 1987*
NORTHERN CALIFORNIA DISTRICT REP

Managed dealership accounts of leading wholesale and retail dental supply companies and laboratories in Northern California; exceeded set sales goal by 20%; monitored product development and market needs.

Barrons, Inc., San Francisco, California   *December 1981 to October 1985*
SENIOR TRAVEL DIRECTOR

Participated in sales presentations and directed inspection trips of proposed destinations for major clients (Datsun, Xerox, Hormel, Olympia Brewing Co., International Harvester, Dodge, Chrysler, Plymouth); provided liaison between clients and hotels, airlines, tour companies, etc.

Wells Fargo Bank, San Francisco, California   *March 1980 to October 1981*
TRUST ADMINISTRATOR

Administered Corporate Pension and Profit Sharing Trusts in compliance with bank policy and legal regulations.

MILITARY:

United States Marine Corps   *March 1975 to November 1979*
CAPTAIN – Honorably Discharged
ASSISTANT LOGISTICS OFFICER (S-4) for 1st Marine Brigade, Company Commander, Combat Trust Company, South Vietnam.

EDUCATION:

BBA – Economics, U.C.L.A., Los Angeles, California 1974

REFERENCES:

Available upon request.

Sandra Nurenberg

400 East 77th Street, Apt. 2625
New York, NY 10162
(212) 734-2648

SUMMARY: Wholly knowledgeable of the travel industry. Experience includes positions in sales and sales promotion in varied phases of the industry. Have lived, worked and traveled in Europe, Latin America, Asia, Africa and 40 of the 50 United States (including Alaska and Hawaii), providing priceless first-hand knowledge about much of the world.

RELEVANT EXPERIENCE:

1992–1996 INTERNATIONAL WOMEN'S CLUB OF COPENHAGEN, Copenhagen, Denmark
President

- ▶ Founded the organization in 1992; founded club magazine in 1993
- ▶ Responsible for all financial affairs of the organization; raised in excess of $300,000 for philanthropic purposes
- ▶ Worked with embassies, tourist offices and airlines to arrange monthly programs and philanthropic projects throughout the world
- ▶ Organized and arranged all tours throughout Scandinavia and Eastern Europe
- ▶ Chaired meetings of 10-member board and monthly meetings for 250 general members; addressed various organizations and associations regarding functions of club
- ▶ Sold 90% of all advertising to, and received donations from, major international corporations and organizations
- ▶ Coordinated editing, proofreading and layout of magazines with staff and printers
- ▶ Wrote press releases for use on TV and radio and in magazines and newspapers

1990–1992 AMERICAN WOMEN'S CLUB IN DENMARK, Copenhagen, Denmark
President

- ▶ Functions similar to those performed with International Women's Club
- ▶ Worked with universities and foundations in Denmark and United States to further club's scholarship program
- ▶ As a member of Danish-American Anniversary Committee, coordinated activities with Danish Foreign Affairs Office
- ▶ Personally presented club's book to the Queen of Denmark prior to her departure for the United States to attend Anniversary
- ▶ Raised funds for and assisted in planning of Bicentennial student group tour of United States, including housing

1987–1988 ECOLE SUPERIEURE D'AFFAIRES et de SECRETARIAT, Brussels, Belgium
Business English Lecturer

- ▶ Taught American business techniques from letter composition to filing systems to 80 women students from 16 countries
- ▶ Gave private consultations to individual students and to interested employers

1985–1986	BELTZ WORLD TOURS, San Francisco, CA

Travel Consultant

- ► Met with retail accounts and individual clients and formulated plans and made arrangements for transportation, hotel accommodations and tours for business and pleasure
- ► Sold Asian travel packages including cruises and steamship lines
- ► Top sales representative for three consecutive months with fewest cancellations
- ► Travelled extensively to Europe and Latin America; coordinated tours with competitive travel agencies

1984–1985   JAPAN EXTERNAL TRADE ORGANIZATION, Chicago, IL

Administrative Assistant

- ► Supervised Chicago showrooms and displays
- ► Arranged special promotions and exhibits for trade shows, state fairs and exhibitions in the Midwest promoting Japanese products
- ► Hired personnel to work special exhibits
- ► Worked with management of various hotels in setting up conferences, banquets and receptions
- ► Created, administered and arranged for public reaction questionnaires to be given out to people viewing products and exhibits
- ► Worked special assignments in Tokyo, Osaka and Vienna

1982–1984   NORTHWEST ORIENT AIRLINES, Chicago, IL

Reservation Sales/Service Agent

- ► Processed reservations and tickets for domestic and international flights; maintained passenger manifests
- ► Handled cancellations; investigated passenger complaints

1977–1982   HERTZ CORPORATION, Chicago, IL

Station Manager

- ► Supervised twelve employees
- ► Coordinated all office procedures including processing monthly accounts, acquisition of office supplies and equipment with the main office

EDUCATION: Northwestern University, Evanston, IL
1979-1980: Liberal Arts/European History

Loyola University, Chicago, IL
1980-1981: Liberal Arts/European History

Florence Utt Business School, Indianapolis, IN
1976-1977: Business Administration

LANGUAGES: Danish, German, French (read and write)

REFERENCES: Available upon request

George Halkiades

100-55 77 DRIVE . FOREST HILLS, NY 11375 . (212) 896-3275

SUMMARY:

More than ten years' experience in retail/customer service management with four years definitive experience in full management responsibility and accountability. Skilled in selection of merchandise to attract local customers, merchandising and cost control. Creative in traffic-stopping displays and promotion with keen eye to profitability. Excellent in customer and employee relations.

HIGHLIGHTS OF PROFESSIONAL EXPERIENCE:

Current   MAXI-DISCOUNT DRUGS, Richmond Hill, NY

Manager

- Solved problem of confusion over price changes by proposing price-coding system to be circulated to managers of eight stores in chain
  - Proposal adopted by general management has developed into orderly presentation of imminent price changes on merchandise to allow all store managers a method to put changes into effect simultaneously

- Developed creative merchandising plan for Christmas sales
  - Proposed codification of Christmas display set-up to enable local managers to effect same or similar merchandising displays
  - Personally supervised set-up for five of the eight stores
  - Through grouping of Christmas items for easy access, merchandise is moving well in every store in chain with profitable outlook anticipated

1984–1991   F.W. WOOLWORTH COMPANY

Manager – Rego Park, NY (1989–1991)

- Developed, instigated and maintained fluid merchandising policy to meet the demands of a changing neighborhood
  - Stocked merchandise to attract different ethnic groups
  - Improved profit picture to turn around operation that was scheduled for closing

- Recommended removal of lunch/fountain operation which was losing money through poor sales and high maintenance costs
  - Instituted expansion of horticultural, shoe and hosiery departments that produced large increases for the year (25% to 50%)

- Initiated merchants' committee of forty local store managers to install special Christmas lighting to improve night traffic, which had declined considerably over four-year period
  - Night business showed large increase over previous year with minimal cost to all concerned

(continued)

F.W. WOOLWORTH (Continued)

Manager – Rye, NY (1988–1989)

- Hired dynamic individual to replace retiring operator of lunch fountain that had been steadily losing sales over long period
  – Lengthened hours of operation; hired additional, competent help
- Developed reputation of being "the place to eat" in Rye, especially at breakfast; sales took upward turn and increased dramatically

Positions of Increasing Responsibility – Various Stores (1984–1988)

- Was accepted into Management Trainee program, which included training in merchandising, office procedures, lunch operations and overall management of store
- Was steadily promoted to Assistant Manager, Advanced Assistant Manager and Specialized Assistant Manager prior to official appointment as Manager of Rye store

1980–1984 GLATT TRAVEL, Hicksville, NY

Tour Coordinator

- Managed arrangements for world-wide tours of 20–30 people
  – Scheduled tours; booked members into hotels; dealt directly with carriers for most timely and economical travel accomodations
- Interacted with people at all levels on a one-to-one basis
- Booked in excess of $20,000 per year in general and customized tours

EDUCATION:

Queens College, Flushing, NY
1980 – Majored in History

REFERENCES:

Available upon request

EDWARD BARTLESVILLE

20 Lincoln Plaza • New York, NY 10023

Home: (212) 247-9827   *Office:* (718) 475-5070

SUMMARY:

Ten years' retail management experience with rapid and consistent record of growth and advancement. Conceptual and creative approach to marketing and merchandising. Sound long- and short-range planning skills. Astute motivator with ability to identify and maximize talent of subordinates.

PROFESSIONAL EXPERIENCE:

1993 to Present   **FEDERATED STORES CORPORATION, Brooklyn, NY**
Director of Merchandise Marketing

➤ Advise top management regarding incorporation of innovative marketing strategies and concepts for all 6 divisions of $600 million corporation

➤ Develop marketing programs to reposition corporation as necessary

- Created 120-store test to analyze customer buying patterns for purposes of maximizing inventory investment (testing validated program implementation in all 489 stores)

- Initiated and implemented merchandise line plan to fully develop previously non-formalized corporate policy (concept to be layered into organization as basis for focusing merchandise purchase in second and third quarters of 1994)

1987 to 1993   **SAKS FIFTH AVENUE, New York, NY**
Senior Vice President   **General Merchandise Manager, Sportswear and Intimate Apparel (1991–1993)**

➤ As member of Executive Committee and Management Board, participated fully in all marketing and merchandising decisions for $500 million organization

➤ Generated 22% volume increase ($102 million to $125 million) and 1.2% gross margin increase (46.3% to 47.5%) through restructuring and redefinition of planning, merchandising, marketing, merchandise distribution, and training and development operations

- Trained, developed and managed 5 divisional merchandise managers and 21 buyers to achieve their professional goals, as well as company objectives

Vice President   **Divisional Merchandise Manager, Intimate Apparel (1990–1991)**

➤ Supervised planning, management, merchandising and marketing operations of $25 million business to achieve annual gross margin objective

➤ Improved division profit ranking from tenth to first (out of 17 divisions) by broadening customer base, reorganizing resource structure and developing effective marketing strategies

➤ Generated 26% sales volume increase ($20 million to $25 million) and 2.1% gross margin increase (49.0% to 51.1%)

Divisional Vice President   **Managing Director, Branch Store**
                                       Fairlane Mall, Detroit, MI (1989–1990)

➤ Assumed total responsibility for start-up and opening of individual store
  - Led and managed all areas (merchandising, operations, personnel and inter-community relations) to achieve sales volume and profit objectives
  - Trained, developed and managed Assistant Managing Director, 6 operational Department Managers, 13 merchandising Department Managers
  - Established environment of full employee input preparatory to store opening, keeping motivation and morale at optimum levels
➤ Generated $14 million in sales volume and 2.6% pre-tax profit during first year of operation

Divisional Merchandise Manager   **Men's Clothing, Boys' Clothing and**
                                       Furnishings divisions (1987–1989)

_1984 to_   **BLOOMINGDALE'S, New York, NY**
_1987_   **Group Manager**   **Men's Sportswear and**
                                              Designer Sportswear (1986–1987)

➤ Promoted from two Buyer positions after starting as Staff Assistant to Divisional Merchandise Manager in 1984

EDUCATION:

SOUTHERN METHODIST UNIVERSITY

_1984_ – M.B.A., Major: Marketing
_1983_ – B.A., Major: History; Minor: Economics
        Dean's List, 8 semesters
        Sigma Phi Epsilon Fraternity

REFERENCES:

Furnished upon request

JAY OLIVER

---

685 Summer Street
Austin, Texas 78745

---

(512) 963-4434 Home • (512) 968-4893 Office

PROFESSIONAL EXPERIENCE

8/93–8/96   **Barton & Sills, Co.**, Houston, Texas
Executive & Corporate Services Department
Account Executive/Research Coordinator

Developed corporate relationships with officers, directors and 10% holders of
public corporations and facilitated trades of large blocks of stock on their behalf
under Rule 144 and 145. Assisted in the financial management of the proceeds
from these transactions.

Researched initial public offerings, mergers and acquisitions and leveraged
buyouts for individual stockholders valued at $5 million or more.

5/92–8/93   **Moore & McBride, Inc.**, Dallas, Texas
Prospecting/Sales Coordinator

Initiated a prospecting program for Rule 144 sales and stock repurchase
programs.

Responsible for facilitating trades, research and operations.

2/88–9/88   **Doyle & DuBois Advertising, Co.**, Dallas, Texas
Account Clerk

Worked with ten radio and television media buyers. Balanced daily disbursement
with computer printout. Audited television and radio invoices for payment.

EDUCATION

7/95–8/96   **Baylor University, Houston**, Texas
M.B.A., Degree in Marketing, 1996.

Summer 1992   **Columbia University**, New York, New York
Graduate courses in Labor Management.

1988–1992   **Emerson College**, Boston, Massachusetts
B.A., Sociology and Psychology. Related courses in Organizational Behavior.

REFERENCES   On request

JOHN STONE

222 Jefferson Avenue • Boca Raton, Florida 33487 • 407-721-0089

• SALES • BUSINESS MANAGEMENT •

Entry-level candidate for Sales or Executive/Management training; educational background in Business Management.

Brief experience in administrative capacity for large commercial building construction company, with demonstrated ability to successfully handle diverse responsibilities and communicate effectively with people at all levels.

SUMMARY OF QUALIFICATIONS:

- Exposure and capabilities in a variety of related areas, including research, project planning, organization, implementation and management.
- Strong communication and interpersonal skills; conducted informational seminars to educate employees on health and safety programs.
- Personnel supervisory experience.

EXPERIENCE:

COMCO CONSTRUCTION, INC., FT. LAUDERDALE, FL   *April 1995 to August 1995*
Project Administrator/Safety Officer
- Organized and put into place a new "Drug Free Workplace" program for the company.
- Researched details and attended seminars to acquire expertise to develop effective program, which resulted in a 17% Workers' Compensation Insurance premium reduction.
- Conducted meeting and seminars to educate employees.
- Implemented systems and procedures for drug testing of new employees.
- Promoted to Safety Officer as a result of program's success.
- Developed and implemented safety standards to comply with OSHA standards and regulations.
- Supervised 20 employees in absence of Project Manager.
- Received three salary increases within a brief period of time for outstanding performance.

BOCA ALE HOUSE, BOCA RATON, FL   *September 1994 to April 1995*
Waiter
- Temporary position after graduation
- Serviced and attended to the needs of customers.

EDUCATION:

LYNN UNIVERSITY, BOCA RATON, FL   1994
Bachelor of Business Management Degree

PART-TIME AND SUMMER POSITIONS TO ASSIST WITH COLLEGE EXPENSES:

NORTH HALEDON TREE SERVICE, NORTH HALEDON, NJ   *Summers 1992–1994*
- Foreman of crew; trained new employees
- Operated and maintained equipment.

JAMES SCANLON PLUMBING AND HEATING, MAHWAH, NJ   *Summers 1989–1991*
- Plumber's Assistant.

HARTZ MOUNTAIN INDUSTRIES, FRANKLIN LAKES, NJ   *Summers 1986–1988*
- Mechanic Apprentice.
- Operated heavy equipment; Performed Administrative support functions, including scheduling, preparation and maintenance of reports.

COMPUTER PROFICIENCY: IBM • WordPerfect • Lotus 1-2-3

REFERENCES: Furnished upon request

Manufacturer's Representatives and Wholesale Trade

ARNOLD JOHNSON

517 Balsam Boulevard
Hyattsville, New York 10965
(914) 415-5177

EXPERIENCE:

8/91 to Present **FOLSOM & BROWN, INC.,** Englewood, NJ
Sales Associate
- Promoting sales of Municipal Bonds by serving as intermediary between dealers and dealer banks.
- Receiving bids and posting bidders on various bid wanteds.
- Arranging Municipal Bond swaps with dealers.
- Managing and selling forty existing accounts while prospecting for new ones.
- Interfacing with many professionals who each have more than twenty years in various areas of the Municipal Bond market.
- Completed an in-depth sales training program (4 months) learning all aspects of the brokerage industry.

– PRIOR EMPLOYMENT EXPERIENCE –

Worked Summers and Holidays all through college to earn money for expenses. Employment included positions as *Assistant to the Foreman* (Summers 1989, 1990, 1991) with Local #46 of the Carpenters' Union; and *Sales Associate* (Summers 1987, 1988) selling cars and trucks for Croton Dodge.

EDUCATION:

University of Cincinnati, Cincinnati, OH
BA Economics...Graduated July 1991

Key Courses: Money & Banking...International Monetary and Financial Management... Fiscal Policy...Statistics...International Economy...Quantitative Analysis... Business Regulations...Computer in Business
Research Project: Comparison Between U.S. Currency & Japanese Yen

Activities: *Varsity Baseball & Varsity Football (Full Athletic Scholarship – both sports)*
AADD – Athletes Against Drunk Drivers
Hospital Volunteer

REFERENCES:

Excellent references provided upon request.

FRANCES McCARTHY

422 Elizabeth Drive
Spring Valley, NY 10549
914-717-9919

SUMMARY OF QUALIFICATIONS

- 13 years of experience in employee benefits communication, administration and planning
- 3 years of experience in medical software sales
- Excellent organizational and communication skills
- Extensive business experience from clerical positions to running a company
- MS in Adult Education and Human Resource Development

PROFESSIONAL ACHIEVEMENTS

HEALTHCARE:

- Administered health and welfare, 401(k) and pension benefits for 430 employees
- Designed and implemented monthly health education and screening programs
- Coordinated HMO mailings to 5,000 employees and reviewed HMO contracts
- Wrote copy for benefit brochures, summary plan descriptions and employee handbook
- Analyzed monthly costs for health and welfare plans
- Responsible for inside sales of medical software to oral surgeons and plastic surgeons

SALES & MARKETING:

- Qualified leads and set up sales demonstration trips for outside representatives
- Increased the number of monthly software sales by nearly 50%
- Arranged participation in 20–30 annual trade shows
- Expanded sales through direct-mail campaigns, telemarketing and cold calls
- Drafted sales training manual
- Assistant editor of full-color holiday catalog and annual product catalog
- Maintained database of over 15,000 doctors

OFFICE MANAGEMENT:

- Managed 2 employees in telephone sales of medical software
- Supervised 2 employees in benefits administration
- Co-owner of retail business with annual sales of $200,000 and responsible for all bookkeeping and accounting functions
- Prepared all monthly sales/travel reports and annual travel budget of $250,000

COMPUTER SKILLS:

- IBM compatible computers, printers, modems
- WordPerfect, Access, Word, Windows '95
- Custom databases

EMPLOYMENT HISTORY

3/92–5/95	Micro-Designs Software Ridgefield, Connecticut	*Sales Coordination Manager*
11/89–3/92	ABCO Distributors Monsey, New York	*Marketing/Market Research*
4/88–11/89	Interior Expressions, Inc. Mahwah, New Jersey	*President*
9/82–4/88	Buck Consultants Harmon Meadow, New Jersey	*Senior Assistant Communication Consultant*
5/81–6/82	Manhattan Life Insurance Company New York, New York	*Benefits Specialist*
9/75–5/81	American Broadcasting Cos. Inc. New York, New York	*Staff Analyst— Benefits Planning*

EDUCATION

MS Adult Education and Human Resource Development
Fordham University—New York, New York

BA Sociology
California State College—Bakersfield, California

JOHN GLADSTONE
55 Hemlock Drive
Boca Raton, Florida 33434
407-421-5567

SALES • MANAGEMENT • BUSINESS DEVELOPMENT

More than 20 years of successful sales/marketing experience, including representing leading U.S. manufacturers of contract furnishings.

Extensive background in the technical aspects of marketing office furniture and equipment, with a proven track record of consistently achieving sales objectives. Firm responsible for developing more than $3 million in annual revenues, and achieving 124% of goal for 1994.

Established and developed territory to give companies a leading position among Architectural and Design firms, as well as corporate end-users.

SUMMARY OF QUALIFICATIONS:

➤ Diversified results-oriented experience in sales/marketing and customer service.

➤ Broad exposure and capabilities in a variety of related areas, including layout, design, budgeting, drafting and technical operations.

➤ Excellent communication and interpersonal skills; developed reputation and strong working relationships in office design community.

➤ Experienced and adept with latest sales/marketing techniques, including Relationship Selling, Time Management, Needs Assessment, Client Profile Evaluation and Commitment Strategies.

➤ Thoroughly familiar with technical aspects of products and services: serves as advisor/consultant to accounts.

EXPERIENCE:

BRADY JACKSON & ASSOCIATES, BOCA RATON, FL　　　　　　**January 1993 to Present**
Manufacturer's Representative

➤ Established business and developed association as representative for several leading manufacturers of contract furnishings, including Meridian, Inc., Egan Visual, ASI/Intrex Corp., and Novikoff, Inc.

➤ Developed Southeast Florida territory through telemarketing, cold canvassing, personal networking and trade shows.

➤ Instrumental in developing new business in excess of $3 million annually.

➤ Acquired major accounts, such as Motorola; successful project involved 150 offices with an estimated sales volume of $1.5 million.

➤ Perform as consultant to accounts to analyze needs, develop solutions and implement installation.

➤ Serve as liaison with factory for ongoing project with American Bankers; estimated sales volume in excess of $5 million.

➤ Conduct sales presentations and educational seminars for major accounts, including product information, competitive evaluation and cost effectiveness.

➤ Provide post-sale support and services to maximize customer satisfaction.

JOHN GLADSTONE, BOCA RATON, FL　　　　　　**January 1990 to December 1992**
Manufacturer's Representative

➤ Represented Contract Furniture Division of Krueger International with complete responsibility for all sales/marketing activity in South Florida territory.

➤ Within first 6 months, successfully closed $2 million University of Miami project, as well, as other substantial sales.

➤ Provided "total quality customer service" anticipating and satisfying customer needs.

➤ Utilized telemarketing and other techniques for new business development.

EXPERIENCE: (CONTINUED)

BUSINESS ENVIRONMENTS, FT. LAUDERDALE, FL　　　　　**February 1983 to December 1989**
Account Executive/Project Manager
- ➤ Consistently ranked at top of sales force for largest retail office furniture dealer in Florida.
- ➤ Complete responsibility for directing all phases of major office design projects from initial customer contact through completion.
- ➤ Successfully completed furnishing of Broward Financial Center in Ft. Lauderdale, FL.
- ➤ Acquired a large number of major accounts, including Personnel Pool of America, which accounted for more than $2 million in sales.
- ➤ Established large and loyal following through high-quality customer service, resulting in client satisfaction and referrals.
- ➤ Superior performance in initial position as Showroom Manager led to promotion as Account Executive/ Project Manager.

TECTONIC RESOURCES, MALVERN, PA　　　　　**November 1981 to May 1982**
(Division of Rouse Associates – Major Architectural Firm)
Consultant
- ➤ Responsible for space planning, interior design, and specification preparation for commercial projects.

H. MITCHELL BUSINESS FURNITURE & INT., CHERRY HILL, NJ　　**March 1977 to November 1981**
Sales Representative
- ➤ Made presentations and closed sales for retail dealer of commercial office furniture and open office systems.

ECONO-MED OF NEW JERSEY, INC., CHERRY HILL, NJ　　　　**November 1973 to March 1977**
Owner
- ➤ Established business of Home Health Care equipment.
- ➤ Assumed complete responsibility for all facets of management, fiscal and operational.

EDUCATION:

OGLETHORPE UNIVERSITY, ATLANTA, GA　　　　　　　　　　**1972**
Bachelor of Science Degree
　Major: Biology
　Activities & Honors:
- ➤ President-Student Government Association
- ➤ Selected: "Who's Who in American Colleges and Universities"
　　　　"Who's Who in American Colleges and Universities - Student Leaders (1972)"

RUTGERS UNIVERSITY, CAMDEN, NJ　　　　　　　　　　**1973–1974**
Continuing Education Courses: Health Care

PHILADELPHIA COLLEGE OF ART, PHILADELPHIA, PA　　　　**1977–1981**
Interior Design Program

REFERENCES:

Furnished upon Request

PAUL RODRIGUEZ

14 Oak Boulevard
Yonkers, New York 10591   *(914) 777-9919*

EXPERIENCE:

9/93 to Present   **BARCLAY BEVERAGES, INC.,** Blauvelt, NY
Sales Representative

Was recruited by this leading beer distributor *(#1 distributor of Heineken in America)* to cover Yonkers, a predominately Hispanic territory.

- Call on restaurants, hotels, bodegas and delicatessens to serve existing accounts and open new ones throughout Yonkers – *the highest dollar-volume Heineken territory in Westchester County.*
- Promote new products; coordinate promotions; set up Point-of-Purchase displays; organize shelves and merchandise products; increase shelf space allocations; collect past-due accounts.
- Interface with retailers within the Hispanic community to represent our products and generate new business.
- Named "Salesman of the Month" November 1994.
- Won numerous sales contests including a trip to Puerto Rico.
- Winner of the "Iron Man" Award.
- Increased sales 23% in the Hispanic community

5/92 to 9/93   **FOOT LOCKER, INC.,** Yorktown, NY
Joined this leading retailer of sport shoes and sneakers in a 6-month Management Training program, progressing to Assistant Manager.

Assistant Store Manager (11/92–11/93)

- Trained, evaluated and scheduled Sales Associates.
- Sold and merchandised products.
- Handled cash receipts.
- Opened and closed the store.

Management Trainee (5/92–11/92)

- Trained in all aspects of retailing, i.e. sales, floor planning, customer service, cash management, merchandising, etc.

– PRIOR EMPLOYMENT EXPERIENCE –

Worked all through High School and College to earn money for tuition expenses (paid 100%). Employment included positions as *Customer Representative* (1989–1990) for **Contri Services**, Elmsford, NY; and *Store Manager* (1984–1989) at **Ice Cream Villa**, Tarrytown, NY.

EDUCATION: **Mercy College**, Dobbs Ferry, NY
BS Business Administration...Graduated January 1992

SKILLS: dBase; Data Entry; Bilingual Spanish-English

REFERENCES: Excellent references upon request.

Marcia Baker

16 COURT STREET • NASHVILLE, TENN. 37254   (615) 624-4434

EXPERIENCE

8/94–present   Mason Machinery, Inc., Nashville, Tenn.

Trade Representative

Traveled and did about 10 trade shows. Responsible for setting up of display booth in addition to demonstration and sales.

8/93–8/94   Jones Video, Astoria, Tenn.
(Retail sales and rentals)

Assistant Manager

Developed and designed successful marketing mailer which increased rentals 20% a month. Designed and implemented effective advertising which resulted in 10% membership increase. Responsible for customer service, sales, rental records, purchasing, bookkeeping and perpetual inventory of retail video store. Familiar with equipment and the mechanical aspects.

1/92–3/93   Corning, Inc., Akron, Ohio
(Manufacturer of lawnmower replacement parts)

Customer Service Manager

Established Customer Service Department and developed its policies and procedures. Traveled 3 months a year working major hardware and lawn and garden shows. Responsibilities included assisting customers and sales representatives, order taking, order expediting, handling complaints, debits and returns. Supervised 4 persons.

6/90–12/91   Ladies Quarterly, Nashville, Tenn.

Advertising Representative

Responsible for 50% increase in advertising space sold for quarterly recreation magazine. Assisted in planning of magazine.

EDUCATION

Pembroke College, Saratoga, N.Y.
Bachelor of Arts Degree
Graduated May 1990

REFERENCES

Available upon request.

DONALD NORTON

62 Eastern Boulevard
Dallas, Texas 75203
(214) 962-1346

BUSINESS EXPERIENCE

January 1992 to *Present*	U.S. Rubber Corporation, Dallas, Texas **District Representative** reporting to General Sales Manager. Sales and marketing responsibilities, through distributor network, covering 13 southwestern states.
December 1988 to *October 1991*	Globe & Co., Inc., Chicago, Illinois Independent tire dealer **Sales Representative** reporting to Branch Manager. Responsibilities entailed sales of on- and off-the-road tires and related accessories throughout northern Illinois.
February 1983 to *October 1988*	Morgan & Little, Inc., Pittsburgh, Pa. **Regional Sales Manager** reporting to the Company President. Responsibilities included sales and marketing of all company automotive products throughout the Midwest geographic area, with frequent trips to other areas to assist in the promotion of these products.
December 1977 to *September 1982*	Texaco Steel, Inc., Scranton, Pa. **Outside salesman** between December 1979 and September 1982 reporting to the District Manager, located in St. Louis. Responsibilities included sales of all company products throughout portions of Missouri and surrounding areas. The period prior to this was an inside salesman with offices in Melrose Park, Illinois.
July 1972 to *November 1975*	Miller Shoe Company, Dallas, Texas **Retail Store Manager** reporting to District Director. Responsibilities included handling of all functions necessary to run a successful retail outlet such as merchandising, banking, bookkeeping and hiring.

EDUCATION

Dallas Area Community College
Associate of Arts, 1972. Major in Business Administration

REFERENCES

On request.

NANCY JONES

47 MAIN STREET
DES MOINES, IOWA 50321
(515) 682-4761 • (515) 719-3000

PROFESSIONAL QUALIFICATIONS

- Detailed knowledge of computer supply and computer graphics markets
- Strong sales background: telemarketing, direct sales, account management, direct mailings, sales promotions
- Experience in word processing, software applications, slide design, knowledge of electronic spreadsheets
- Ability to write sales proposals, promotional copy, research papers, correspondence, evaluations
- Knowledge of advertising techniques and implementation of marketing plans

BUSINESS EXPERIENCE

SALES REPRESENTATIVE, Farmers Research Service, Inc. (F.R.S.), Des Moines, Iowa Trained by FRS executives to develop new business with Fortune 500 companies for state-of-the-art computer graphics/slide equipment division. Responsible for territorial management, seminars, product demonstrations, key account management, telemarketing and direct sales. Other duties: sales proposals, correspondence, competitive analysis, direct mailings.

Key Accounts – IBM, INTERNATIONAL HARVESTER, AMERICAN CANCER SOCIETY, FARM CREDIT BUREAU

JUNE 1995–PRESENT

SALES/MERCHANDISING ACCOUNT EXECUTIVE, Keane Electronics, Inc., Des Moines, Iowa Responsible for computer supply sales to retail buyers in Iowa/Kansas/Nebraska area. Maintain $60,000/month quota while assisting buyers with merchandising concepts. Other duties: sales proposals, account management, territorial development, new product suggestions, monthly sales promotions.

JANUARY 1994–JUNE 1995

EDUCATION

University of Nebraska, Currently attending courses leading toward an MBA in management.

University of Nebraska, December 1993. BSBA in advertising/marketing. Internship at ADLAB as account executive.

REFERENCES

References upon request.

Franklin Pierce

90 Plandome Road
Fort Lee, New Jersey 07506
Phone: 201/724-9818 • Fax: 201/724-3010

SUMMARY

Professional marketer seeking position that can utilize experience and skills • Strong academic training in business management • Practical experience in sales and marketing • Adept sales strategist with compelling person-to-person selling abilities • Solid oral, written, and presentation expertise • Effective time- and territory-management skills • Established record of proficiency, creativity, leadership, organization, and problem-solving know-how • Goal-oriented person with proven ability to accept assignments and deliver desired and effective results

EXPERIENCE

Sales Representative
JOHNSON & BIGELOW, INC., • WOODBRIDGE, NJ   *March 1994 to present*

Sell packaging equipment and related steel and plastic strapping material for this Fortune 100 corporation to manufacturing companies in the New York, New Jersey, and Connecticut tri-state area. Deal with top management, including vice presidents and owners.

Accomplishments:

- Implemented a time- and territory-management system that resulted in consistent generation of new and repeat business.

- Commended for securing a $175,000 three-year blanket order from Con Edison, considered extraordinary in contrast to average orders of $3,000.

- Ranked as 1 of the 2 winners out of 30 in the *Grow Your Business* sales contest, which was conducted to motivate bringing in new business.

- Was one of seven winners in the *New Product Introduction Sales Contest.*

Founder and Sales Manager
GOLF PRODUCTS, INC. • HAWTHORNE, NJ   *June 1988 to March 1994*

Started and managed this company that specialized in selling embroidered polo shirts and silk-screened T-shirts and other golf fashioned apparel to retail stores nationwide. Built a sales force of 42 sales representatives covering 50 states. Organized trade show participation and developed new business in five major markets. Established a customer base of 1000 accounts including major stores such as Macy's, JC Penney, Nordstrom, and other retail stores in the US and overseas. Developed sources of merchandise and coordinated all operations. Computerized a manual paper system, improving efficiency and increasing profitability.

Accomplishments:

- Achieved sales of $150,000 in the first year of operation with double growth in the second year. Implemented a telemarketing system that focused on qualified market segmentation and increased sales by 35%.

EXPERIENCE (continued)

Sales Representative
CANON/MCS • PARAMUS, NJ   *May 1986 to June 1988*

Sold fax machines and consistently exceeded 100% of sales quota. Developed principle of account segmentation to increase sales. Penetrated major accounts such as Ralph Lauren and Penguin Publishing.

Accomplishments:
• Ranked highest in sales among 40 salespeople in New Jersey. Won President's Circle Award in 1986 and 1987. Received award for outstanding presentation skills at the company's sales training program.

EXPERIENCE CONCURRENT WHILE ATTENDING COLLEGE

Salesman
TMB SPORTSWEAR • POUGHKEEPSIE, NY   *September 1982 to May 1986*

Started this sportswear company as a freshman in college. Sold T-shirts and boxer shorts door-to-door in over 20 major college campuses in the northeast. Financed 75% of college education costs.

EDUCATION

Bachelor of Science in Business Administration Cum Laude   *May 1986*
Concentration in Marketing, Minor in Psychology
MARIST COLLEGE • POUGHKEEPSIE, NY

References available upon request

JOAN DAVIS

421 WEST 93RD STREET
NEW YORK, NY 10023
(212) 444-8020

EXPERIENCE: *Radius, Inc.*   *3/90–present*
Account Representative
- Managed sales of Radius manufactured hardware and software to resellers and end-user accounts within the Metro New York area.
- Consistently exceeded management objectives and revenue quotas assigned by senior management.
- Generated widespread demand for Radius products at an end user level, including small to medium sized businesses and Fortune 500 accounts.
- Responsible for training of Radius authorized dealers to help promote brand awareness and benefits of products.
- Responsible for corporate presentations.
- Grew territory 19% when region growth was -12%.
- Nominated for Rep of the Year award within Radius for Fiscal years 1992 and 1993.
- Completed diverse sales courses, including Learning International's Professional Selling Skills.
- Participated in trade shows on a regular basis.

Businessland, Westport CT   *5/89–3/90*
Marketing Representative
- Responsibilities included marketing efforts directed toward new account base.
- Provided consultative assistance to customers in system and application-related problems.
- Coordinated account strategy sessions, monitoring effectiveness of implemented marketing programs by providing sales direction with strategic planning. Held follow-up sessions with feedback and positioning detail.

Computerland, Woodcliff Lake NJ   *10/87–5/89*
Sales Representative
- Began career as retail representative, selling to walk-in traffic. Exceeded quota by 150%.
- Developed marketing programs to increase walk-in traffic and attendance in seminar series.
- Promptly promoted to Account Representative, Outgoing Sales, covering small to medium sized businesses.
- Consistently exceeded goals set by senior management.

SKILLS:
- Successful sales and marketing experience with understanding of the sales process.
- Excellent presentation skills with experience in client presentations.
- Adaptive training skills with proven success in training curriculum development.
- Precise in written communication with rapport for successful client and sales representative relationship-building.
- Transferable skill set.

EDUCATION: St. Bonaventure University, Olean, NY.
Bachelor of Business Administration, 1987. Major: Marketing.
Minor in Computer Science
3.4 / 4.0 GPA

REFERENCES: Furnished upon request.

GEORGE MERRICK

5 Ostrich Place, East Brunswick, N.J. 08520 Tel.: (609) 676-7214

PROFESSIONAL ACHIEVEMENTS

Regional Sales Representative   **PBS Building Systems, Inc.**
- Member of PBS Building President Club (1990/91).
- PBS Building Systems Salesman of the Year Award (1990/91).
- Runner-up in new call contest (1992).
- Produced over twelve million dollars in sales in four years.
- Consistently met and exceeded sales objectives.
- Developed the pharmaceutical market from scratch. Within nine months booked an $800,000 project.

Sales Representative   **Pitney Bowes, Inc.**
- Pitney Bowes Rookie of the Year Award (1985).
- Member of the Pitney Bowes Prestigious Sales Leadership Club (1985, '87, '88, '89) – 125% of quota or better.
- Member of the Pitney Bowes Pacemaker Sales Leadership Club (1988) – 165% of quota or better.
- Considered one of the top five sales reps in an office of forty-five sales reps.
- Met or exceeded quota goals every year.
- Managed, trained and directed new sales reps to develop new business in my territory.
- Recognized as a self-starter, maintenance free sales rep.
- Achieved superior track record in developing and booking new business.

EMPLOYMENT EXPERIENCE

July 1990–Present   PBS Building Systems, Inc., Shrewsbury, N.J.

December 1985–July 1990   Pitney Bowes, Inc., Princeton, N.J.

EDUCATION

1984   East Stroudsburg University, East Stroudsburg, Pa.
B.A. Chemistry

MEMBERSHIPS

International Society of Pharmaceutical Engineers (ISPE)
International Facility Managers Association (IFMA)
American Society of Hospital Engineers (ASHE)
American Hospitals Association (AHA)

REFERENCES

Available upon request.

DAVID R. CHOSACK

987 Chicago Street
St. Louis, Missouri 63101
(314) 548-4375

EXPERIENCE:
1990–present

MONROE GLASS INC., St. Louis, Missouri
Sales Representative

Position/Responsibilities: St. Louis District Office.
Managed and generated sale of glass containers to: food, soft drink, beer, and wine businesses in Missouri. Directed all sales office functions including cost control, budgeting, credit, inventory levels, inside staff.

Accomplishments:

- Built relationship, sold as *brand new* accounts:
  - Every State Pepsi Bottler, including Pepsi-Cola allied Beverages.
  - Canada Dry franchises throughout state, including National Beverage Brands, Div. of Curtice-Burns, St. Louis.
  - Coca-Cola Bottlers: franchises in Kansas City, St. Joseph, Springfield, Jefferson City. Owned respectively by Associated Coke, Northeast Coke, Wometco Enterprises, Andersen Beverage.
  - F.X. Matt Brewing, St. Louis Brewing, Aurora Brewing, Cairo Bottling.
  - Bev-Pack, Independence, Mo. (producers of Clarkson, British American, Waist Watchers brands).
    Note: With above accounts usually attained first-year initial sales of $200,000 or more.

- Initiated selling and qualification programs beginning sales in new product categories such as seltzer, processed food.

- Increased number of active accounts from 13 to 34 in 2½ years.

- Attained and held volume with accounts despite lower selling prices offered by domestic and Canadian competition.

- Kept claims, short payments, pallet balances at low ratio to sales.

- Moved greatest amount of aged corporate inventory under commission incentive contest.

Volume:
Sales in territory in 1989: $947,000...1993: $3,177,000.
Units/truckload deliveries nearly tripled between 1989 and 1993.

Perspective:
Was brought into underdeveloped region with directive to penetrate market, build corporate identity and image, and to attain large gains in units and dollars. This was accomplished.

1983–1990	OPTIMUM CAN CO., Newark, New Jersey **Sales Representative** in N.J./N.Y./Conn. area.

Created first-time, and maintained, metal and fiber container sales to: C&C Beverages, Pergament Paint, Progresso, P&G, Tenneco, Cott, Shasta, Pabst, Rheingold, Ciba-Geigy, Sapolin, Globe Products, Faberge, Clairol, Mennen, Pfizer. Managed territory and had responsibility for all areas impacting on profit (cost), e.g.: inventory, pricing, credit, budgeting, sales forecasting. Managed office contact staff. Coordinated Engineering, Technical Service Departments.

Average 22% units increase/yr. 1983–1990.
Sales in 1984: $8.0mm.; 1988: $11.5mm.; 1989: $14.6mm.

Excellent record converting prospects to accounts.

1978–1983 AMERICAN GROUP, N.Y.C., N.Y., AMERICAN CAN CO., Metal Container Div., Pittsburgh, Baltimore Districts, after Upper N.Y.S. training.

Composite and metal can sales; steel pail sales to food, soft-drink, beer, and general line customers (aerosol, motor oil). Accounts: Heinz, PPG, Musselman, Knouse Foods, Pittsburgh Brewing. Responsibilities, units and dollars, and accounts parallel above but on smaller scale.

Sales Gain: $2.5mm to $4.2mm from 1979 to 1983.

EDUCATION: Lafayette College, Easton, Pennsylvania. B.A. Economics, 1978

REFERENCES: Furnished on request.

Claudia McKenna

190 St. Charles Drive
Yonkers, N.Y. 10761
(914) 962-9831 • (914) 961-7900

Business Experience:

1992-Present   Teleaudio, Inc., White Plains, N.Y.

Account Executive – Package, market, sell American and international programming to cable, syndication and theatrical distribution. M.S.G. Cable Network, telerep, Katz, WTBS, etc.

1988-1992   On Film, Inc., New York, N.Y.

Sales Manager – Sold and produced industrial films. Involved with the complete production. Some clients: IBM, Electronic Associates, Exxon.

1982-1988   Chapman and Cunningham, Inc., Princeton, N.J.

Account Executive – Sold and coordinated marketing communication projects with clients. (New product introductions, sales and marketing meetings, test marketing, new packaging and marketing promotion). Total responsibility from inception to completion. Coordinated projects with clients; supervision over creative, budget and production areas. Some clients: IBM, Chesebrough-Ponds, Proctor & Gamble, Coty.

1980-1982   Steinman Communications, Inc., Newark, N.J.

Account Executive – Supervised complete production of audio-visual programs. Some clients: American Gas Association, Thomas R. Crowell Publishing.

1976-1980   Reed and Smith T.V. Sales, Inc., New York, N.Y.

Sales Executive – Purchased TV films and 40 feature films, and negotiated the sales of films to foreign stations for syndication.

1973-1976   Talent Associates, Boston, Mass.

Business Affairs – Participated in negotiations and administration of TV talent, packages and sales for Network and Syndication, acquired contracts that included pricing and budgeting, price control and sales report for about 60 network and syndicated shows.

Education:

MBA, 1982 Advertising & Marketing – N.Y.U.

BA, 1973   English – Emerson College, Boston

References:

Available upon request.

John Emerson

150-03 Oak Street
Flushing, New York 11366

EXPERIENCE

National Air Filter　　　　　　　　　　　　　Great Neck, New York
Sales Representative　　　　　　　　　　　　　1992–Present

- Sell high efficiency air filters for heating and air conditioning equipment
- Sell to major manufacturers, distributors, municipalities, health care facilities, government agencies, pharmaceutical industry and academia
- Responsible for a 6-county territory in northern New York and Connecticut

Accomplishments
– First quarter sales for 1993 were doubled in relation to 1992 sales
– Developed 3 new accounts with incremental sales potential of $200,000

Lincoln Plastic and Chemical Company　　　　　Astoria, New York
Sales Representative　　　　　　　　　　　　　1989–1991

- Sold all forms of plastic including rod, sheet, tube and film; silicone sealants, adhesives, cleaners and polishes
- Sold major manufacturers, OEM's, distributors, municipalities, health care facilities, government agencies, and academia
- Responsible for N.Y./Metro territory

Accomplishments
– Increased sales by 15% in the last fiscal year; developed 5 new accounts with annual sales potential of $50,000 each

Almac Plastics　　　　　　　　　　　　　　　Brooklyn, New York
Sales Representative　　　　　　　　　　　　　1987–1989

- Sold plastic window assemblies to major transit authorities and school bus companies
- Assistant to Transportation Sales Manager

EDUCATION

Queens College of The City University of New York　　Flushing, New York
Bachelor of Arts, February 1987　*Major:* History

Learning International Professional Selling School　　Boston, Massachusetts
Certificate of Accomplishment in Selling Skills, January 1989

REFERENCES　Furnished upon request

JEFFREY NEWHOUSE

17 Lois Lane • Stormville, New York 14221
914-555-4411

SUMMARY OF QUALIFICATIONS

Experienced sales professional skilled in account management, business development, new product introductions, merchandising, customer relations, and electronic communications.

PROFESSIONAL EXPERIENCE

BURDINE HEALTH, New York, NY   1977–Present

A multinational marketer of pharmaceutical (Demerol) and over-the-counter (Bayer Aspirin) health products. Formerly a wholly-owned subsidiary of Kodak, Burdine was sold to Miles, Inc.

1989–Present	Senior Sales Representative/Key Account Manager, Buffalo, NY
1979–1989	Senior Sales Representative/Key Account Manager, Houston, TX
1977–1979	Sales Representative, Houston, TX

- Extensive experience calling on all classes of trade including retail food, wholesale drug, and mass merchandiser headquarter accounts.
- Introduced and merchandised new products and line extensions.
- Trained and managed part-time personnel calling on retail accounts.
- Coordinated retail food coverage with P.I.A., a national merchandising broker.
- Developed retail shelf management systems utilizing planograms, and carried out resets.
- Established local advertising and promotional programs with accounts.
- Addressed customer service concerns with a strong customer orientation.
- Presented formal annual business development plans and recommendations to accounts.
- Named "Achiever" eleven years for annual quota attainment.
- Named "Silver Achiever" for territory sales excellence in Eastern Region, 1991.
- Designated "Territory Manager of the Year" for West Central Region, 1987.

SAV-ON-DRUGS (now Walgreens), Houston, TX   1976–1977

Retail Manager-In-Training – Merchandising, customer service, purchasing, shipping and receiving

U.S. GEOLOGICAL SURVEY, Houston TX   1972–1973

Water Resources Assistant—Field work and analysis of water samples

COMPUTER AND LANGUAGE SKILLS

Working knowledge of personal computer account analysis and sales applications including WordPerfect, Lotus 1-2-3, modem communications for downloading and printing data, and electronic mail communications.

Proficient in spoken and written Spanish; Served voluntary two-year mission to Peru.

EDUCATION

B.S., Business Management and Marketing, Brigham Young University, Provo, UT, 1976

DAVID BENCKE • 300 East 93rd Street • New York, NY 10028 • (212) 737-6620

OBJECTIVE: MEDIA SALES – PRINT/BROADCASTING

SUMMARY: Results-oriented salesman with proven ability for productive effort. Broad background in self-education through employment in different types of industries as well as extensive travel throughout United States, the Caribbean, Latin America and Europe. Excellent verbal skills. Proficient in French. Strong in interpersonal relations.

RELEVANT EXPERIENCE:

1991–1996   TREND NEWSPAPERS, INC., Boston, MA
Account Executive
- Serviced established accounts; contacted and sold new accounts
- Presented prestige concept of publication to prospects; assisted clients in ad design and composition
- Worked with clients in establishing new format for ads when publication changed size from tabloid to magazine
- Maintained excellent customer relations with established accounts through reinforcement of magazine concept

Concurrent   TIME/LIFE LIBRARIES, INC., Boston, MA
Telephone Sales Representative
- Developed sales of Home Improvement Series through phone contact with people in their homes
  - Established 19 new accounts in 4 days (200 calls, 50 pitches – working 4 hours per day)

1990
(Christmas Season)   BARNES & NOBLE BOOKSTORE, Boston, MA
Sales Clerk
- Maintained company policy of instant and courteous assistance to customers; set up displays for best attraction; helped with inventory

OTHER EXPERIENCE:

1990   73 MAGAZINE, INC., Peterborough, NH
Book Production Assistant
- Edited manuscripts and other copy; proofread and corrected galleys; selected type; produced rough pasteups; participated in research

1983–1989   SUMMERTIME AND PART-TIME JOBS WHILE GOING TO SCHOOL
- Lumber Industry, Missoula, MT – sawmill assistant
- Management Consulting Firm, Durham, NH – groundskeeper
- Construction Industry, Lee, NH – swimming pool installation
- Laundry Industry, Portsmouth, NH – delivery driver
- Prescott Park Arts Festival, Portsmouth, NH – art instructor
- Also: crewed on 65 ft. ketch; housepainter, Alaska; landscape gardener; grape harvester in France

EDUCATION: UNIVERSITY OF NEW HAMPSHIRE, Durham, NH
1989 – BA, English; Minor: French

ALLIANCE FRANCAISE, Paris, France
1987 – French

EDWARD SALSON

144-30 Ford Brooks Road Citadel
California 95610
(916) 539-8486

Business Experience

October 1991–
March 1996

Gibson Color Systems, Sacramento, California
Offset preparatory firm located in San Francisco with a Sacramento Sales Office.

Salesperson – Developing and servicing accounts handled out of the Sacramento area. Estimated cost of preparatory work including separating and stripping job into position. Handling color correcting press proofs and detail work pertaining to a given job.

December 1989–
September 1991

Shank Graphics, Chicago, Illinois
Detroit Litho and Gravure separator with a Chicago office.

Sales and Sales Service – Responsibilities included servicing established accounts and opening up new accounts. Did all the estimating for the Chicago office.

February 1987–
December 1989

Baronet Litho Company, Chicago, Illinois
Small commercial printer. Equipment included a 60-inch four-color press. Plant had complete facilities including stripping, platemaking and bindery and mailing department.

Assistant to Plant Manager – Handled all jobs received from salespeople. Made out job tickets and job layouts. Followed through on all jobs in various stages of production. Ordered paper and other items necessary to produce final product.

Education

Rochester Institute of Technology
Earned A.A.S. degree in Photographic Science, 1984
Earned B.S. in General Printing, 1986

References

Will be furnished upon request.

Elizabeth Borden

18 Lasalle Court
Los Angeles, California 90072
(213) 682-1465

November, 1991–present

Schwartz Brothers, Los Angeles, California
NATIONAL ACCOUNT EXECUTIVE

Sales and implementation of restaurant equipment, supplies, durable goods, and disposable products to national chain and franchise establishments engaged in restaurant, hospitality and health care fields as well as directing new corporations not presently involved in restaurant and/or lodging fields.

Establishing new vendor sources for diversification of product mix for present and future customers. Establishing markup that will show the largest profit margin for the company as well as some 450 local and national sales force.

Training of sales personnel to initiate programs that have been established through corporate headquarters.

December 1982–October, 1991

Henry Hall, Inc., Carmel, California
DISTRICT MANAGER

Acted as field representative for various stores that were without proper management and needed to obtain a more stable condition. Included in this area was the revamping of office procedures, sales orientation and employee sales motivation and general merchandising as well as display of stores.

The recruiting, hiring and training of personnel in the phases of management trainee, assistant manager as well as promoting of qualified personnel.

All phases of merchandising that consisted of ordering, markdowns, records of damaged goods to manufacturers. Also, the safety and security of employees and customers on or near store premises.

December, 1979–December, 1982

James Personnel, San Diego, California
AREA SUPERVISOR

Responsibilities were the hiring and training as well as supervision of other employment counselors. Interviewing and rating of job applicants for employment.

Types of job applicants ranged from general clerical to advanced degrees seeking positions in business and industrial fields. Duties also entailed recruiting for specific job openings listed by various companies throughout the San Diego area.

Education

BA, 1979 San Diego State College
Major: Psychology

References

Available upon request.

DAVID HOFFMAN

222 ELM STREET • WHITE PLAINS, NEW YORK 10552
914-555-2810

EXPERIENCE:

7/89–Present   **KRAFT, General Foods, Inc. Woodbury, New York**
Sales Representative

Direct account responsibility for Military and Royal Farm retail chain stores.
Responsible for several other retail accounts in the Metropolitan area.
Achieved 100 percent effective coverage, Winner of the Metropolitan category challenge.

Building the Business
Regularly achieved tonnage plan.
Met and exceeded objectives on new items, special programs and focus priorities.
Gained maximum account support for all Kraft products including authorizations, features, and plan-o-grams. Developed and implemented programs to improve account volume and shares.

Managing an Account
Regularly developed and delivered analytically based sales presentations.
Established positive business building relationships with account decision makers including top management.
Developed/maintained account strategic plan and tailored programs accordingly.

Analysis, Problem Solving, and Priority Setting
Analyzed product profile to identify maximum volume and profit opportunities.
Developed plans and programs to solve problems and capitalize on opportunities.

Completed Internal Professional Development Workshops, including Effective Presentation, Professional Selling Skills, Advanced Sales Training, and Managerial Training Techniques.

12/87–7/89   **Otto Brehm, Inc., Yonkers, New York**
Supervisor

Monitored the proper loading and maintenance of fleet vehicles to conform to Department of Transportation specifications and regulations.
Maintained warehouse supplies, products, inventory reports, and deliveries.
Supervised staff of warehouse employees, including scheduling and accounting of hours.

EDUCATION:

9/84–12/87   State University of New York College at New Paltz, New York
Bachelor of Arts Degree – Organizational Communications and Marketing

9/82–5/84   Westchester Community College, Valhalla, New York
Associate of Liberal Arts Degree – Marketing

AFFILIATIONS:

1984–1990   United States Naval Reserve – Aviation Airman E-3
Omega Psi Phi Fraternity, Inc., Mount Vernon Council on Youth Development
Mount Vernon Youth Football, Coaching Staff

REFERENCES: Available upon request

Jeremy Gibbons

186 Intracostal Highway
Boca Raton, Florida 33448
(305) 965-9328

Ten years' professional experience in engineering salesmanship.

EXPERIENCE:

Senior Consultant

The Southern Sun Inc., Boca Raton, Florida – 1985 to date

This position involves the professional selection and sales of real estate investments, requiring knowledge of tax laws and shelters as well as applicable real estate laws and geographical growth trends.

Sales Engineer

Hobart Air Compressor Corporation, Highland Beach, Florida – 1981/1985

This position required the sales of industrial air compressors and their intrinsic components. These components included regulating, drive, and air drying systems and their auxiliary support accessories. As technical salesman, incorporated the attributes of an applicable engineer, sales representative and a field service engineer. A successful sale required the paralleling of stipulated specifications with the most reliable, effective and economical systems. Frequently assisted with engineering, assembling, and authoring of facility expansion or new plant construction specifications. Often, the installation of new equipment demanded the coordination, instruction, and supervision of mechanical and electrical contractors. Subsequent start-up and troubleshooting required the establishment of a working relationship with plant and maintenance personnel.

Student Trainee

Miami Naval Laboratories, Miami, Florida – 1976/1981

In conjunction with five-year cooperative program, participated in developing, assembling, plotting, and recording data while working with engineers in the research and development of shipboard fire fighting systems, high-strength steels and titanium for submarine hulls, and damping materials for sonar dome application.

EDUCATION:

Miami University, Miami, Florida – Mechanical Engineering
B.M.E. June 1981 (Dean's List).

AFFILIATIONS and LICENSES:

Associate Member – American Society of Mechanical Engineers, F.A.A. Airframe Mechanics License, Florida Teaching Credential, Florida Real Estate Association.

References furnished upon request.

HOWARD K. DONALDSON

1170 East Sycamore Lane
Columbus, Ohio 43211
(614) 279-5341

EMPLOYMENT RECORD:

Apex Chemical Co., Inc.
Columbus, Ohio   1991–present
SALES REPRESENTATIVE

Sales and service to area industries, food processing plants and manufacturers. Product lines sold include water treatment processes for cooking towers and boilers, polymers, oils, greases, various acids and alkalines and cleaning systems for food processers.

Responsibilities include maintaining current accounts and opening new business. Also included is providing technical information to customers, water testing and sample surveys.

Southern Star Bank
Louisville, Kentucky   1979–1991
ASSISTANT BRANCH MANAGER

In 3 years was responsible for building branch sales from $200,000 per year to over $1,500,000 in 1990. Budgeted a further growth in 1991 of 50%. Duties also included responsibility for day-to-day management of the branch.

Marketing Group: Was responsible for preparation, production and distribution of all retail point-of-sale materials including brochures, flyers and posters. Helped develop cross-sell programs, tracking and evaluation of results: preparation and analysis of MIS for tracking new and old product performance.

EDUCATION:

Lexington State College	BA	1976, Finance
Kentucky State University	MBA	1979

References: Furnished on request

Hailey Bronson

555 Alamo Road, Englewood Cliffs, NJ 07632 (201) 415-5515

BACKGROUND SUMMARY

SALES/MARKETING REPRESENTATIVE. Fourteen years' experience providing marketing and sales services to Fortune 500 Companies, Medical Institutions and Government Agencies. Industry experience includes: Communications, Advertising, Medical and Publishing. Proven track record. Consistently exceeded sales quotas. Areas of related expertise include: New Business Development, Sales Presentations, Demonstrations, Negotiations and Financing. Have PC/Mac training and computerized typesetting experience.

CAREER HISTORY

DAKIN INC., NJ

Marketing Representative, 1993–Present

Sold and marketed Dakin product line. Provided best marketing solution of product mix and display for each account. Maintained and serviced customer base; opened new business (in excess of 90 accounts). Top performer in New Account Contests; Flintstones Contest. Top 20% of sales force.

Awards: Quota Member, 1993–1994. Presented by National Sales Club of America

QMS, NY

Account Manager, 1990–1991

Responsible for design and sale of QMS intelligent printing systems. Provided solutions to corporations' departmental requirements based on studying clients needs. Performed approach calls, surveys, demonstrations, and proposal writing to obtain quotas. Focused on major account business. Wrote national account agreements with Hearst Communications, Gralla Communications and Condé Nast Publications.

Awards: Quota Member, 1990; Major Account Award, 1990.

COMPUGRAPHIC CORPORATION, NY

Sales Consultant, 1984–1990

Responsible for sale of pre-press computer systems which included hardware, software, and word processing capabilities. Performed approach calls, surveys, demonstrations and proposal writing to obtain quotas. Studied prospective clients needs and proposed appropriate systems. Provided training, service, and financing. Clients included Fortune 500 companies, advertising agencies, commercial typographers, and publishers.

Awards: Quota Member 1989; Presidents Club 1986–1988.

TAB PRODUCTS COMPANY, NY

Sales/System Representative, 1980–1984

Responsible for marketing sophisticated computer storage/computer filling systems with view toward maximizing efficiency and space. Products included: Business forms/equipment, computer accessories, computer landscaping and mobile computer storage systems. Created marketing and mailing programs, surveys, layouts and proposal formats. Studied customer applications and tailored systems to meet company needs. Opened over 50 new accounts with major medical facilities and major corporate accounts, including Mobil Oil Company and the United Nations, significantly upgrading sales volume.

Awards: Quota Member, 1980–1983; Presidents Club 1982–1983.

EDUCATION

B.S., Business Administration, Northeastern University, MA.

References Furnished upon Request

141

Territory and Regional Sales Managers/Account Managers and Executives

Dorothy Paulsen

230 West 62nd Street • New York, NY 10128
(212) 779-7171

EXPERIENCE

1990–Present HALLMARK CARDS, INC.

Sales Development Specialist   New York, NY

Direct 10 sales executives in all market development activities within a 4-state district. Establish specific territory for brand conversions, remodels, relocations, and expansions of card stores. Forecast sales and perform site evaluatons. Analyze trade areas to determine new points of distribution. Evaluate prospective retailers and assist in lease negotiation. Assess the strategic positioning of individual stores in the market. Achieved 100% of the year's objectives in a 5-month period.

District Retail Trainer   Danbury, CT

Designed retail training programs to improve customer service, merchandising, selling skills, and product knowledge for 250 Hallmark Card Shops. Organized all district-level retail classes, seminars, and meetings. Developed and implemented marketing promotions. Prepared training program used by 7 other districts.

District Sales Trainer   Danbury, CT

Conducted all phases of field sales training within the district. Reviewed sales executives and set developmental objectives. Introduced new products and programs to the sales force. Served as national trainer at corporate headquarters and worked on national task force for new greeting card line.

Sales Executive   Long Island, NY

Expanded a $5.0 million territory consisting of 20 card shops. Formulated business plans and marketing strategies for stores. Won R. B. Hall Award in 1992 for achieving the highest yearly sales increase in the district. Created promotional plan selected for initial launch of new product.

Sales Representative   Queens, NY

Managed a $2.5 million territory consisting of 25 card shops. Earned R. B. Hall Award in 1990. Received District Market Development Award for third and fourth quarters.

1988–1989 THE GAP AND GAP KIDS

Store Manager   New York, NY

Opened the company's flagship store with sales of $6.0 million. Recruited, hired, and trained staff of 60. Supervised 5 assistant managers. Awarded Store Manager of the Year in 1988 for exceeding sales goals and reducing operating expenses.

EDUCATION

1983–1987 UNIVERSITY OF NORTH CAROLINA   Chapel Hill, NC

BS in Business Administration, May 1987. Concentration in Marketing. Full academic scholarship. Dean's List. Worked 30 hours per week during school. Served as orientation counselor.

ADDITIONAL

Proficient in PowerPoint, Excel, and Quattro Pro. High School Valedictorian. Interests include travel, running, tennis, and movies.

WILLIAM FIELDS
90 Blue Ridge Road
Darien, Connecticut 06831
(203) 621-4414

EMPLOYMENT: **PITNEY BOWES, INC.**
3/86–Present   *Senior Account Executive (8/91–Present)*
Account Executive (3/87–7/91)
Associate Trainee Executive (3/86–3/87)
As a Senior Sales Representative for Pitney Bowes, have become knowledgeable in a wide variety of products including electronic mailing systems, inserters, computerized shipping applications, and customized furniture systems. During the past 8 years have had the opportunity with management to promote and launch new products and marketing ideas. In October of 1989 was consulted to put my sales and marketing successes on video for the U.S. sales team. Geographic locations with Pitney Bowes have included: Dallas, Manhattan and White Plains. These areas held large Pitney accounts including United States Tennis Association, MCI, Northwest Airlines, NYNEX, Tambrands, General Electric, Ralph Lauren Polo, New York Telephone.

Accomplishments:
- Attended Sales Leadership Conference 1994 – Boca Raton, Florida, Pacemaker
- Attended Sales Leadership Conference 1993 – Phoenix, Arizona, Pacemaker
- Pacemaker Status Top 1% of country
- Northeast Sales Representative of the Year, 1992 and 1993
- Northeast Leasing Leader of the Year, 1992 and 1993
- Attended Sales Leadership Conference, Puerto Rico, 1990
- Attended Sales Leadership Conference, Hawaii, 1989
- Surpassed corporate quota during the past 8 years – 125%
- Participated in Pitney Bowes Northeast Involvement Team
- One of top 18 representatives selected for extensive training program, 1988
- Named Sales Representative of the Month 22 times

BODY WORKS GYM, Denton, Texas
9/82–3/86   *Sales Manager* **(While Attending College)**
As gym sales manager was responsible for 4 sales representatives and their on-site training. This position also enabled me to work with upper management to solve gym facility and sales problems. Worked 20–60 hours per week.

EDUCATION: **North Texas State University,** Denton, Texas
Bachelor of Business Administration, 1985
Major: Marketing/Sales
- 100% self-generated college tuition and expenses

ACTIVITIES:
- North Texas State University Northeast Alumni Coordinator
- United Way Representative
- New York Real Estate Association
- Lambda Chi Fraternity
- Extensive World Traveling
- Powerlifting Competitor – American Drug-Free Powerlifting Association

ROGER CLIFT
1 Harrison Drive • Scranton, Pa. 18524
(717) 142-3891

PROFESSIONAL PROFILE

Product Knowledge
Public Relations

National Sales Meetings Presentations

Public Speaking Ability
Real Estate License

EMPLOYMENT HISTORY

SENIOR TERRITORY MANAGER – *July 1985 to Present*
Chelsea Choins & Locks, Allentown, Pa. (A Division of U.S. Steel)

Started as Sales Trainee in Buffalo territory serving as inside Sales and Customer Service Rep; handled quotations, processed and expedited orders, and provided safety inspections.

Promoted to Territory Manager in July 1986 in the Upper Ohio Valley Region (sales volume over $2 million).

Administrative activities include establishing client contact with distributors, OEM, and User accounts; conducting sales meetings at the distributor level and in-service safety seminars and inspection surveys at the user levels; introducing new products nationally; serving as liaison between inside sales management force and distributors; implementing hardware sales blitzes at the consumer level.

Promoted to Senior Territory Manager in August 1989.

BUSINESS ANALYST – *March 1982 to July 1985*
American Bank & Co., Business Information Division, Scranton, Pa.

Served as Business Analyst and Credit Information Representative with responsibility for preparing credit reference reports on companies containing the following information: business entity's trade record, financial position, history, and nature of operation.

Established client contact with companies in the western New York area, southern New York State, and northern Pennsylvania.

ASSISTANT MANAGER TRAINEE – *December 1981 to March 1982*
GS Rubber Co., Akron, Ohio

Started as Sales Trainee for their retail outlets and accepted into the Management Training Program.

REAL ESTATE SALESMAN – *November 1981 to March 1982*
Hemlock Farms, Hawley, Pa.

EDUCATIONAL BACKGROUND

STATE UNIVERSITY OF NEW YORK, Buffalo, New York
B.A. Economics – 1980
   Varsity Hockey – 4 years
   Concurrent Employment...Credit Clerk, Customer Service
            Department of Niagara Mohawk Power Corp.

REFERENCES

Available upon Request

CHARLOTTE GREEN

200 East River Drive
Smyrna, Delaware 19977
(302) 741-7038

WORK EXPERIENCE

CALDWELL INDUSTRIES, INC., Wilmington, Del.

July 1993 to present   *Area Sales Manager*

Major responsibilities range from managing the growth of a dealer network to solicitation, qualifying, and closing of national and government accounts. Train and support dealer's sales representatives, both in the field as well as at structured dealer training sessions, to ensure goal attainment.

Major achievements include:

- National recognition for 1995 Area Sales Manager of the Year.
- Consistently maintained a position of over 150% of quota.
- Personally secured and maintained contracts with 10 Fortune 500 companies.
- Within a 6-month period signed 6 major dealers who had previously represented a competitor, thereby significantly increasing my company's market penetration.

BUFFALO SAVINGS & LOAN BANK, Buffalo, N.Y.

July 1991 to July 1993   *Sales Representative*

Major responsibilities included establishing new merchant Visa/Mastercard accounts. Managed assigned territory by providing client assistance and educated merchants in the use of computerized authorization systems. Duties also included profitability studies, sales forecasting, and cost analysis.

Major achievements included:

- Award for having highest profitability rate per transaction in the New York Region Market.
- Numerous awards for top district sales personnel.

WHITE CLOUD PAPER CO., Atlanta, Ga.

September 1990 to July 1991   *Sales Representative*

Major responsibilities included development of consumer goods retail volume.

Major achievements included:

- Excellent performance rating for both new volume created and indirect customer contact response.
- Exceeded 100% of quota.
- Improved customer relations.
- Significantly increased numbers of client companies.

XEROX, INC., Rochester, N.Y.

September 1989 to September 1990   *Sales Representative*

Major responsibilities included ensuring business forms and equipment in a territory with a zero account base, enabling reinstatement of accounts lost due to former mismanagement of product lines.

Major achievements included:

- First sales representative to sell large equipment in this branch in approximately a year.
- Consistently exceeded sales quotas.
- Successfully completed Special Communications training program.

MIM'S DEPARTMENT STORES, Buffalo, N.Y.

September 1986 to September 1989   *Department Manager*

Major responsibilities included initially working as assistant buyer in forecasting department volume, procurement, and control of inventories. Promoted to department manager, where responsibilities included performance development, performance reviews/recommendation of advancement of over 10-person staff.

Major accomplishments included:

- New inventory control, which allowed tighter control and improved accuracy for all branches of responsibility.
- Improvement of interdepartmental employee relations.

EDUCATION:

B.A. – Marketing, June 1990
University of Buffalo

B.S. – Business Management, June 1986
York College, Pa.

REFERENCES:

Available upon request.

PAUL BARON

55 STALLION DRIVE

NEW HAVEN, CONNECTICUT 06468

HOME: 203-462-9190

WORK: 203-917-7474

A senior sales and general management professional with over 13 years of management experience with a strong background in building, managing, and motivating sales organizations. Demonstrated skill and achievements in exceeding assigned revenue goals, reducing expenses, and establishing alternate channels of distribution. Exceptional core strengths in the following areas: sales and sales management training, new business and national account development, and strong interpersonal, organizational and negotiating skills.

EMPLOYMENT

VOICE MAIL SYSTEMS INCORPORATED, ATLANTA, GA　　　　　　1991–Present
Regional Sales Director – North Central Region

National voice processing services company that specializes in fulfilling the interactive messaging, facilities management and interactive voice response needs of the Fortune 500 as well as medium-sized businesses. Responsible for $23,000,000 in annual sales, including the management of a head-count of 46 that consists of District Managers, Account Executives, National Account Executives and Administrative positions.

Accomplishments
- Consistently achieved the Regional revenue, margin and expense plans.
- Effectively merged WISC, ASYNC and Voice Mail into a streamlined sales organization.
- Led the country in selling new customers in 1992, 1993 and 1994.
- Developed and implemented numerous sales programs that increased sales and then became National programs.
- Created and taught Voice Mail's new-hire sales training program in 1992.
- Monthly, quarterly and annual recognition programs are consistently and effectively used to create a healthy competitive environment.
- Conducted numerous sales incentive programs that created an environment for self-motivation and sales success.
- Winner of numerous National awards including top Region in 1992 and 1993.
- Qualified for "Achievers Club" in 1992, 1993, and 1994.

WANG INFORMATION SERVICES CORPORATION, LOWELL, MA　　　　1988–1991
Regional Sales Director

National voice processing services company that specializes in fulfilling the interactive messaging, facilities management and interactive voice response needs of the Fortune 500 as well as medium-sized businesses. Reported to the General Manager. Responsible for $14,000,000 in annual sales with P & L accountability, including the management of a headcount of 50 that consisted of Sales Managers, Sales Representatives, Consultants, Customer Support Representatives and Administrative positions in the East, Midwest, and Western United States.

Accomplishments
- Grew annual revenue from $12,000,000 in 1989 to $16,000,000 in 1990.
- #1 Region in 1989 and 1990 at 105% and 112% respectively
- Monthly, quarterly and annual recognition programs were consistently and effectively used to create a healthy competitive environment.
- Conducted numerous sales incentive programs that created an environment for self-motivation and sales success.
- Along with over 60% of the Region's sales force, qualified for "Achievers Club" in 1989, 1990 and 1991.
- Developed and implemented numerous Regional sales and marketing programs that increased sales and then became National programs.

WANG INFORMATION SERVICES CORPORATION (continued)

- Reduced expenses and increased sales in two failing branches in 1989.
- Led the country in selling new customers in 1989, 1990 and 1991 with 100+ each year.
- Developed and implemented a direct mail campaign that generated $750,000 in new annual revenues for a cost of only $4,000.
- Consistently exceeded 55% gross margin.
- Conducted a regional "Demorama Contest" that significantly enhanced the Region's sales presentation skills.

District Sales Manager   **1985–1988**

- Grew the Tri-State District from zero revenue and no headcount in 1985 to the #1 District in 1988 with annual revenues of $6,000,000.
- #1 District in 1988 at 115% goal.
- #2 District in 1987 at 124% goal.
- Increased revenue 77% from 1986 to 1987.
- Hired, trained and coached the only two WISC Sales Representatives that were promoted to District Sales Manager.
- Qualified for "Achievers Club" in 1986, 1987 and 1988.
- Recipient of numerous Regional and National awards for sales performance.

THE WESTERN UNION TELEGRAPH COMPANY, UPPER SADDLE RIVER, NJ   **1982–1985**
District Sales Manager

National telecommunications company that specialized in providing a wide range of voice data systems, electronic mail products, satellite communications and variety of integrated solutions to the Fortune 500 marketplace. Reported to the Branch General Manager. Responsible for $10,000,000 in annual sales, including the management of 10 Sales Representatives, 2 Customer Representatives, and a support staff. Additional responsibilities included training, developing and implementing sales programs, and sales administration.

Accomplishments
- Achieved in excess of 115% of assigned revenue goals for 3 consecutive years, and was awarded District Manager of the Year-1983.
- Produced the #1 Salesperson of the Year 2 out of 3 years within an area that consisted of 60 field sales representatives.
- Qualified for "Achievers Club" in 1982, 1984, and 1985.
- Recipient of numerous Regional and National awards for sales performance.

THE WESTERN UNION TELEGRAPH COMPANY, UPPER SADDLE RIVER, NJ   **1977–1982**
Experience Prior to 1982

Joined Western Union as a Communications Sales Representative in 1977, then promoted to Senior Account Representative and later to a Major Account Representative.
Career highlights include qualifying for 4 "Achievers Clubs" and winner of 8 National and numerous Regional awards including Salesperson of the Year 1978.

EDUCATION

NORTHEASTERN UNIVERSITY, BOSTON, MA   **1972–1977**
B.A. in Marketing
Graduated with a 3.1 GPA and honors

References furnished upon request.

DWIGHT MARLBORO

442 OCEAN AVENUE • ST. PETERSBURG, FLORIDA 33604 • (813) 666-1240

QUALIFICATIONS SUMMARY

Sales experience has been exclusively with large chain drug and chain food warehouse accounts in the categories of fragrance & HBC. Qualified and capable of handling every aspect of key account/national account management. Interested in professional consumer sales field with an employer who rewards commitment with pay and/or promotion, looking for a long-term career development relationship with eventual management goal.

CAREER HISTORY

Maybelline, Inc.   August 1993–present
Division Account Manager   Tampa, Florida

➤ At Yardley Limited Company, a division of Maybelline, Inc., was responsible for the management of all major warehouse accounts in the state of Florida, such as Eckerd Drug, Publix, Winn Dixie and Albertsons. Large wholesalers included.

➤ Product line includes the Yardley Bath Shoppe line and commodity bar soap. Territory Volume, $1.5mm.

➤ Excellent working knowledge of WordPerfect and Lotus 1-2-3.

Revlon Classic Cosmetic & Fragrance Group   January 1989–June 1993
Field Account Manager   Baltimore, Maryland

➤ Responsible for large chain food and chain drug warehouse accounts including Rite Aid, Giant Food, Kerr Drug, and The Cosmetic Center. Territory Volume, $3.5mm.

➤ Handled all aspects of key account management including the corporate buyer, merchandising managers, category buyers, advertising supervisors, in addition to making extensive presentations before Headquarter Management.

➤ Supervised 2 merchandisers.

Shulton, Inc. (A Proctor & Gamble Company)   March 1985–November 1988
Key Account Manager   Clearwater, Florida

➤ Responsible for Exclusive Management of Eckerd Drug Headquarters. Product line included Old Spice and Pierre Cardin fragrances, Breck Hair Care, etc.

➤ Handled special promotions, seasonal events, advertising and pricing strategies, roto and tab setting recommendations as well as "selling" both marketing and merchandising ideas overall as critical core of essential job.

Block Drug Company   March 1981–February 1985
Key Account Manager   Tampa, Florida

➤ Sold consumer products with such key accounts as Publix, Winn Dixie, Kash n' Karry as well as Albertson's buying headquarters, managing a $3 million territory, supervising 3 merchandisers.

EDUCATION   B.A. Degree in Marketing, December 1980
                    The University of South Florida, Tampa, Florida

REFERENCES   Furnished upon request.

RICHARD J. LAZARUS

12 Roadside Avenue
Beechwood, Ohio 45208
(513) 862-1783

SALES/MARKETING

EMPLOYMENT

1995–present **LAMBERT LABORATORIES, Cincinnati, Ohio**
Territory Manager/Midwestern Region

Full sales responsibility for a high-volume area territory that includes Ohio, Illinois, Indiana, and Kentucky. Territorial volume: mid-six-figure range. Product line consists of state-of-the-art urological products and equipment that sell for as much as $13,000 each.

- Increased territorial sales by approximately 35% in the first year through organizing educational seminars, cold canvassing and making presentations at medical conference/conventions.
- Provide intensive training to technical support personnel as well as urologists.
- Effective in increasing the company's share in a highly competitive marketplace.
- Provide ongoing input to the home office relative to product improvement, new product ideas and feedback from the urological profession.
- Work closely with physicians demonstrating products in actual clinical situations.

1989–1994 **EIMER ARMAND, Cleveland, Ohio**
Sales Representative

Sold a full line of laboratory equipment and supplies to hospital and private clinic laboratories. Territorial responsibility: western Pennsylvania and Ohio.

- Within 3 years increased territorial sales from $400,000 annually to $1.3 million despite several territorial reductions.
- Acknowledged as a leading sales producer through membership in the President's Team—representing production in the top 10% of a 400-person sales force.
- Joined the company as a Customer Service Representative. Became fully familiar with distributor's product line and was promoted to Sales Representative.

1988–1989 **CHUBB & SONS, Cleveland, Ohio**
Claims Adjuster

Independent responsibility for the adjustment of physical damage and personal liability claims.

1986–1988 **AETNA INSURANCE CO., Cleveland, Ohio**
Claims Representative

Dealt with customers regarding personal lines claims (homeowners, bodily injury, etc.).

EDUCATION
B.S., 1986
Case Western Reserve University

REFERENCES
Personal and business references available on request.

JEFFREY WEBSTER

210 MARKET LANE • SYRACUSE, NEW YORK 13251 • (315) 642-1890

GENERAL BACKGROUND

Seventeen years of sales growth and achievement in the medical field, having established strong rapport with professional practitioners. Have developed long-lasting personal and professional relationships throughout northern New York, allowing marketing penetration and sales results unavailable to many others.

EXPERIENCE

1989 to present

Field Sales Executive – Upstate New York Region
Fidelity Insurance Co., Hartford, Connecticut

Involved in market development and total sales of specialized professional services to ophthalmic field. Traveled throughout upstate New York, Vermont, New Hampshire, and Western Massachusetts, calling on contact lens specialists comprised of Ophthalmologists, Optometrists, and Opticians.

Responsibilities:
- Promote and implement sales of unique reinsurance and prepaid insurance programs for soft and hard contact lens.
- Administer territory sales plan and budget, forecast sales and objectives, and prepare annual expense budget.
- Instruct the practitioners and their staff on methods of selling insurance to their patients and benefits of using the program as a management tool to assure patient contact and control.

Achievements:
- Succeeded in gaining the support of 60% of the 850 contact lens specialists in the territory.
- Never missed a day's work in 6 years or exceeded projected costs of sales (expenses) during that period.
- Increased sales overall from $66,000 to $465,000 annually, maintaining an annual average of 38% increase.
- Upon recent introduction of new "Pre-Paid" program, succeeded in obtaining 350 new patient applications per month.

1983–1989

Medical Sales Representative – New York Territory
Baker Labs, Newark, New Jersey

- Sold prescription soaps, lotions, bath oils, shampoos, and drugs, detailing their use, indication, and application to physicians, nurses, pharmacists, therapists, and purchasing agents throughout all of upstate New York.
- Had direct sales responsibility to hospitals, drug wholesalers, chain drug headquarters, health clinics, nursing homes, and governmental agencies.
- Initiated direct sales and promotion to the territory, increasing volume from 0 to approximately $100,000 annually in 4 years.

WORK EXPERIENCE – Continued

1980–1983 **Medical Sales Representative** – Syracuse Territory
Century Labs, Lincoln, Nebraska

- Promoted and sold pharmaceuticals and non-prescription drugs for treatment of upper respiratory diseases and allergies.
- Sold to purchasing agents of hospitals, chain drug headquarters, drug wholesalers, and governmental agencies, covering greater central and the north country area of upstate New York.

1975–1980 **Territory Representative** – Syracuse Area
Essex Pharmaceuticals, Carmel, California

In-depth involvement in promotion of various prescription pharmaceuticals, proprietary drugs, over-the-counter health and beauty aids, hospital diagnostics, and central service supplies.

Extensive sales and marketing in 4 medical specialties: Ophthalmology, Dermatology, Radiology, and Anti-Tubercular Therapy.

Responsibilities:
- Sold contact lens products, skin care medications, ophthalmic solutions, X-ray diagnostics, post-operative disposables, and anti-tubercular drugs.
- Called on: hospitals, governmental agencies, optical wholesalers, drug wholesalers, chain drug headquarters, independent pharmacies, physicians, opticians, optometrists, and hospital resident programs.

Achievements:
- Opened new territory introducing entire product line to the area. Increased sales from $4,000 to $125,000 annually while opening 135 new accounts.
- Merchandised countless pharmacies and health and beauty aid departments, setting up contact lens solution sections and converting cosmeticians to utilizing O.T.C. products as makeup base.

EDUCATION

Syracuse University
B.A. Chemistry, 1975

REFERENCES

Are available upon request.

William Morrow

33 Naples Drive
Clay, N.Y. 13041
(315) 629-1062

EMPLOYMENT

5/91–present ESSEX POWER CO., Syracuse, N.Y.
Medium-sized manufacturer of pneumatic and hydraulic cylinders and related components ($40 million annual sales).

Territory Manager

Responsibilities: Generate sales volume to show growth for territory at a reasonable profitability percentage with a good product mix ratio. Consult with customer engineering on proper design and use of products, and with maintenance personnel for repair, replacement and service. Ensure continued customer satisfaction. Follow up on all inquiries and call on existing accounts on a call frequency based on potential. Keep controllable expenses at a minimum. Keep complete, accurate records for each account.

Customers: OEM's, machine tool builders, and user accounts (all types of manufacturing requiring automated processes).

Contacts: Project and Design Engineers, Maintenance Supervisors, and Purchasing Agents.

Territory: New York State from Syracuse east to Vermont and Massachusetts line, north and south from Canadian border to the Pennsylvania line.

Volume: Built territory from $75,000 in 1990 to $300,000 in 1992. Had 32% increase for 1st quarter of 1995 before having territory reorganized.

Accomplishments: • For second quarter of 1996 in new territory, had 13% increase over 2nd quarter of 1995.
   • Top sales for presses in the company and was second highest for air motors for 2nd quarter sales period.

9/90–3/91 JOHNSON RESEARCH, Newark, N.J.
Small manufacturer of welding parts ($10 million annual sales).

Outside Sales Representative

Generated sales throughout the Hudson Valley-eastern New York area, calling on maintenance departments, paper mills, and manufacturing facilities. Position was on a straight commission basis (worked simultaneously for Sklar Tools).

12/90–5/91   SKLAR TOOLS, Yonkers, N.Y.
               Small distributor of maintenance items, tools, fasteners, etc. ($15 million annual sales).

               Outside Sales Representative

               Generated sales in entire Hudson Valley-eastern New York area, calling on maintenance departments, manufacturing facilities, OEM's, and automotive garages. Worked on a straight commission basis up until 3/91, at which time received a draw salary, commission, and company car.

2/86–9/90   MAJOR SUPPLY CO., Glens Falls, N.Y.
               Automotive and industrial products distributor of fasteners, chain, binders, cable, truck accessories, and other maintenance items.

               Sales Representative

               Sold and serviced existing accounts, generated new business, called on delinquents, introduced new products, and trained other salesmen. Customers included industrial accounts, utilities, municipalities, large truck fleets and school bus garages. Contacts were purchasing agents, maintenance departments, stock room personnel, and service managers. Territory was Hudson Valley (Plattsburgh, Glens Falls, Albany). Built territory from zero base to approximately $300,000. Became key account salesman servicing customers that owner personally handled.

EDUCATION

Siena College, Albany, N.Y.
A.A.S. Business Administration (1985)
Dean's List, *Who's Who in American Junior Colleges*

REFERENCES

Will be furnished upon request

DAVID SUMMERS

65 MEADOW DRIVE
SOUTH BEND, INDIANA 46623
(219) 241-3824

EXPERIENCE:

October 1990
to Present

ACME SPORTSWEAR DISTRIBUTORS
South Bend, Indiana

Regional Sales Manager: Direct factory rep responsible for annual sales in excess of $1,000,000. Manage all stocking-distributor and direct-dealer accounts in Illinois, northwest Indiana, and southeast Wisconsin. Responsibilities include opening new distributor accounts, building dealer distribution, forecasting, establishing quotas, training distributor and dealer sales personnel, merchandising/designing custom displays, conducting sales seminars, implementing advertising, sales aids and product promotions, coordinating and working trade shows, and solving on-site consumer complaints and problems.

November 1984
to September 1990

AMERICAN MARKET CO., INC.
Division of Warner-Lambert Company
Terre Haute, Indiana

District Sales Manager: Was responsible for recruiting, training and managing Retail Reps in five territories located in northern Illinois and eastern Iowa. Also had key-account responsibility for all drug-and-sundry wholesalers, and for drug, hardware, and mass-merchandiser chains.

September 1982
to October 1984

PACIFIC INDUSTRIES, INC.
Division of National Home Products
Chicago, Illinois

Field Salesman: Entry-level outside sales position. Had sales and service responsibility for retail grocery, drug, mass-merchandiser, and hardware stores. Territory included the northern suburbs of Chicago.

EDUCATION:

B.A. 1984 University of Chicago
Chicago, Illinois

REFERENCES:

Available upon request.

RALPH EMERSON

19 New Beard Drive • Rendge, NH 03461 • (603) 262-1461

Experience

July 1995–present

Nelson Assoc., Inc.
REGIONAL SALES MANAGER – NY, NJ, CT, NH, VT

Start-up situation for Florida-based manufacturer of new fabric protectant. Responsibilities include building customer base among furniture dealers, interior designers, hospitals; doing market research to identify potential customers and competitors; starting to build sales force; attending trade shows.

May 1993–June 1995

Evans Roger Fabrics, Inc.
TERRITORY SALES MANAGER – U.S. and Canada

Increased sales force from 17 to 22. Reorganized territories and developed sales force. (Company now has best sales force in its market niche.) Did market research to identify potential customers and products. Produced lavish color catalog, the company's major marketing tool. Made presentations to important customers. Prepared and implemented marketing strategies.

Sales representative for Canada from 1993–1994. Appointed Territory Manager in January 1995.

1983–1993

David Burns, Ltd.
Talent Agency based in Montreal and Toronto.
MANAGER, TORONTO OFFICE

Responsible for preparing and implementing strategies, contract negotiations, union relations. Organized office and supervised staff of 2.

Developed and preempted new markets by expanding into theater and French-language productions. Increased office revenues by 25% during industry recession in 1992. Improved quality of client roster until fewer than 1% of applicants were accepted for representation. Dealt with people of varied temperaments and backgrounds. Served as guest speaker to drama students.

1977–1979

Arrow Employment Co., Inc.
Temporary Labor Supply Co., Montreal
DISPATCHER

Responsible for soliciting new accounts, servicing existing ones, in charge of up to 100 men. Succeeded in doubling the office revenues within 2 years, though office staff was reduced from 3 to 2.

Sumer Jobs
1980; 1981

Avis Rent-A-Car, Montreal Airport Office
CAR JOCKEY AND FILL-IN FOREMAN

Education

UNIVERSITY OF NEW HAMPSHIRE
M.B.A. 1994 (evening courses)

CONCORDIA UNIVERSITY, Montreal
B. Communications, Major in Management 1982

UNIVERSITÉ DE MONTREAL
French courses, summer 1976

Honors and Awards

CONCORDIA UNIVERSITY
Academic Honors List every year, Ranked first in graduating class
Fluent in English and French

References available upon request.

JUNE BROWN

30 Broad Street
Atlanta, Georgia 30397

home: (404) 821-5994
work: (404) 532-4148

KEY QUALIFICATIONS:

- Over fifteen years' successful sales, sales management, and marketing experience in highly competitive and technical markets.
- Superior record in developing account/distributor networks, and training/motivating/ directing an effective sales force.
- Effective problem-solving abilities—knowledgeable in customer relations, market conditions, and technological trends.
- Excellent communication skills—ability to interface effectively with all levels of personnel and management.
- Familiar with creating and implementing successful corporate marketing/advertising strategies.
- Consistent record of increasing levels of sales, profitability, and responsibility.

AREAS OF KNOWLEDGE AND EXPERIENCE:

- Strategic Planning
- Policy Determination
- Sales Administration
- Sales Forecasting
- Sales Hiring/Training
- Trade Shows/Promotions

- Field Service Management
- Distributors/Sales Reps.
- Dealer Contracts
- Territory Layout
- Marketing/Pricing
- Customer Relations

BUSINESS EXPERIENCE:

1990–Present **Knepper Manufacturing Co., Atlanta, Ga.**
Regional Marketing and Sales Manager

Primary responsibilities and accomplishments as follows:
- Planning, directing, coordinating, and supervising all sales activities ($11 million); developing and implementing product/marketing strategies; formulating appropriate budgets/sales forecasts. Involved with Strategic Planning and familiar with MBO and current management techniques.
- Establishing goals for field managers, marketing services, and related personnel/ services. Supervising/evaluating subordinate personnel.
- Maintaining effective customer relations; liaison with manufacturers, distributors/ accounts.

1986–1990 **Everlast, Inc., Atlanta, Ga.**
Territory Sales Manager

Responsible for general management of sales operation with P&L accountability for assigned area. Developed sales forecasts by product line and geographic sales area. Increased sales from $1.3 million to $3.8 million/year.

1983–1986	**Marshal & Murphy, Inc., Atlanta, Ga.**
	Field Sales/Marketing Services Manager

Established planning and control activities for managing field representatives, training and motivating. Coordinated, directed, and evaluated all administrative functions and responsibilities associated with implementation of marketing programs for field personnel.

1980–1983	**Kossack, Inc., Atlanta, Ga.**
	Product Manager

Coordinated product line planning, marketing, and pricing. Direct involvement in implementing successful promotional programs for assigned products. Developed cost reduction programs on existing product lines.

EDUCATION:

University of Georgia
- MBA in Marketing, 1989
- MBA in Management, 1987
- BA in Marketing, 1986

PROFESSIONAL SOCIETIES:

American Marketing Association
American Management Association
Gamma Lambda Chapter of Delta Mu Delta, National Honor Society in Business Administration

REFERENCES:

Available on request.

GRACE HARPER

61 LAWSON LANE
SILVER SPRING, MD 20946
(301) 621-2297

REGIONAL SALES MANAGEMENT

Versatile, articulate executive, with demonstrable capacity to undertake, develop, and direct business projects based on sound goal-setting and planning. Have solidly increased sales and profits of every business with which associated.

Entire career concerned primarily with sales, sales promotion, and personnel, some with management-level responsibilities covering comprehensive range of business activities – investments, leasing, product, management. Strong administrator of diverse activities requiring heads-up ability. A creative marketing strategist; formed and maintained direct sales teams, improving motivation and selling techniques. Able analyst, imaginative and resourceful.

EXPERIENCE

Real Estate – Sales, Sales Management, and Investment
Hotel Chain – Sales, Management
Consumer Product – Sales and Marketing

1977–present   Leeds & Co., Baltimore, Md.
Sales Representative

Solely responsible for the southern New Jersey and Delmarva Peninsula sales and marketing of an electric-heating products line to mass merchandising accounts, department stores, and electrical distributors. Brought this line from an unknown entity to a leader in the field.

- Constant field-activity in personal selling, and meeting with buyers and merchandise managers.
- Conducted sales seminars on product and selling technique.
- Wrote all marketing and sales bulletins.

1972–1977   Rodgers, Smith & Co., Camden, N.J.
Vice President

Co-founder of this second largest real estate investment-syndication firm, selling participations in real estate ownership.

- Created sales force of over 80 people from scratch.
- Coordinated sales promotion and advertising.
- Responsible for investigation and critical evaluation of real estate offerings and building operations; financial analysis, management appraisal, legal and tax consequences.
- Associated activities involved lease negotiations, S.E.C. regulations, commission arrangements.
- Created and managed rental campaigns for income-producing properties.

1970–1972   Pat Berger Associates, Inc., Newark, N.J.
             Vice-President

             Instrumental in establishing real estate syndication sales on a higher and broader level of operation.

             ♦ Joined company at its inception as salesperson, advancing to position of Vice President, with full responsibility for managing all sales activities, selection and training of salesforce, formulation of marketing strategy, responsible for more than 100 sales personnel.

             ♦ Shared responsibilities in all other functions similar to those outlined above at Rodgers, Smith.

1963–1970   Jonas Hotels Management, Springfield, Mass.
             Director of Sales

             Responsible for all sales at the Shelton Hotel, Springfield, Mass., and the Hotel Theresa, New York City

             ♦ Planned and executed advertising campaigns with local newspapers and radio stations.

             ♦ Met with corporate executives soliciting commercial room sales and banquet functions.

EDUCATION

University of Maryland
B.A. Business Administration, 1963

University of Maryland
Real Estate Seminars, 1965

REFERENCES

On request.

PETER CHU MING

10 ASHLEY AVENUE
NORWICH, NY 10523
(914) 592-6320

EXPERIENCE

BAKER INDUSTRIES, New York, N.Y.   8/91 to Present

District Sales Manager – Responsible for administering company policy and supervision of District Sales force in the merchandising of Industrial and Automotive supplies to achieve forecast. Primary responsibility is to hire and train representatives to successfully sell Industrial and Automotive parts and supplies.

Direct Responsibilities:
- To supervise, motivate, and coordinate a staff of ten sales representatives.
- To continue sales training by field visits utilizing the "coach" concept.
- To break district goals down into territory goals and administer their success.

Accomplishments:
- Key account intensification program.
- Establishing an Automotive Distributor network.
- Expansion of account base.

REVLON COSMETICS, Rochester, N.Y.   7/84 to 8/91

Territory Manager – Sold, merchandised and established promotional programs in all retail stores, including department stores, JC Penney and Sears in the Rochester, Buffalo, and Syracuse markets. Established communication with salespersons, buyers, merchandise managers and general merchandise managers in territory.

Accomplishments:
- Maintained accounts despite a national department store trend to more prestigious houses.
- Selected to give a presentation at the department store National Sales Meeting.
- Initiated a new "Stock to Sales" concept to increase purchases with Revlon.
- Acted as a troubleshooter with problem accounts out of territory. Created and presented merchandising plans to these accounts.
- Trained new sales personnel.

MENDELSON BROTHERS, Yonkers, N.Y.   8/75 to 6/84

Stationery and Greeting Card Buyer – Promoted to Cosmetics after one year, a larger department with 40 salespeople and a heavier promotional activity program. Primary function was to administer all phases of department operation as if it were a separate business to include responsibility for net profit performance.

MIMI'S DEPARTMENT STORE, Yonkers, N.Y.   3/73 to 7/75

Buyer – Managed and sold in many departments including: Stationery, Greeting Cards, Luggage, Silverware, Notions, and Christmas Specialties.

EDUCATION

Monroe County Community College
A.A.B., Merchandising, 1972

REFERENCES

Available upon request.

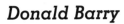

309 W 76 Street
New York, N.Y. 10001
(212) 787-4617 • (212) 719-6000

Donald Barry

EMPLOYMENT HISTORY

7/89–Present COLGATE MARKETING GROUP, INC., New York, N.Y.
(knit tops, novelty printwear)
Vice President of Marketing and Regional Sales Manager
Supervise sales force of 15, servicing major national accounts, such as: J.C. Penney Co., Montgomery Ward and Hills Department Stores. Chairperson of the Advisory Committee, responsible for the creation and merchandising of all lines.

6/87–6/89 LEVITT MILLS, INC., New York, N.Y.
(underwear and knit tops)
Sales Representative
Sold to major chains, discounters, and screen printers. Involved in merchandising and setting up major chain programs.

10/84–6/87 JONES AND SMITH, INC., New York, N.Y.
Sales Representative
Sold and serviced major chain accounts (Sears Roebuck and Co., J.C. Penney Co., and Montgomery Ward). Have knowledge of all facets of chain operations.

EDUCATION

1980–1984 Ohio University, Athens, Ohio
Received a Bachelor of Science degree in Public Relations, with concentrated areas in marketing research and English. Was a member of the Sigma Delta Chi Fraternity. Was the Business Associate on the Athens Magazine staff. Did some public relations work for the Athens County Children's Services. Played intramural sports.

REFERENCES

References will be furnished upon request.

Peter E. Bazarcus

132 Centre Street
Arlington, Virginia 22275
(703) 661-2490

PROFESSIONAL EXPERIENCE

Fifteen years' experience in Sales and Marketing, including developing national accounts calls for both export and import sales. Attained increased sales and revenues. Developed sales agency network in New England (Mass., Conn., R.I.), upstate New York (Buffalo, Rochester, Syracuse), Baltimore, and Chicago. Sales and marketing calls made on national accounts, foreign freight forwarders, and custom house brokers.

Responsible for Sales and Agency Staff of approximately twelve employees. Professional background has been selling services in the Transportation Field (Steamship and Trucking).

EMPLOYMENT HISTORY

Royal Cargo, Inc.
Washington, D.C.
Vice-President, Sales Manager
1992–present

Report directly to President.

Responsible for increasing sales and revenues to our market lanes serviced by Royal Cargo, Inc.

Responsible for making national accounts sales calls with sales staff and agents in New York, New Jersey, New England, Baltimore, and Chicago.

Cunard Lines, Inc.
Baltimore, Maryland
Manager, Wines & Spirits
1987–1992

Reported to Senior Vice-President of Marketing.

Responsible for increasing sales and revenues for all wines and spirits carryings from the Continent, United Kingdom, and Mediterranean.

Holiday Steamship, Inc.
Baltimore, Maryland
Assistant Director of Sales
1980–1987

Reported to General Manager.

Responsible for increasing sales and revenues to the trade lanes in the Carribean and West Indies.

Responsible for New York sales team and agency networks in New Jersey, New England, and Baltimore.

EDUCATION

University of Maryland
1985–1987

REFERENCES

Upon request

JOHN TUMINO

25 NORTHRIDGE ROAD, OLD GREENWICH, CONNECTICUT 06870

Home: (203) 637-6653   *Office:* (203) 980-8573

Professional Experience:

1995–present   GILLIAM LABS, Danbury, Connecticut

Special Project

Responsible for the compilation, maintenance, and automation of an inventory control system for the purpose of depreciating fixed assets.

1994–1995   BENTON & MATHISON, New York, New York

Account Manager

Was responsible for servicing existing accounts and acquiring new accounts for firm. Trained Account Executive in branch office in the areas of canvassing, sales strategy, operational procedures and policies.

- Obtained 32 new accounts and recovered 23 dormant existing accounts. Increased sales by 21.5 percent.
- Instituted sales brochure, proposal agreement, marketing surveys, and monthly telemarketing to improve the efficiency of the firm.
- Attended conventions in Washington, D.C. and Philadelphia to further my knowledge of product and expand future potential market.

1992–1994   MARTIN'S DEPARTMENT STORE, Danbury, Connecticut

Selling Specialist

Generated sales activity for wide range of merchandise. Extensive activity in the areas of inventory, advertising, and merchandising. Determined proper assortment and coordinated departmental changes to increase sales.

Education: B.S. Business Administration; concentration in Marketing; New York University
Cumulative Average 3.3   Major 3.6
Member of Delta Mu Delta Business Honor Society

Professional Affiliations: American Marketing Association

Special Skills: Fluent in Italian.

Professional References: Available upon Request.

ROBERTA DONNELLY

P.O. Box 715 • New City, NY 11547
(914) 522-4141

EXPERIENCE

12/93–present

GENERAL DEVICES LTD.   **Yonkers, NY**
Manufacturer of innovative digital audio products.

Account Executive
Create markets for the integration of a unique digital audio technology with existing products and systems. Determine potential applications, establish initial contact, promote need for audio to enhance customer's system, and orchestrate implementation of product.

- Won General Devices' first opportunity to participate in a mass transit stop-announcement system.
- Generated new product applications in markets such as industrial equipment, amusement, safety, and transportation.
- Streamlined sales process to key industry. Improved utilization of manufacturer's representatives.

6/88–12/93

PHOTOCIRCUITS CORPORATION   **Glen Cove, NY**
Market leader in printed circuit board manufacturing.

7/90–12/93

Account Manager
Managed all facets of business relationships with new and existing customers. Supervised Technical Service Engineers and directed Customer Service, Production Control, Manufacturing, Engineering, and Quality to achieve total customer satisfaction. Accounts included Motorola, OKI Telecom, Panasonic, Compaq, and Texas Instruments.

- Expanded account base from $6 million to $19 million over an 18-month period by increasing market share at existing customers and penetrating new market areas.
- Guided future company growth by studying marketplace and predicting needs for process capacity expansion, new equipment, additional services, and lower cost manufacturing methods.
- Resolved critical product reliability issue by leading a team of manufacturing managers, engineers, and executives. Succeeded in retaining $4 million in business.
- Developed Photocircuits' first relationship with Japanese automotive transplant operations. Overcame cultural and technical obstacles to achieve high volume production.
- Conducted technical marketing presentations to customers to communicate improvement plans, design guidelines, quality systems, and new manufacturing processes.
- Cultivated company-wide quality system vital to relationships with key accounts.

6/88–7/90   **Technical Service Engineer**
Primary technical interface with Ford Electronics. Designed production tooling for manufacturability and cost effectiveness, quoted new business, ensured conformance to specification, tracked product yield, and monitored field performance.

- Provided technical service on design and quality issues through biweekly visits to customer assembly site.
- Participated in formal design reviews. Suggested cost-saving alternatives, ensured manufacturing feasibility and high yield.
- Reduced customer defect from greater than 3,000 to 200 parts per million by identifying root causes and facilitating implementation of corrective actions.

EDUCATION

9/85–6/88   **RENSSELAER POLYTECHNIC INSTITUTE**   **Troy, NY**
Bachelor of Science, Mechanical Engineering
Phi Beta Phi Sorority, Big Brothers/Big Sisters.

Spring, 1985   **UNIVERSITY OF GRANADA**   **Granada, SPAIN**
Spanish studies abroad.

REFERENCES   Furnished upon request.

Robert Lopez

7 El Centro Avenue • Austin, Texas 78765
(512) 214-7756

QUALIFICATIONS SUMMARY

➤ Possess strong written and verbal communication skills; interact and work well with people at all levels.
➤ Strong initiative; accustomed to a heavy workload without supervision. Results oriented.
➤ Analytical and creative; able to define problem areas and provide effective solutions.
➤ Considerable leadership experience in business and in civic and social organizations.

EMPLOYMENT EXPERIENCE

7/95–present   Willow and Eager, Inc., Austin, Texas

Account Manager. Responsible for telemarketing and obtaining information required for cost analysis for client projects. Conducted on-site sales presentations.

5/88–6/95   Queens Lithographs, Inc., Austin, Texas

Regional Marketing Consultant. Supervised marketing and customer service representatives during client transactions. Designed office space for marketing representatives. Planned and directed marketing strategy for North Texas. Increased scope and volume of product sales using telemarketing and personal visits.

Marketing Representative. Represented Queens at local and national conventions. Helped design pricing plan. Responsible for increasing sales of school photography products. Wrote newsletter for School Division customers.

Customer Service Representative and Account Executive. Responsible for special handling of client requirements, logistical arrangements, price quotes, and expediting rush orders. Acted as liaison between clients and lab. Provided customers with advice and information on all aspects of photography. Promoted additional services during business development.

5/83–9/84   Wal-Mart Inc., Austin, Texas

Assistant Manager. Responsible for retail sales of photography equipment and for inventory maintenance.

11/78–11/84   **United States Naval Reserve.** Honorable Discharge.

EDUCATION

1984–1987   BFA, University of Texas
Kappa Pi Honorary Art Fraternity. Dean's List.

1981–1983   Associate Degree of Applied Science, Photography – May 1983
Amarillo College, Amarillo, Texas
Received partial academic scholarship, with balance of college expenses self-financed. Dean's List.

1990   Dale Carnegie Course – Graduate Assistant

MEMBERSHIPS
Professional Photographers Association of America.
Texas Professional Photographers Association.

References furnished upon request.

ALBERT CHAPMAN

44 MARJORIE LANE
SIOUX CENTER, IOWA 51150
(712) 645-5291

EXPERIENCE:

10/92–Present ACCOUNT MANAGER
Van Proof Business Machines, Inc.
Sioux Center, Iowa

While developing business in new and existing accounts, achieved 100% of quota in 1993 ($250,000) and 107% of quota in 1994 ($300,000). In recognition of being #1 in branch sales for 1993 and 1994, was promoted from Sales Representative to Territory Manager to Account Manager. The branch went from last to first in the district during this time.

In addition to sales, trained new sales representatives in sales techniques, sales strategies, and account analysis.

9/90–10/91 ASSISTANT BUYER
Barton & Thomas, Sioux Center, Iowa

In the Men's Jeans Department, with an annual volume of $4,500,000, was responsible for placing orders and forecasting. Coordinated and controlled the flow of merchandise between the main store and 10 branch stores. In addition, trained, supervised, and evaluated merchandise assistants.

6/87–9/90 MANAGER
Jade Gifts & Cards, Reno, Nevada

As Manager, assisted owner in purchasing, selling, and merchandising in $350,000 retail business.

EDUCATION: Iowa State University, B.S., June 1986
Major: Business Administration-Marketing
(Worked at part-time positions throughout school)

PROFESSIONAL ORGANIZATIONS: Delta Sigma Pi, Professional Business Fraternity.
As Financial Committeeman, coordinated campus publicity and fund-raising events.

REFERENCES: Submitted on request.

ROBERT STEVENS

1573 Palm Springs Blvd.
Miami, Florida 33182
(305) 890-5261

– EXPERIENCE –

FLORIDA NATIONAL BANK, Miami, Florida   1992–Present

Account Manager – World-renowned banking institution maintaining a reputation of excellence in the area of finance. Responsibilities include: independent maintenance of 1,000 client accounts encompassing a territory of 10 southeastern states; in concert with field manager and sales representatives: generating new business; direct contact (80% travel); servicing existing accounts; operational problem analysis and resolutions; establishment of new business sources and determination of cost profitability; monitoring volume of sales; coordinating receipt of banking materials to conduct training and instructional seminars for clients; preparation of marketing, sales volume and penetration reports; direct incentive and promotional presentations; attendance at sales and management banking seminars.

CHARTER, INC., Orlando, Florida   1991–1992

Group Manager – Location represented $5 million per annum in sales; responsibilities included: management of 5 departments (5 department managers, 100 employees) efficiently and effectively ensuring productivity and profitability; merchandising; display; personnel; compilation and budgeting of payroll; cost analysis; financial reports.

WILLIAM SMITH ASSOCIATES, Atlanta, Georgia   1986–1990

Assistant Manager/Fashion Coordinator – Coordinator for 4 corporate facilities; responsibilities included: personnel (hiring, training, counseling, and termination); payroll; display planning; purchasing; planning, coordination and presentation of fashion seminars.

– EDUCATION –

University of Miami
Miami, Florida
BA, 1986
Major: Business Management
Minor: Psychology

REFERENCES AND ADDITIONAL INFORMATION AVAILABLE UPON REQUEST.

Joan Jackson

64 Charles Street
Byron, Pa. 16917
(814) 914-4076 · (814) 628-3579

EXPERIENCE

6/93–Present Major Financial Data Bank, Byron, Pa.
ACCOUNT MANAGER
Responsibilities include introducing new products and services to present and potential subscribers. Coordinate tasks with Dayton-based Administration, Marketing, Product Development, and Operations staffs.
- Winner of sales awards for 3 consecutive years for exceeding quotas.
- Built a professional staff by recruiting, interviewing, hiring, and training Account Representatives.
- Developed a cohesive, highly motivated Area Team by providing coaching and directing long-range and short-range planning sessions.

5/91–6/93 Financial Data Base, Inc., Erie, Pa.
ACCOUNT REPRESENTATIVE
Sold services to decision makers in a variety of market segments. Provided ongoing and advanced training to subscribers. Persuaded subscribers of the benefits of information services by developing applications.
- Increased revenue base by building use and adding terminals.
- Authored "Marketing Guide to the Financial Industry."

4/86–5/91 Johnson Clearing House, Pittsburgh, Pa.
SALES REPRESENTATIVE
Sold specialized reporters in the legal marketplace. Serviced subscribers by keeping them abreast of new publications.

EDUCATION

1986 B.A., Psychology Major
St. Andrews College, Lancaster, Pa.

REFERENCES

Available upon request

Helen Rowland

46 Robin Lane Rd.
Toledo, Ohio 43612
Phone: (419) 936-6215

EMPLOYMENT EXPERIENCE

Marsh Food Service, Inc.
Toledo, Ohio

National Accounts Manager
April 1995 to present

Originally employed to reorganize and train an existing sales staff. Position was expanded to include both national account and street sales as well as customer service and operations. This position entailed formalization of job descriptions, initiation of training programs, and establishment of procedural formats. Eventually the position included handling all matters pertaining to multi-unit food service customers at corporate levels. Promoted to position of National Accounts Manager.

Loft Candy Co., Inc.
Toledo, Ohio

Director of Sales and Marketing
August 1992 to April 1995

Initially employed to manage sales through an established national sales organization consisting of 31 brokers. Promoted in 1982 to Director of Sales and Marketing for the U.S. Responsibilities included enlargement of the sales organization, hiring and training of sales personnel, streamlining of the company marketing effort, design and sale of specialty promotions for advertising, and account trouble-shooting. The company market included retail, wholesale, vending, and military.

Life Savers, Inc.
Akron, Ohio

Key Account Manager
September 1987 to July 1992

Employed as a sales representative to service Lebanon, Cumberland, Dauphin and Perry counties in Pennsylvania. Responsible for sales of the various Life Saver candy products to wholesalers, and to both individual and chain retailers. Promoted in 1988 to Key Account Manager for the Philadelphia-Harrisburg area. As KAM for that territory, responsibilities included training of sales personnel, conducting sales meetings, introduction of new products and direct sales work. Ranked as #1 KAM in the U.S. for Life Savers, never lower than #5 of approximately 50.

Allen's Furniture
Allentown, N.Y.

Store Manager and Designer
July 1986 to September 1987

Employed to manage the transition of this retail furniture store from purely sales to custom design and sales. Responsibilities included retraining of retained personnel and the hiring and training of new designer/sales employees. Duties also included selection of product lines, design and implementation of store displays, and custom design work for customers. Ultimately managed store and all outside operations.

Biltmore Interiors (Ethan Allen Furniture)
Akron, Ohio

Interior Designer
April 1979 to July 1986

Employed after completion of education in Interior Design. Work included assisting in the interior design of the newly opened store and continuing interior design for store customers.

EDUCATION

School of Interior Design
Toledo, Ohio 1979

REFERENCES

Available upon request.

John Foster

410 East 79th Street • New York, NY 10128 • (212) 445-4144 (H) • (212) 555-9190 (W)

WORK EXPERIENCE:

Sprint Corporation – 380 Madison Avenue, New York, NY   *6/94–Present*
Senior Business Services Representative

- First sales representative in region to sell Sprint Link (dedicated access to the Internet).
- Successfully selling Sprint's DRUMS service to postproduction community.
- Illustrate consultative selling approach through vertical marketing of Frame Relay.
- Selected acting Branch Manager while incumbent was vacationing.
- Trained in LANs, Bridges, and Routers via NorthEastern's Corporate Education Series.
- Extensive training in X.25, Frame Relay, ATM, and Internet applications.

MCI Telecommunications – 3 International Drive, Rye Brook, NY   *11/92–5/94*
Account Executive

- Successfully sold switched and dedicated services to both existing and new commercial users.
- Achieved 148% of sales quota for 1993.
- Responsible for $5,000 monthly revenue quota.
- Analyzed customer's telecommunications services and proposed appropriate alternatives.
- Formally trained in data communications and sales strategy.

Chrysler Financial Corp. – 660 White Plains Road, Tarrytown, NY   *11/90—10/92*
Account Adjuster

- Performed collection duties to prevent delinquent payments.
- Responsible for consignment funds of repossessed automobiles.
- Analyzed account status and recommended repossession when appropriate.

Field Representative

- Performed customer service duties in lease department.
- Issued final invoices on mature accounts.
- Audited dealer inventories and researched discrepancies.

EDUCATION:

State University of New York at Albany   *5/86–5/90*

- BA Degree in European History.
- Minors in Political Science and English.
- Dean's List – 3.1 GPA - 3.7 in major.

COMPUTER SKILLS: Proficient in WordPerfect, Windows, ACT!, Lotus 1-2-3, and Excel.

References Furnished upon Request

Sales Managers and Executives

Ellen Feinberg

800 Canoe Brook Drive
Grand Rapids, Michigan 49520
(616) 688-7452 · (616) 233-8784

EXPERIENCE

August 1992 to Present

SALES ADMINISTRATOR –
Air Travel, Inc.
Grand Rapids, Michigan
- Planning & Initiation—Demonstrated organizational ability through effective time management and assigning precedence to diversified duties. Created telemarketing program to generate leads for field reps. Consulted with sales promotion agency to develop new brochure. Represented company as a vendor at major conventions. Organized all social functions for corporate clients.
- Client Contact—Developed and implemented strategies for presenting new services to different market segments. Assisted Vice-President in maintaining a sales volume of $3.5 million per year through continued telephone public relations campaigns, face-to-face presentations, and written correspondence. Prepared written pricing proposals for client evaluation. Handled client complaints and resolved service problems.
- Corporate Management—Acted as operations and sales liaison to identify problematic trends and propose solutions. Monitored corporate sales goals by analyzing sales figures and profit margins. Prepared sales meeting minutes and reports for upper-level management. Administered lead program and supervised office staff.

February 1992 to August 1992

CONTRACTS ADMINISTRATOR –
Nelson Publishing, Inc.
Detroit, Michigan
Issued international and domestic subsidiary rights contracts for company and its many publishing divisions.

July 1991 to January 1992

ENTERTAINMENT AGENT –
Carnegie Entertainment Bureau
Detroit, Michigan
Sold lecture engagements to colleges and universities. Wrote promotional correspondence, negotiated contractual deals, and collected accounts receivable.

EDUCATION

Bachelor of Arts in Rhetoric and Communications at Michigan State University, magna cum laude, May 1991.

Vice Chairperson, Michigan Speakers Forum. Budgeted funds of $50K for programming lectures and allocating to other student groups. Negotiated with agents and arranged all engagements. Directed a staff of 30 in publicity, ticketing, and stage management.

Publicity Chairperson, Michigan State University Concert Board. Publicized concerts via radio, newspapers, and posters. Wrote ad copy, designed posters, and delegated work assignments.

ASSOCIATIONS

Member, National Association of Female Executives
Coordinating Committee, Raoul Wallenberg New Leadership Society of the Simon Wiesenthal Center

REFERENCES

Submitted on request

HARRISON MILLER

17580 Redwood Circle
Tacoma, Washington 98052
(206) 932-4414

AREAS OF DEMONSTRATED EFFECTIVENESS

- Developing innovative sales strategies to expand market share
- Opening and developing new accounts, as well as new business segments
- Establishing effective long-term business relationships with key accounts
- Increasing performance of existing accounts through hands-on account management
- Recruiting, training and motivating people to work together as an effective team

PROFESSIONAL EXPERIENCE AND ACHIEVEMENTS

Belsons, Inc. Seattle, WA   April 1988 to present
A worldwide supplier of Northwest evergreen products.

Director of Sales & Marketing, Sherwood Forest Farms Division (April 1993 to present)

- Responsible for $5.1 million in sales; control marketing budget of $400,000. Personally handle company key accounts, representing 30% of gross annual revenue.
- Developed and implemented marketing plan for division which accounted for 46% increase (1.6 million) in sales over 2 years.
- Established company's first inside sales force, which included hiring, training, supervising and evaluation.
- Initiated and developed all direct mail pieces and sales brochures; direct mail pieces generated higher than industry-average returns.
- Instituted nationwide advertising campaign. Researched trade publications in new market segments; advertising in these publications increased incoming leads by 20% and opened new markets for division.
- Successfully diversified customer base and expanded company's geographic coverage to traditionally weak Eastern Seaboard through targeted direct mail and follow-up plan.
- Instituted client referral incentive program resulting in 50% more new customers than projected for 1994, highest lead-to-final-order performance of all programs; saved company $12,000 in advertising costs.
- Developed and implemented inactive account regeneration program, resulting in $120,000 in gross sales revenue and saving company $8,000 in advertising costs; increased customer retention through hands-on account management.
- Instrumental in placing division on line with computer system and contact management software (Market Force), increasing productivity and customer service efficiency.
- Responsible for efficient movement of seasonal inventory nationwide within tight shipping window. Act as liaison between brokers and production facilities.
- Established company newsletter to project image of accessibility.

National Sales Manager, Belsons, Inc. (April 1988 to March 1993)

- Responsible for $3.5 million in sales; reported directly to the company president.
- Hired to establish, train and supervise sales force.
- Developed all sales and merchandising programs as well as promotional materials and sales brochures.
- Called on key European accounts in Holland and Germany; increased European key account container business by 10%.
- Expanded domestic wholesale floral business through new prospecting techniques and multiple pricing techniques.
- Developed "grocery pack" marketing concept that allowed entry into the national grocery chain business; concept subsequently copied by competitors. Single-handedly opened H.E. Butt Grocery, King Soopers, Albertsons, Jewel Food Stores, Publix Supermarkets, and Gardener's Eden, which ultimately accounted for 80% of total gross sales.
- Developed "palletized" marketing concept that allowed entry into wholesale club stores and retail nursery outlets. Single-handedly opened Home Depot S.E., Sam's Wholesale Club, Price Club, and Pace Membership Warehouse.
- Established and supervised nationwide broker network for grocery and club accounts.

Arndt Investments, Seattle, WA   December 1986 to March 1988

Provided interim property management for family-owned real estate investment company.
Responsible for liquidation of all properties and dissolution of business.

Maidenform, Inc.   March 1984 to November 1986
Manufacturers Representative, Chicago, IL

- Worked closely with buyers of key accounts developing merchandising plans and open-to-buy for sale of product line. Achieved an overall 20% increase in floor space at Marshall Fields by introducing innovative new merchandising concept.
- Responsible for hiring, training and supervision of merchandising staff. After 5 months in Chicago territory, promoted to Denver area to increase business.
- Selected by company as trainer for new sales representatives nationwide.
- Achieved 28% increase in military account revenues in one year through creative pricing structures; concept now used by company nationwide.
- Increased business in territory by 24% in first year during a period of only 3% to 4% growth nationally.

Savin Corporation, Elk Grove Village, IL   July 1982 to February 1984
Sales Representative

- Developed new business and corporate accounts in large territory; opened 4 corporate accounts during first 3 months that resulted in multi-machine contracts.
- Recognized companywide for largest sales month for introduction of new product line.
- Received Salesman of the Month Award 8 times.
- Received National Creative Selling and Central Region Top Ten Awards.

EDUCATION

Bachelor of Arts, Augustana College, Rock Island, IL   June 1982

Major: Business Administration   *Minor:* Political Science

STANLEY Y. THORSON

12 Central Street, South
Omaha, Nebraska 68114

(402) 456-0976 (Home)   (402) 451-4555 (Work)

BACKGROUND SUMMARY

Sales and marketing professional with 19 years of progressive business experience. Specific strengths in:

Product Marketing	Sales Training
Planning and Implementation	Problem Solving
Sales Management	Recruiting
Key Account Sales	Marketing Services

EXPERIENCE

1994–Present **HUTTON & ROGERS, Omaha, Nebraska**
Sales Manager

Author of business plan. Forecasting of all sales and gross profit targets. Management of 30-member sales force accounting for $25 million sales volume. Key account business-to-business sales of office equipment, stationery, furniture, and printing. Hiring and training of new salespeople. Development and coordination of vendor/customer promotions.

Major accomplishment: Introduction of information supply product categories directed to the automated office systems market. These products will account for $1.5 million in additional business for 1996.

1992–1994 **LEEDS REAL ESTATE, INC., Omaha, Nebraska**
Sales and Market Development Account Executive

Responsible for market planning; liaison with developers, financial institutions, and investment groups; analysis of investment properties; major property sales; financial structuring of development projects; commercial management; retail site selection and feasibility; lease negotiation and preparation. Possess Broker's License.

Major accomplishment: Leasing and management representation of 93-acre industrial park.

1988–1992 **PRINCESS PRODUCTS, Chicago, Illinois**
Sales Manager

Sales responsibility for a national giftware manufacturer/distributor. Forecasted and developed sales quotas; established pricing structure; created incentive programs; developed and executed sales presentations to key account chains, department stores, supermarkets, and buying groups; supervised trade shows; developed and produced sales support catalogs; supervised direct mail programs; trained sales personnel; managed 16-member sales force, 4-member administration staff, and independent manufacturers' representative organizations.

Major accomplishment: Developed merchandising programs that successfully opened channels of distribution to supermarket chains.

1984–1984   **ROBERT HALL, INC., Chicago, Illinois**
Group Product Manager

Directed all consumer marketing functions; bottom-line responsibility; supervised preparation of marketing plans; administered operations, promotion and advertising budgets; initiated new product development; established criteria for fixturing and packaging; liaison with advertising agency; managed market research and test market functions; hired and trained marketing personnel.

Major accomplishment: Increased market share during 1986 to 1988 by an average of 12% for all retail product lines.

1977–1984   **ESSEX, INC., Chicago, Illinois**
Senior Product Manager

Developed marketing plans; managed market research function; developed sales strategies; determined manufacturing allotments and pricing; administered and directed 7-figure advertising budget; liaison with agency on production of print and broadcast advertising.

Major accomplishment: Opened new markets, accounting for an additional $11 million in sales.

EDUCATION

M.B.A. Marketing, University of Chicago
B.S. Accounting, University of Chicago

AFFILIATION

Sales Executive Club of Chicago

BENJAMIN WILSON

612 Water Street
Seattle, Washington 98157
(206) 759-1887

PROFESSIONAL EXPERIENCE

1994 to 1996   FAIRBANKS, INC., Seattle, Washington
Sales Manager

Directly responsible for sales and marketing for new manufacturing company including: setting up markets for new consumer product; contacting major accounts including K Mart, Walmart, and Super X Drugs; arranging advertising for TV, radio, and printed media; holding training programs for new Sales Representatives and Brokers for product knowledge and presentation experience; projections and sales forecasts for five-year period.

1990 to 1994   EASTERN WORLD IMPORTS, Vancouver, Canada
U.S. Sales Manager

Company headquarters were in Vancouver with office in Seattle. Set up markets throughout Northwest for foreign imports from China, Japan, Korea, Thailand, and Taiwan. Products included sporting goods, hunting and fishing, team sports, lawn and garden, hardware and tools, electronic equipment (VCR, TV, and radio), toys, model airplanes, boats, etc. Called on buyers of national accounts and coordinated with Buyers and Merchandising Vice-Presidents and their Advertising Departments to set up promotional materials with all media.

Also set up and conducted sales training programs for in-store demonstrations, and forecast sales for new products being introduced into U.S.

1986 to 1990   HARPER & NORTON, Seattle, Washington
Western Regional Sales Manager

Introduced textbooks and curriculum (English, Mathematics, and Science) to department heads and coordinators from elementary through senior secondary levels. On college level worked with departmental deans and curriculum coordinators.

Set up educational seminars working with the educators, demonstrating techniques of using textbooks. Worked with state government agencies to receive title funding for educational programs. Called on local and state libraries to set up major reference and educational programs. Trained new product representatives.

1981 to 1986   L-MART STORES, Tacoma, Washington
Buyer

Responsible for purchasing lines of sporting goods, lawn and garden goods, tools and hardware. Handled year-round buying of domestic and foreign products in above product lines. Managed sales forecasting and promotions, advertising, inventory control, etc. Attended trade shows both domestic and foreign.

1977 to 1981   PORTLAND HIGH SCHOOL, Portland, Oregon
                Teacher

                Taught Biology, General Science, and Chemistry in a classroom setting. Served as
                Head Football and Baseball Coach. Won three State Championships in baseball.

1973 to 1977   UNITED STATES AIR FORCE
                Special Services Officer

                In charge of recreational activities in N.C.O. Officers Clubs, servicemen's centers,
                theaters; set up all sports activities and Base entertainments.
                Highest Rank: Captain
                Honorable Discharge

SUMMARY   • Strong in human resources; ability to establish and maintain positive, productive
                  rapport with customers, management, and subordinates.
                • Excellent sales record in both domestic and foreign markets.
                • Experienced trainer and motivator; instill pride resulting in quality performance
                  and achievement.
                • Work well with clients in problem-solving situations; strong closer.
                • Good organizer with proven ability in getting assignments accomplished and in
                  encouraging others to cooperate.

EDUCATION   UNIVERSITY OF CALIFORNIA, San Francisco, California
                Masters Degree in Business Sales and Marketing Research, 1973

                UNIVERSITY OF CALIFORNIA, Los Angeles, California
                Bachelor of Science, 1972
                Major: Chemistry, Biology, General Science
                Minor: Coaching, ROTC Air Force Program

REFERENCES Available upon request

LINDA RUSHMORE

106 Roger Lane
Syracuse, N.Y. 13212
(315) 415-1144

EXPERIENCE

BUSINESS SYSTEMS, INC., Syracuse, N.Y. *1994–Present*
General Sales Manager
- Responsible for National Sales Force consisting of three Regional Sales Directors, fifteen Sales Consultants, and two Telephone Sales Representatives.
- Responsible for Field Sales Administration (three managers) and the implementation of sales policies and procedures.
- Develop and implement business plans, operating budgets ($3 million), commission plans, and override incentive plans.
- Set quotas, establish performance criteria, and use reporting procedures that I established for quantitative analysis of sales results.
- Recommend pricing and marketing strategies.
- Coordinate activities among sales and engineering, technical sales, production, and field service to assure effective communication with these departments.

WESTERN COMPUTER SYSTEMS, Rochester, N.Y. *1990–1993*
Branch Manager
- Increased branch revenue over fifty percent in FY91 and FY92 and put P & L in solid black position. Led company in new accounts and developed new business with existing client base.
- Responsible for P & L, budgeting, and forecasting.
- Researched, planned, and implemented company entry into the micro market.
- Negotiated agreements with hardware companies, identified and arranged dealerships with software companies, and developed the overall micro marketing strategy.
- Recruited first-rate marketing and technical staff and expanded services offered by branch.
- Directed marketing effort toward concept sale vs. product sale; developed sales literature and customer user aids.
- Designed Prospect Database, directed mail compaigns, and conducted product seminars.

NIAGARA LAND, INC., Rochester, N.Y. *1986–1989*
Marketing Representative
- Responsible for $900,000 annual timesharing revenue.
- Planned and directed territory seminars, prepared branch operating budget, directed branch mail campaigns, and helped train and develop new marketing representatives.
- Developed new marketing strategies for products and outlined accompanying selling techniques.

Financial Analyst
- Designed and prepared FY88 Operating, Headcount, and Capital Budget Business Plan.
- Conducted Post Acquisition Audit on company subsidiaries and initiated subsidiary monthly performance reports.
- Prepared Three-Year Business Forecast, reviewed and summarized industry pricing surveys, and prepared quarterly reports for Board of Directors meetings.
- Designed business models for budgeting and forecasting.

STATE FARM INSURANCE CO., Wayne, N.J.   *1980–1986*
Planning Administrator and Senior Research Consultant
◆ Prepared Operating Business Plan and Quarterly Reports.
◆ Researched and developed leading business indicators.
◆ Developed models to simulate divisional operating strategies.
◆ Prepared economic forecasts and competitive analysis reports.
◆ Scheduled and monitored divisional planning activities for corporate annual and long-range plans.
◆ Designed questionnaires, conducted market surveys and branch office location analyses for operating divisions.

ELLENVILLE COLLEGE, Middletown, N.Y.   *1979–1980*
Lecturer in Statistics and Market Research

EDUCATION

University of Rochester – Graduate School of Business
   Master of Business Administration, 1979
   Concentration in Business Economics
   Financed graduate study through loans and part-time employment

St. John's University
   Bachelor of Business Administration, 1977
   Economics Major
   Business Manager of Newspaper, Economics Club. Financed studies through New York State Regents Scholarship, part-time and summer employment

REFERENCES

Available upon request.

WILLIAM BURTON
16 RAYMOND STREET
PHILADELPHIA, PA. 19121
(215) 628-4813

Sales representative, with more than 16 years of diversified sales experience, seeks a position leading to management.

EMPLOYMENT HISTORY

July 1990–present   Audio Productions, Inc.
Sales Manager   Philadelphia, Pa.

A Telex Company – selling service throughout the Tri-State Area.

Responsibilities include directing 9 sales reps: Training, hiring; setting up a bonus and incentive program. Handle any problem accounts; hold weekly sales meetings. Also review each sales rep's weekly report.

April 1989–May 1990   American Express, Inc.
Collection Consultant   New York, N.Y.

Called on Credit Managers and Controllers of large manufacturing companies. Handled their accounts receivables for collection. Sales volume between $150,000 to $200,000 per month.

December 1983–March 1989   Barker TV Corporation
Sales Representative/Assistant Sales Manager   Philadelphia, Pa.

Initial responsibilities as sales rep included working closely with real estate interests and building managers to install cable television in various uptown apartment houses. Promoted to Assistant Sales Manager and given the responsibility for recruiting, hiring, and training a staff of 12 field sales reps.

Was successful in increasing Barker TV's penetration of the cable television market.

September 1980–November 1983   Xerox, Inc.
National Account Sales Representative   Philadelphia, Pa.

Sold copying machines to 14 major accounts. Consistently exceeded quota for each month in the employ of the company.

EDUCATION

B.A., Business Administration, University of Pennsylvania

PERSONAL DATA

Area Preference: Southeast Pennsylvania area
Personal and business references available on request.

ABBY CHARLES

80 Central Park West
New York, New York 10014
212-349-1138

Summary

Major career achievements and satisfactions have come from positions with responsibility for the identification and resolution of problems. Skilled in decision-making, including the organization and analysis of data, evaluation of alternative solutions, selection of the optimal approach, and negotiation for the implementation of the decision. Experience in both line and staff positions and strong interpersonal skills. Results-oriented, learn quickly, and enjoy challenge. Accomplishments in all positions are substantiated by rapid salary growth.

Experience

July 1983–Present   *Manager, Academic Market Development, Book and Information Services,* Walton and Champion Companies, Walton, New York. Sales analysis and strategic planning for existing academic market (college and university libraries). New product development, including market research, evaluation of external new ventures proposals, initiation of new products and services, financial analyses, and design of marketing offer. Exploration and recommendation of new market segmentation, development of marketing strategies for these segments, preparation of financial projections, and implementation of accepted proposals.

June 1980–June 1983   *Gift and Exchange Librarian,* Barnard Libraries, Rochester, New York. Establishment of a department to administer the acceptance and review of gifts to the University libraries. Preparation of a uniform gift policy and procedure manual for ten campus libraries. Negotiation and administration of the exchange of materials with foreign libraries, particularly in the Soviet Union and Latin America. Negotiation with dealers for the sale of unneeded material. Supervision of ten employees.

Education

M.S.L.S., DeWitt University, January 1982.
M.A.T., Manchester University, June 1978   Majors: History and Education.

Honors

Dean's List all semesters
Phi Beta Kappa
Beta Phi Mu honorary

Interests

American architectural history and historic preservation; creative photography.

References

Available upon request.

CATHERINE BLACK

Telephone: (215) 463-2114
75 Oakdale Terrace
Philadelphia, Pa. 19012

BUSINESS EXPERIENCE *(10/95–Present)*	MONASH, INC., Philadelphia, Pa. *National Sales Manager* (management consultant) Responsible for all sales—direct mail, retail, wholesale, premium, etc. Organized and directed commission sales representatives.
(1/95–10/95)	BAKER L. MAJOR, INC., Philadelphia, Pa. *Director of Sales and Marketing* Responsible for all marketing and sales, including: textbooks, trade, wholesale, telemarketing, direct mail, book stores (chain and individual), stationery, card and gift, sporting goods, foreign book rights, subrights, trade shows, special sales (premium and bulk), clubs, etc. Assisted in editorial selection and list planning. Planned and directed all advertising, publicity, trade shows, conventions. Re-established and expanded commission rep sales force.
(2/91–1/95)	ANDERSON MAP CO., Newark, N.J. *General Manager and Product Supervisor* Distributor of maps, books, souvenirs, pens, office supplies, toys, novelty items, etc. Established, trained, and directed sales force. Increased sales from $50,000 in 1980 to $400,000 by the end of 1994.
(5/87–2/91)	McGRAW-HILL, INC., New York, N.Y. *National Sales and Marketing Manager* Increased sales by 25% in the first 6 months, partly through the establishment of a distributor network, and 50% within the first year. Created and directed a house and commission sales force. Set up first active sales promotion department.
(10/84–5/87)	SIMON & SCHUSTER, INC., New York, N.Y. *Assistant Sales Manager and Supervisor of Major Accounts* Responsible for sales to major accounts, premiums, and the direction of sales representatives. HARPER & ROW, INC., New York, N.Y. *Trade Sales Representative* (New York City, Long Island, New Jersey) Increased sales volume by 25% on Long Island. Increased sales volume by 50% in New Jersey. Premium Sales Manager added to sales responsibilities in 1983.
EDUCATION	University of Maine – Bachelor of Arts, 1978 Long Island University – 30 credits earned toward MBA, 1981
REFERENCES	Furnished upon Request.

ARTHUR BRODER

204 Juliet Road, Portland, Maine 04137
(207) 761-4691

Profit Generator • Innovative Merchandiser
National Accounts Manager • New Markets Specialist

2/94–Present MOUNTAIN & SHORE PRODUCTS, INC., Portland, Maine
Merchandising/Sales Director
- Profitably increased sales from $806,000 to $1.5 million with existing accounts in 10 months, by remerchandising products and introducing new point-of-sale displays and materials.
- Developed and coordinated Herman's merchandising program, increasing sales from $335,000 to over $1 million.

8/84–10/93 EVERLAST SPORTING GOODS, Rockland, Maine
National Sales/Key Accounts Manager
- Initiated consumer products division and personally generated $8 million in sales to national and regional accounts.
- Penetrated new markets by introducing new merchandising programs and recruiting national sales forces, increasing annual sales by 65%.
- Designed sales promotions for national target accounts resulting in $2.75 million annual sales to Sears, K-Mart, J.C. Penney, and major catalog showroom chains.
- Broadened private label sales from $300,000 to $2.5 million by fulfilling the program needs of competitors.
- Reversed an annual $800,000 manufacturing loss by innovating a half-price sale of "non-salable" merchandise, to a $400,000 gross profit.

11/81–7/84 SLEEPING BAG CORPORATION OF AMERICA, Raleigh, North Carolina
National Sales Manager
- Sold and developed mass-merchandiser market, increasing sales $700,000 first year.
- Recruited, trained, and managed 90 manufacturer's reps.

9/74–11/81 JOYCE INTERNATIONAL CORPORATION, Durham, North Carolina
Regional Sales Manager
- Revitalized sales force with poorest performance record, achieving first place position nationwide for two years.
- Generated $1.25 million annual sales to major chains.

EDUCATION

Davison College, North Carolina, B.A. Degree 1974

REFERENCES

Available upon request

RICHARD COLE • 66-25 100th Street • Forest Hills, N.Y. 11375 • (212) 897-7311

SALES MANAGEMENT (TEXTILES)

1989–Present **President**, SPECIAL IMPRESSIONS
Flushing, New York

- Achieved $800,000 average annual sales
- Supervised manufacture of T-shirts, including selling, financing, marketing, and establishing overhead
- Direct reports at the Lindenhurst Plant were:
  1) Production Manager
  2) Shipping Manager
  3) Bookkeeping Department
  4) Accountant
  5) 5 Salespeople
  6) 50 Employees of the cutting and sewing department
- Improved working relationships with mills and cut & sew staff, resulting in reduced cost of manufacturing by approximately 10%
- Developed working relationships with wholesale distributors, chain stores, department stores, media sales promotion situations, sales reps, individually owned T-shirt retailers, and boutiques
- Managed and extended credit to customers when warranted
- Promoted independent contractor reciprocation
- Liquidated company July, 1990

1986–1989 **Sales Manager**, GOTHAM KNITTING MACHINERY
Glendale, New York

- Handled in-house sales
- Gained 35–40 new accounts, at an average billing of $50,000 each
- Maintained gross sales of $5 million
- Delegated work to 4–5 salespeople worldwide
- Traveled to mills throughout country in order to evaluate machinery needs and update and service existing system
- Established long-lasting customers through good will and public relations
- Worked part-time during senior year in college
- Resigned from firm to go into business for myself

EDUCATION

BS (Sociology/Psychology), Queens College   1986
Far Rockaway High School   1981
    Dean's List, 2 years
    Student advisor to school newspaper, *The Phoenix*

SPECIAL INTERESTS

Languages: French – read/speak   Spanish – read
Member, New York City Chamber of Commerce Board
1986–Present:
    Basketball Coach for last four years, Forest Hills Jewish Center
    Basketball League for 17 year olds

RICHARD A. REESE

48 CASS AVENUE
FALLS CHURCH, VA. 22040
(703) 947-6121

EMPLOYMENT HISTORY

1993 to present   Omega Corporation
                        Falls Church, Va.

Vice President/Sales Management: Responsibilities include contacting and negotiating with mid-size Japanese manufacturers. The company is an importer of numerous diversified products. Once imported, these products are sold by our distribution network of manufacturer's representatives. Responsible for hiring these representatives. Major accomplishment with this company has been the establishment and structuring of a U.S. sales force. Prior to this, the emphasis was solely on consulting for foreign firms wishing to sell their products in the U.S.

1989 – 1993   Jason Synthetics, Inc.
                       Washington, D.C.

Sales Vice President: The company is a manufacturer of synthetic materials. In the past, company (in business 30 years) operated exclusively as a contractor for various jobbers. Accomplished establishment of a direct sales force nationwide calling on the wholesalers directly. Able to eliminate many jobbers and increase profit margins accordingly. Also accomplished widening of the market for our products by personal canvass of new industries where possible application for products might exist.

1985 – 1988   E. F. Hutton
                       Washington, D.C.

Registered Representative: Licenses: N.Y.S.E., A.S.E., N.A.S.D., C.B.T.

1982 – 1985   Smith & Johnson
                       Washington, D.C.

Sales Manager/Registered Representative: Responsibilities included the hiring and training of new reps for this OTC brokerage company. Formed joint-participation sales efforts with other OTC firms for the purpose of placing new issues with the public.

EDUCATIONAL BACKGROUND

University of Virginia, BS Degree-Marketing, 1982

REFERENCES

Furnished upon request.

Ellen Lume

59 Ridgeway Avenue
Danbury, Connecticut 06856
203-742-3301
203-628-1690

EXPERIENCE

April 1994–Present

Anderson International Fragrances, Inc., Danbury, Connecticut

Manager, Sales Administration

Primary functions are as follows: Directing all phases of sales support and customer service activities including pricing; prioritizing laboratory activities and establishing production priorities; identifying markets, both product and geographic, for development; designing promotional and sales literature; providing major contributions to annual profit plan; providing statistical information necessary for accurate sales forecasting; reviewing monthly sales analysis for variations in customer and product sales and/or profitability.

February 1992–March 1994

Newberry & Castle, Danbury, Connecticut

National Sales Manager

Directed selling of fruit juice concentrates, essential oils, and aroma chemicals to potential and established customers. Also overall responsibility for identifying and developing business in new accounts and territories and establishing brokerage arrangements and sales representation for areas not directly covered. Generated over $400,000 in new sales annually and an additional $100,000 through brokers and other representatives.

January 1991–January 1992

Jones & Kimball, Inc., Darien, Connecticut

Basic Products Sales Coordinator

Internal Sales Coordinator responsible for the various activities involved in the sales of essential oils and oleoresins. These included pricing, identifying existing and potential markets and assisting in directing the sales force.

November 1985–December 1990

Libby & Kraft, Inc., Newark, N.J.

Flavor and Fragrance Division

Manager, Marketing Service, April 1988–December 1990

Overall pricing responsibility for all product lines, FD&C and Natural Colors, Flavor, Fragrances, Essential Oils, Oleoresins; screened, evaluated, and prioritized all laboratory work; developed and implemented marketing strategies; supervised all customer communications and contracts; contributed to sales projections and forecasts; central coordinating function.

Account Executive, June 1987–April 1988
> Direct sales responsibility for the Metropolitan New York, New Jersey, and Connecticut areas, as well as all of New England. Sought and developed new accounts and enhanced business to existing accounts. Increased territorial sales by 15% (over $100,000) in ten months of direct selling. Promoted to Marketing Service Manager.

Sales Service Manager, **Flavors and Essential Oils**, November 1985–June 1987
> Handled all customer service and pricing matters for flavors and essential oils product lines. Promoted to Account Executive.

September 1982–November 1985

Marx & Morris, Inc., Newark, New Jersey

Sales Administrator
> Handled all internal sales activities for assigned geographic areas.

PERSONAL BACKGROUND

Education   University of Connecticut
                Bachelor's Degree in Business Administration, 1982.

References   Provided upon request.

PAUL BRADLEY

76 WESTERN AVENUE • FT. LAUDERDALE, FLORIDA 33341 • 305-253-4452

QUALIFICATIONS SUMMARY:

Vice President with more than 12 years of experience planning and directing sales/marketing programs for major U.S. Corporations. Currently, heading a sales division of an international corporation with transaction volume in excess of $75 billion.

Extensive business knowledge of the U.S. and Latin American markets. Developed a bilingual and culturally oriented sales entity that helped to launch a new product in the Caribbean market, and produced, within the first year, a $6 million sales performance.

Known for skills and expertise in market strategy, planning, implementation and administration of marketing programs. Increased sales for one product line 400% in 1 year, by developing an innovative distribution channel including Manufacturer's Reps, Value-Added Integrators and Key influencers. Substantial supervisory experience in personnel and the resolution of both technical and non-technical problems.

Successful track record of building and expanding market share, appointing distributors and representatives, strategic market planning and contract negotiations.

PROFESSIONAL EXPERIENCE

CREDIT CARD INC., MIAMI, FL   **NOVEMBER 1994 TO PRESENT**
Vice President
- Report directly to Senior Vice President of world's largest merchant bank card processor, holding a 30% market share.
- Plan and implement marketing strategies for portfolio of electronic credit services.
- Maintain and renegotiate existing clients.
- Areas of responsibility in vertical marketing program, generating $2.5 billion annually, include department stores, discount stores, health and beauty merchants and the optical industry.
- Achieved significant inroads into innovative program involving major universities nationwide.

AGFA FILM COMPANY, MIAMI, FL   **JUNE 1991 TO NOVEMBER 1994**
Director and Regional Business General Manager – Latin America   *May 1993 to November 1994*
- Promoted to position to direct sales/marketing activities of Edicon Systems Division in Latin America.
- Recruited, trained and developed strong bilingual and culturally oriented sales organization that was responsible for producing more than $3 million in sales.
- Responsible for entire scope of operations, sales, marketing, channel development and channel management.
- Extensive market analysis for product group, resulting in increased sales and profits.

Director of Sales   *December 1991 to May 1993*
- Directed sales/marketing activities for the Eastern and Mid-West groups in North America.
- Responsible for product planning, marketing programs and strategies.
- Successfully increased portfolio with new and more diversified products.
- Achieved 400% increase in sales performance in 1992, from $2 million to $8 million.
- Organized and developed completely new distribution channel, including Manufacturer's Reps, Value-Added Integrators and Key Influencers, accounting for the success in this program.
- Participated in various international marketing programs.

Manager – Access Control   *June 1991 to December 1991*
- Planned, implemented and managed program to launch new products and solutions into the domestic marketplace.
- Coordinated activities with Product Management and Marketing teams within the organization.
- Achieved a 200% increase in new sales in a 6-month time frame.

ADT SECURITY SYSTEMS, INC., ROCHESTER, NY   **OCTOBER 1983 TO JUNE 1991**

National Accounts Manager   *April 1989 to June 1991*
- Total responsibility for account management worldwide.
- Clients included multi-national corporations, including Eastman Kodak, Bausch & Lomb and Xerox.
- Developed programs to create "sole source" relationships for entire product offering to be implemented globally.
- Consistently surpassed corporate sales goals, and ranked in the top 1%.

Sales Manager – Upstate New York   *January 1987 to April 1989*
- Directed sales activities for 6 major cities, accounting for more than $8 million in annual revenues.
- Supervised activities of 12 Account Representatives.
- Responsible for P & L, cash and earnings for entire commercial sales effort.
- Involved with system design, budget planning, training and implementation.

Account Sales Representative   *November 1985 to January 1987*
- Sold systems ranging from small micro-based controls to enterprise-based integrated security management solutions.
- Major development accounts included, Eastman Kodak, General Motors and University of Rochester.

Commercial Sales Representative   *May 1984 to November 1985*
- Responsible for enlarging the customer base, as well as retaining current accounts.
- Designed and implemented large integrated protection systems for commercial clients.
- Ensured that products and services met corporate goals for performance and profitability.

Residential Sales Representative   *January 1984 to May 1984*
- Increased sales in residential market by generating new leads and following up new client referrals.
- Surveyed homes and sold protection systems, as well as monitoring and maintenance plans.

Administrative Assistant   *October 1983 to January 1984*
- Designed and implemented systems for the commercial market with the sales team.
- Coordinated project applications and installations with the project management team.

EDUCATION:

MONROE COMMUNITY COLLEGE, ROCHESTER, NY   **1983**
AAS Management/Fire Protection Technology
G.P.A. 3.4

American Management Association
Executive Management Development Program

ACHIEVEMENTS:

1994 – 180% of Annual Operating Plan
1993 – 200% of Annual Operating Plan
1992 – 195% of Annual Operating Plan
1991 – 200% of Annual Operating Plan
1984 – 1994 President's Council Top Performers

REFERENCES:

Furnished upon request.

ALBERT ROMANO

6200 NEVADA AVENUE • WASHINGTON, D.C.   (202) 916-5417

SALES/MARKETING EXECUTIVE
With General Management Experience

**EMPLOYMENT
RECORD**

1993–1996   **APRÉS NUIT, INC., Washington, D.C.**
President
Profit and loss responsibility for a manufacturer of better lingerie.
- Established business from inception and within 12 months company became profitable.
- Oversaw the sales and marketing as well as administrative functions of business. Was instrumental in penetrating the better department store and specialty store chain markets nationwide.
- Developed a nationwide sales force-manufacturer's reps and in-house people. Personally called on major customers.

1983–1993   **BEAUX ARTS INC., Washington, D.C.**
Vice President, Sales
Full sales and marketing responsibility for a manufacturer of better women's lingerie. Volume: 8-figure range.
- Recruited, hired, trained, and supervised a national in-house sales force of more than 20.
- Increased sales by 2½ times after assuming the position of Vice President, Sales.
- Participated in the merchandising of the line resulting in an upgraded fashion image.
- Contributed to the company's profitability through the marketing of "promotional" merchandise, maintaining factory in full production.
Joined company as a sales representative (Philadelphia, Baltimore and Washington), promoted to Sales Manager and, ultimately, Vice President, Sales.

1971–1983   **DEUTCH & ROGERS, Baltimore, Md.**
Sales Representative
Called on apparel manufacturers in the mid-Atlantic area with a full line of industrial sewing threads and zippers. Ranked among the top producers in a 30-person sales force.
Developed new markets for the company including the men's clothing industry in the Philadelphia metropolitan area—resulting in a substantial increase in territorial volume.

EDUCATION   B.A., Haverford College, Pennsylvania 1971

REFERENCES   Personal and business references available on request.

Market Research and Entry-Level Marketing

HENRY ROBERTS

35 Franklin Road • White Plains, New York 10605 • (914) 489-6103

OBJECTIVE	Entry-level market research position that offers opportunity for dedicated corporate service as well as personal growth.
EXPERIENCE	*White Plains Chamber of Commerce and Industry*
	White Plains, N.Y.
6/93–12/93	Marketing Department – Internship
	– Surveyed members to assess critical business problems
	– Developed Small Business Members Directory
	– Provided general direction and advice to members on Chamber services
	– Assisted in Chamber Corporate Relocation Project
	– Participated actively in Small Business Council Meetings
6/92–6/93	*Stevens Publishing Company* – New York, N.Y.
	Computer Operator
	– Operated Tandem Model 16, Data General Eclipse 330
	– Revised and maintained tape library, data logs
	– Conferred with various departments pertaining to scheduling jobs
	– Began as temporary employee; currently on a permanent part-time basis
Full Time *12/90–6/92*	*National Bank of Westchester* – White Plains, N.Y.
	Computer Operator
	– Operated IBM System 3 Model 10, System 34
Part Time *9/90–12/90*	– Supervised in absence of shift manager
	– Scheduled jobs, trained new operators, performed bank reconciliation
Summer *1987–1990*	*Westchester Country Club* – Harrison, N.Y.
	Club Service Manager
	– Supervised two co-workers, waited on customers in Pro Shop, caddied intermittently
	– Devised system storing members' equipment, maintained golf carts and practice range
EDUCATION	Bachelor of Science, January 1994, Fordham University
	College of Business Administration, Bronx, N.Y.
	Major: Business Administration
	Concentration: Marketing
	Associate in Science, May 1991, Westchester Community College
	Business Administration – Management
	Valhalla, N.Y.
	Earned 80% of college expenses.
EXTRA-CURRICULAR ACTIVITIES AND INTERESTS	Marketing Society, Budget Committee, Concert Committee, Jogging, Golf, Intercollegiate and Intramural Football
REFERENCES	Available upon request.

IRENE C. NEWMEYER

HOME ADDRESS: 84-84 Dalny Road · Jamaica, New York 11432 · (718) 523-1904
SCHOOL ADDRESS: 4309 Hortensia Avenue · San Diego, California 92130 · (714) 297-9952

**JOB
OBJECTIVE**

A position offering challenge and responsibility in consumer affairs, marketing or advertising research.

EDUCATION

1992–1996

THE UNIVERSITY OF CALIFORNIA

Graduating in May 1996 with a B.A. Degree in MARKETING AND CONSUMER BEHAVIOR. DEAN'S LIST DISTINCTION.

Field of study includes: marketing and advertising theory and research, economics, business law, calculus, mass communications, statistics, psychology, sociology, and research methodology.

COURSES: Social and Managerial Concepts in Marketing, Consumer Behavior, Product Policy, Advertising Theory and Policies, Sales Force Management, Marketing Research.

SENIOR RESEARCH SEMINARS AND PROJECTS:
- Children and Advertising
- Marketing Research – Cash vs. Credit Retail Analysis
- Portrayal of Women in Magazine Advertising (Role Model)
- Persuasive Impact of Liquor Ads in Print Media
- The Male Contraceptive Pill: Product Development and Marketing Strategies, including Advertising
- Independent study on *advertising effectiveness*

**WORK
EXPERIENCE**
Summers
1995

CALIFDATA CORPORATION – San Diego, California
Administrative assistant in Sales Department. Trained in basic sales and organizational procedures. Responsible for record keeping, expense reports, public relations, correspondence, inventory updates, and billing.

1994

GRAHAM MILLS – La Jolla, California
Basic sales and management training. Responsible for billing, orders, inventory maintenance, shipping arrangements, and deliveries.

1993

THE PRESS CLUB (Office) – San Diego, California
Extensive experience in inventory control, contracts, billing, correspondence, and public relations.

**EXTRA-
CURRICULAR
ACTIVITIES**

Down South – responsible for soliciting advertising as well as writing copy and layout for "Intro to California."
Active with Freshman Orientation Programs. *UCSD Marketing and Management Club* – involved with structuring innovative lecture series in career opportunities in related fields and designing community "Intern" Program. California Consumer Board – Volunteer.

REFERENCES   Available on request.

Nancy Cohen

3 Pin Oak Lane
Hartford, Conn. 06112

(203) 997-1221 *Day*   (203) 238-9524 *Evening*

WORK EXPERIENCE:
(part-time summer)

1993   **Salesperson.** The Proving Ground, West Farms Mall, Farmington, Connecticut. Sold men's clothing, helped in coordinating clothing, wrote sales, helped display merchandise, dressed mannequins, did inventories.

1992   **Cashier.** Genovese Drugs, Bloomfield, Connecticut. Sales, priced, and displayed merchandise.

1992   **Salesperson.** Sym's Department Store, Elmsford, New York. Women's department. Worked in dressing room, priced and organized merchandise.

1991   **Receptionist/Researcher.** Arthur Vincent Contracting Co., Inc. Answered phone, set up interviews, researched zoning maps for land on which to build, opened and closed office.

1991   **Cashier/Salesperson.** Millwood Chemist (pharmacy), Millwood, New York. Responsible for maintaining store, displayed and priced cosmetics.

EDUCATION: **Bachelor of Science in Business Administration, 1994**
University of Hartford, Barney Business School, West Hartford, Connecticut

Associate of Arts in Liberal Arts, 1991
University of Hartford, College of Basic Studies, West Hartford, Connecticut

ACTIVITIES: Social Committee, one year

American Marketing Association, two years

Campus Assistant (gave tours to incoming freshmen and worked at information desk), two years

REFERENCES: Available on request.

James Rivera

15 Maple Street
Youngstown, Ohio 44575
(216) 765-7035 home
(216) 765-6229 work

EMPLOYMENT

7/94–7/96   **U.S. RUBBER CO., INC.**   Youngstown, Ohio

Marketing Research Analyst. Responsible for providing objective and reliable information to senior management, with data obtained from pre- and post-product surveys, marketing program evaluations, pricing studies, and advertising and merchandising research projects. Developed new computer pricing programs for competitive pricing analysis and risk analysis simulation. Directed research staff for survey programs. Conducted major metropolitan market evaluations for sales personnel training.

7/93–7/94   **GENERAL TIRE AND RUBBER**   Akron, Ohio

District Manager – Dealer Sales. Responsible for dealer sales of tires and related products in Ohio and western Pennsylvania. Sales quota attainment $3,000,000 +. Developed and trained new and existing independent dealers. Assisted dealers in all financial and operational functions.

5/92–7/93   **REYNOLDS RUBBER CORPORATION**   Detroit, Michigan

Product Marketing Associate. Assisted in the development of the marketing plans for passenger, light truck, and performance tires. Developed new product marketing plans, sales strategies, and sales forecasts for the Comp T/A tire line. Created a computer assisted regression analysis forecasting system for all new product lines. Assembled and computed daily sales and inventory analysis reports. Conducted marketing strategy review meetings. Developed and implemented special task force programs for new products.

1990–1991   **J. & G. MARSHALL ASSOCIATES**   Dearborn, Michigan

Industrial Coordinator. Responsible for the design, manufacturing, and packaging of industrial hardware. Organized and executed product installation at customers' premises.

Summers 1989–1990   **BICYCLES UNLIMITED**   Bloomington, Indiana

Co-Owner and Operator. Responsible for advertising, bidding, hiring, training, supervising employees, and maintaining financial records. Company grossed $25,000 to $30,000 per summer. Paid for college tuition and additional expenses.

EDUCATION

1990   B.S., University of Indiana, Bloomington

REFERENCES   Furnished upon request.

SALVATORE BIANCO

600 Rosedale Avenue • Larchmont, New York • (914) 946-7357

SUMMARY: Eight years of diversified experience in clinical and immunological cancer research. Candidate for Master's degree in marketing. Master's degree in immunology and Bachelor's degree in biology/chemistry.

EXPERIENCE:
1982 to Present

INMAN INSTITUTE, New York, NY
Senior Research Assistant (1987 to Present)
- Conduct experimental immunological research (in-viro and in-vitro)
- Write experimental papers
- Direct laboratory and staff of approximately 15 MDs, PhDs, technicians, students and volunteers
- Prepare annual budget of $250,000
- Administer $100,000 annual laboratory purchases from pharmaceutical companies
- Write grant papers
- Interview job applicants

Research Assistant (1982 to 1987)
- Developed formally adopted creative procedures for performing perfusion techniques in live animals
  - Performed immunological preparation associated with liver and pancreas transplantation surgery in dogs and cats
  - Performed microsurgery in rats
  - Ran Alpha Feto Protein Immune-Electropheresis of serum proteins from patients suspected of having liver malignancy
- Responsible for some laboratory administration laboratory administration

EDUCATION:

NEW YORK UNIVERSITY, New York, NY
Present – MBA candidate, Marketing
1991 – MS, Immunology

BOSTON UNIVERSITY, Boston, MA
1982 – BS, Biology/Chemistry

UNIVERSITY OF ROME, Rome, Italy
1982 – Summer courses at School of Medicine

FAIRLEIGH DICKINSON UNIVERSITY, Teaneck, NJ
1981 – Summer course in Advertising

EXTRACURRICULAR ACTIVITIES:

Worker in University Hospital Volunteer Plan
Orientation advisor and guidance counselor

LANGUAGES: Italian – read/speak

CARLETON K. ROBERTSON

16 Bell Street
Harris, Minnesota 55941
Telephone: 218-583-9313

EXPERIENCE:

**Senior Market
Research Analyst**

FAL CORPORATION, New Falls, Minnesota   1987–present

Responsible to the Manager of Market Research for collection and analysis of information in business areas of interest to the corporation. Survey and evaluate literature and interpret trends where relevant. Organize investigations, analyze, report findings and recommendations to management.

Recommended a course of action for establishing R&D objective. Researched and developed a half-billion-dollar market related to current product lines. Market segmentation pinpointed R&D goals.

Suggest market opportunities, consult on new products, evaluate production and supply statistics. Interpret economic news.

**Senior
Associate Analyst**

JOHNSON AND CO., Raleigh, North Carolina   1979–1987

Engaged in all functional responsibilities necessary to answering critical questions for Fortune 500 clients. Advanced from Market Analyst to Senior Associate Analyst. Developed more than 50 major studies calculated to have yielded millions of dollars to corporate customers.

Studies were sponsored to audit and define consumer and industrial markets; help plan and test new products and services; evaluate sales and distribution operations; appraise acquisitions or divestitures; plan production facilities proximate to markets.

Personal research has effectively:
◆ Evaluated the distributor network of a proposed $15 million corporate acquisition.
◆ Determined the advisability of a client divesting a $10 million sales division.
◆ Delineated the market for production of a proposed $19 million turnkey process facility.
◆ Measured share of market and isolated areas for penetration for a $100 million dollar supplier of specialty materials.
◆ Developed statistical and qualitative audits of industries segmenting profitability of product markets. Used by sponsors to plan multimillion-dollar productions and define goals.

Field Underwriter

STATE INSURANCE, Greg Plains, Nebraska   1976–1979

Marketed personal lines of coverages. Trained for and received New York State licensing. Conducted telephone and in-person prospecting. Sold concepts and underwrote life, health, and disability protection to meet estate plans.

Sales Manager	FIELD BROS. IMPORTERS LTD., New York, New York 1963–1976

Administered territorial sales and marketing activities. Successfully motivated the several forms of customers to stock and promote sales of a broad line of packaged goods. Cultivated associated distributor personnel's cooperation and gained their interest in promoting coverage and sales volume.

Achieved near saturation distribution in a market containing over 2,000 accounts. Was successful in converting this near virgin territory to a highly profitable market with improved volume of over 800%.

Projected company policies, sales supports and product uniqueness to the industry and in distributor meetings.

EDUCATION: B.B.A., Major Economics, University of Miami, Coral Gables, Florida, 1963

REFERENCES: Available upon request.

CHARLES DEXTER

451 FENNEL LANE • POMPANO BEACH, FLORIDA 33428 • 407-554-7172

ENTRY LEVEL • SALES/MARKETING • EXECUTIVE TRAINING

Diversified business experience in customer relations/service and accounting support functions. B.B.A. Degree in Marketing, Management and Advertising. Brief career encompasses some supervisory experience, as well as assuming full responsibility for day-to-day operations of small business enterprise.

SUMMARY OF QUALIFICATIONS:

➤ Exposure and capabilities in a variety of related areas, including accounting, order processing, billing and other office support functions.
➤ Computer efficient: Working knowledge of data processing, spreadsheet and word processing programs.
➤ Strong communication and interpersonal skills.
➤ Retail sales experience, as well as prospecting new business through "cold calling."

EDUCATION:

FLORIDA ATLANTIC UNIVERSITY, BOCA RATON, FL   1994
Bachelor of Business Administration Degree
Major: Marketing
Activities: ➤ As a founding member of Sigma Alpha Mu Fraternity, helped to establish and develop organization into the leading fraternity on campus, with membership of 40.
➤ Performed as disc jockey for campus radio station WOWL, 1610 AM.

EXPERIENCE:

SIEMENS NIXDORF PRINTING SYSTEMS, BOCA RATON, FL   **January 1995 to Present**
Accounts Payable Assistant
➤ Responsible for coding and paying invoices, preparing and disbursing checks.
➤ Monitored system for errors and resolved procedural problems.
➤ Reviewed employee expense reports.

GLORIA JEAN'S GOURMET COFFEE, BOCA RATON, FL   **August 1994 to January 1995**
Franchise Representative
➤ Acted as liaison between franchise owners and corporate offices.
➤ Processed orders and provided efficient, timely response to whatever requests or problems franchise presented.

Helped finance college expenses through full- and part-time employment:
➤ Crate & Barrel, Boca Raton, Fl.: Sales Associate, set up store displays, supervised new employees.
➤ Ramada Hotel, Boca Raton, Fl.: Front Desk, registered guests, made reservations, assisted in sales/marketing office.
➤ Silk Greenhouse, Clearwater, Fl.: Sales Associate, received merchandise shipments, maintained inventory.
➤ Smugglers Cove Miniature Golf, Clearwater, Fl.: Night Manager, full responsibility for supervision of operations.

COMPUTER SKILLS:

• IBM and compatibles • Microsoft Word • AS400 J.D. Edwards • MSA • WordPerfect • Lotus 1-2-3 • Microsoft Excel • Microsoft Publisher

REFERENCES:

Furnished upon request.

RAYMOND W. CLANCY · 6518 Grant Place · West New York, N.J. 07093 · (201) 867-7777

OBJECTIVE An entry-level position relating to sales and marketing in a major growth organization. The position would make use of education, negotiating and analytical skills.

WORK EXPERIENCE

3/95 to Present NEW JERSEY NATIONAL BANK, West New York, N.J.
BUYER: Responsibilities include purchasing, cost/price analysis, product comparison studies:
- Purchase capital equipment, i.e., video, microfilm, word processors. Negotiate for best service and quality at the lowest price. Achieve significant savings resulting in approximately 14% per month.
- Prepare various monthly and year-to-date savings reports, i.e., fixed, variable and average unit cost, vendor error ratio, and invoice error ratio reports. Prepared various management reports relating to budgeting, market trends, estimates and price comparisons.
- Purchase electrical, plumbing, chemical, and carpentry items for the Real Estate Management Division of Bankers Trust. Reviewed previous vendor usage, established purchasing standards, negotiated contract agreements, approved master vendor list. Improved purchasing operations resulting in 15% savings per month.
- Conduct product/price comparison studies. Advise management as to best selection. Serve as representative of managers negotiating special purchases. Establish bank standards for future purchases.
- Attended various training seminars, e.g., Lotus 1-2-3, Negotiating Skills, Persuasive Strategies in Writing.

8/92 to 3/95 AETNA INSURANCE
New York, N.Y.
UNDERWRITER: Completed 2-year management trainee program that included rotation within various departments. Specific job responsibilities included the following:
- Supervised 4 employees in the analysis of high-risk special property insurance.
- Analyzed reports submitted by 8 branch offices evaluating sales, allocation of financial risk and validity of forecast method. Documented findings and wrote recommendations to senior management.
- Conducted extensive observations of field sites. Prepared reports concerning prospective investments, evaluating each property for risk and profitability.

EDUCATION Candidate for MBA, dual major in Corporate Finance and Marketing. Rutgers University 41/63 credits completed. *Graduation Date:* Spring 1996

B.A., *Major* – Psychology; *Minor* – Economics
Rutgers University, May 1992

CLUBS/ORGANIZATIONS

ADK/AMC Winter Mountaineering School – Assistant Director
Catskill Mountain Club – Leader, Planning Committee
Bicycle Touring Club – Trip Leader

REFERENCES On Request.

Thomas Josephs

435 Drew Street
Cleveland, Ohio 44135
Home Phone: (216) 349-4561

CAREER OBJECTIVE:

Immediate Goal: Marketing Trainee

Long-Term Goal: Progression to Marketing Management function, with involvement in training, advertising and market research.

EXPERIENCE:

7/95–present Globe Printing, Cleveland, Ohio

Sales Representative – product marketing, market research, forms design, credit collection.

9/92–7/95 Y.M.C.A., Shaker Heights, Ohio

Assistant Equipment Room Manager – issuance and collection of equipment, interim manager, public relations, security.

Program Aide – assisted counselors and instructors in weight-training program, set up equipment and miscellaneous work.

5/92–11/93 Glen's Department Store, Cleveland, Ohio

Sales Clerk – recorded sales, assisted customers, inventory management, stock work, created displays.

Earned 75% of college expenses from summer and part-time jobs.

EDUCATION:

B.S. in Marketing, May 1995
Ohio State University

Major areas of study

Marketing Research	Consumer Behavior
Marketing Management	Business Writing
MIS and Computers	Managerial Environment
Communication Theory	Business Statistics I & II

COLLEGE ACTIVITIES:

Dean's Honor List
American Marketing Association, 1994–95
Junior Varsity Basketball
Intramural Athletics

REFERENCES:

Will be furnished upon request.

BARRY WESTIN

52-32 Sycamore Street
Forest Hills, New York 11375
718-345-6731

EXPERIENCE

1984–present   *Product Manager, Ronson Management Research, Inc., New York City.*

P/L responsibility for $500,000 marketing budget used in direct mail, space advertising and telephone sales. Wrote annual marketing plans and forecasted product pro-forma statements. Doubled 1985 revenues to $1.6 million by segmenting existing markets and pinpointing new ones. Integrated marketing and financial data to rank markets according to profitability. Heavily used cost accounting and advanced marketing research techniques. Supervised copywriters, artists, printers, and media buyers in advertising and sales promotion campaigns.

1982–1984   *Marketing Research Analyst, Rolands Mail Order House, Milwaukee.*

Developed statistical program for evaluating new customer credit applications. Used analysis of variance techniques to correlate customer demographics with payment history. Determined optimal mailing sequence for catalog and direct mail response. Determined user needs. Wrote MIS specifications for corporate programming staff.

EDUCATION

1982–1984   *Graduate School of Business, Milwaukee University*

M.B.A. Concentrated in Marketing and Financial Management. Secondary interests in Organizational Development.

1976–1981   *University of Detroit, B.S.*

Majored in Systems Analysis Engineering and Operations Research.

HONORS

Recipient of Astor Scholarship at Milwaukee University,
and Michigan State and Morgansteiner Scholarships at University of Detroit.
Graduated with honors.

LANGUAGES

Speak both French and German fluently.

REFERENCES

Provided upon request.

ELLEN ROGERS

16 JAMES STREET
TRENTON, N.J. 07621
(609) 414-2622

EXPERIENCE:

6/94–Present   APEX DRUG, INC., Trenton, N.J.

Product Manager – DYNAMITE (Household Insecticide)

Full management responsibility for diverse TNT product line (14 items). Primary activities include brand planning, advertising/promotion, volume/P & L projection, cost management, and new product/line extension development. Promoted to Product Manager 1/96. Prior to that was Assistant Product Manager—BC (Powdered Analgesic) and DENTROL (Denture Adhesive). Responsible for business analysis and assisting in brand management. Wrote and presented marketing plans. Strongly contributed to planning and implementing line extension. Developed and executed consumer and trade promotion events. Evaluated and recommended business building alternatives.

12/92–6/94   AMERICAN FOODS, INC., Trenton, N.J.

Marketing Assistant – *BUTTERSWEET* MARGARINE.

Analyzed market share, consumer research, and sales performance data. Involved in sales and financial forecasting. Implemented consumer and trade programs. Managed marketing budget. Developed all sales/merchandising material. Spent 2 months as sales trainee covering a cross-section of trade outlets.

6/90–12/92   ACR, Jersey City, N.J.

Account Manager

Developed and presented marketing proposals directly to national packaged goods advertisers such as Bristol-Myers, Nestle, Colgate-Palmolive, Oscar Mayer and others. Other responsibilities included analysis of market segments and profiles, payout projections, testing and measuring alternative advertising strategies.

EDUCATION:

12/90   Bucknell University
M.B.A. – Marketing

5/88   Lehigh University
B.S. – Marketing

Achievements: President-Advertising Society; Member-Business Society, Dean's List; offered Graduate Assistantship (Full Scholarship)

REFERENCES: Available upon request.

Barbara Albright   17 Waterford Street, Roselle, New Jersey 07521 • (201) 555-1786

PROFESSIONAL EXPERIENCE:

1994–Present   DARTMOUTH INK & DYE CORP., Hoboken, New Jersey
Product Manager

Responsible for implementation of a start-up operation of a new product line – toners and developers for copiers/duplicators. Significant achievements in the operation led to my promotion from sales representative to my present position one year after introduction of the product.
- Was responsible for opening new dealerships and national accounts in the New York Metropolitan area. First year sales were in excess of $1 million.
- Initiated investigation and analysis of market potential, which helped to realize first-year sales goals.
- Represented the company at national trade shows and organized and ran company open houses at both branches to feature the new product line.
- Designed and implemented training program for dealer salespeople, telemarketing campaigns, and new hires.
- Presently manage a department of 5 people – both sales and sales support.

1992–1994   NELSON PHOTOCOPIER, INC., Westbury, N.Y.
Senior Sales Representative
Sold large copier/duplicator systems and electronic typewriters to 80 major accounts on Long Island. Consistently overachieved my sales plan by 50% each year.

1990–1992   ACME ALARM, INC., Rochester, N.Y.
Security Systems Sales Representative

Marketed burglar, fire alarm, and CCTV systems in Manhattan. Was 189% of plan and was awarded the "Rookie of the Year" award – Eastern Region (1991) for the highest volume of sales for a new employee on the East Coast.

1987–1990   ROCHESTER SCHOOL DISTRICT, Rochester, N.Y.
Spanish Teacher – Middle School

Duties included curriculum planning, test evaluation, organizing community events, and heading the Spanish Club.

1982–1987   ROCHESTER SCHOOL DISTRICT, Rochester, N.Y.
Substitute Spanish Teacher

EDUCATION: University of Rochester
M.A. in Liberal Studies, 1987
Member of Chi Epsilon Delta Honor Society 3.72 GPA
University of Rochester
B.A. in Spanish and Education, 1982

REFERENCES: Submitted on request

Khanh Van Chen

488-1/2 State Street
San Francisco, California 94063
(415) 555-2345 • (415) 555-1600

Career Qualifications Summary

Ten years' hands-on learning experience, with a successful record of performance, and highly effective skill in Product Marketing and Design.

Expertise for supplying innovative adaption to new and existing product lines, and ensuring the most productive and profitable solutions to business needs.

Designed every facet of product presentations. Education of sales personnel. Creation of new marketing plans and advertising campaigns. Full knowledge of production. Identifying and penetrating new markets.

Hiring, training, supervising, and terminating personnel.

Total expansion of Marketing and Sales.

Professional Experience

Barton's Shades & Awnings, Inc.   **1994–present**
San Francisco, California
Manufacturers of Interior and Exterior Window Treatment Products

Product Manager, Custom and Readymade Sun Tamer Exterior Shading Products, Galaxy Sun Controller
                Blinds

Accomplishments and duties include complete product marketing and management of new product lines. Devised and implemented marketing programs for products. Wrote and designed complete product manuals for many Barton product lines. Educated and motivated national sales force. Set up national networks of dealers and contractors to sell, install, and service products. Designed dealer and sales programs, and implemented new strategies for penetrating new markets. Created and supervised direct mail campaigns. Designed and improved new and existing product literature and sales aids. Managed advertising campaigns for consumer and trade publications. Budgets, sales forecasts, and profit/loss responsibility.

California Sporting Goods, Inc.   **1990–1994**
Carmel, California
Manufacturers of Consumer Recreational Products

Operations Manager

Chief duties included design and marketing of new products. Updated and improved on existing lines. Successfully handled such areas as taking a product from inception and seeing it through to national market, using the most advanced marketing procedures. Supervised many direct mail programs including market research. Organized trade shows and conventions. Total profit/loss responsibility. Oversaw complete operation. Supervised sixteen employees.

Rogers Custom Canvas Co.   **1989–1990**
Sausalito, California
Manufacturers of all types of canvas products on a custom/production line basis.

Owner/Operator

Chief duties included wholesale and retail sales, estimating costs, buying, product design and marketing of products on a local/national basis. Product lines include: canopies (interior and exterior), marine covers, cushions, tarpaulins, and all types of industrial canvas/textile goods. Supervised eight employees. Complete profit/loss responsibilities.

Education

1988–1990 University of San Francisco, California

References

Submitted on Request

Advertising and Sales Promotion

Samuel J. Taylor

300 Riverside Drive
New York, New York 10025
212-797-3149

Four years' experience as copywriter for leading publisher, as well as freelance writing of film reviews over the past five years.

EXPERIENCE:

May 1992– Present

Copywriter. Curtis-Hall, Inc., Publishers, Bergenville, New Jersey.

Create and write direct-mail advertising for premium sales and professional books; do layouts, designs and paste-ups for cover material; train new copywriters; condense copy from full-size publications into "mini" books for premium sales.

September 1991– Present

Freelance Film Reviewer, for various news media.

Write reviews on educational films for radio and newspaper presentation.

Currently writing publishing plan to expand interactivity of reviews.

Developing CD ROM of film reviews for online service.

EDUCATION:

M.F.A., June 1991, New York University.
B.A., June 1989, Cornell University.

SPECIAL HONORS

Phi Beta Kappa
University Scholarship Award – 1987 and 1988.

REFERENCES

Will be furnished upon request.

LYNDA ANSBRO

29 Alan Road
White Plains, New York 10603
(914) 946-2982

OBJECTIVE: Entry-level position in the field of sales and promotion or advertising.

EDUCATION: Mercy College, Dobbs Ferry, New York
B.B.A. Degree, Concentration in Marketing
May, 1996

**RELATED
COURSEWORK:**

Seminar: Women in Business
Sales & Promotion
Sales Function
Management Info. Systems

Computer: BASIC
Advertising
Consumer Behavior
Multi-National Marketing

**RELATED
EXPERIENCE:**

- Coordinated promotional campaign for White Plains Hospital's new perinatal building. Developed creative strategy, prepared 30-second radio commercial, utilized various types of direct mail, organized creative strategies aimed toward the recruitment of high school students for volunteer work.

- Assisted in marketing research project for Mercy College Career Development Center; gathered pertinent data, quantified and recorded it.

- Created and conducted Management Information Systems project for Jay Products Inc., Hastings, N.Y. Identified system problems, suggested alternatives, follow-up study.

Helped finance college through the following employment:

9/92–present: Cashier
Finast Supermarket, White Plains, N.Y.

1991–1992:   Head Cashier
The Pizza Plaza, White Plains, N.Y.

ACTIVITIES: American Marketing Association
Mercy College Martial Arts Club

REFERENCES: Available upon request

GREGG D. LEWIS

1085 WARBURTON AVENUE, APARTMENT 808
YONKERS, NEW YORK 10701
914/423-5858

EXPERIENCE

MILLER PRODUCTS, DIVISION OF MILLER-WALLER, INC.   MAY 1985 to PRESENT

Sales Promotion Manager

Coordinate promotions for brand and sales management. Includes: budgeting, planning, creative and complete implementations of plans.

Manage department of four. Responsible for all sales promotional materials: artwork, printing, displays, premiums, sampling and couponing.

Negotiate for services of mailing and sampling executions, fulfillment houses and coupon-clearing organizations.

Successfully introduced Dri XX Spray, Dri XX Roll On Deodorant and Dew Drops with Fluoride: developed and executed promotion plan and strategy.

Promotion budget of $10,000,000.

BEAUTIFUL HAIR, INC.   FEBRUARY 1983 to MAY 1985

Product Promotion Manager

Responsible for all retail promotion programs in the Hair Color and Toiletries Division: trade promotions, collateral material, pricing, sales objectives and advertising plans by sales region.

Developed promotion plans and executed them for new products: trade strategy, sampling, couponing, ad sales materials. New products include Essence Shampoo, which grew to number three in shampoo market.

Worked closely with research, production planning, legal, graphic suppliers and ad agency.

Promotion budget of $12,000,000.

Heavy business travel.

Assistant Product Promotion Manager   MARCH 1981 to FEBRUARY 1983

Assisted the Production Promotion Manager in all areas explained above.

Sales Representative   JANUARY 1979 to FEBRUARY 1981

Managed merchandise shows for company in local markets. Responsibility for sales volume in 150 direct and indirect accounts. Worked closely with company research in new product tests including: implementation of new product sales plans, weekly audits and test analysis.

EDUCATION

University of North Carolina, 1974–1978
B.S. in Business Administration/Marketing

REFERENCES

Provided upon request.

BRUCE CAMPBELL

2100 Broadway • New York, N.Y. 10023 • (212) 777-4210

EXPERIENCE

1984–Present   *Manager, Advertising and Sales Promotion*
Carlton Publications, New York, N.Y.

In charge of all phases related to publication of six trade magazines with nation-wide distribution to industrial corporations.

1983–1984   *Manager, Advertising and Sales Promotion*
Collins Research Corporation, Bear Lake, N.Y.

Directed all operations involved in advertising and sales promotion, with staff of eight, in this company that produced electrical meters and various electrical components used in radios and television sets.

1982–1983   *Advertising Manager*
Hersey-Starling Electronics Division, New York, N.Y.

Integrated and supervised activities involved in publicity and sales promotion of products, including transistors, receivers, television picture tubes, digital display devices and digital integrated circuits.

1972–1982   *Manager, Advertising and Sales Promotion*
William Meyers Associates, New York, N.Y.

Organized and executed advertising and sales presentation programs for the promotion of this company's products, which included pipe fittings and meter valves, thermostats and various control devices.

1961–1972   *Valve Design Engineer*
Marine Motors, Seagirt, N.Y.

Designed valves for use in marine equipment. Conducted research for improvement in design and construction of these valves.

1957–1961   *Assistant Project Engineer*
Cylinder Design Dept., Zurtis Motor Design Corporation, Alison, N.J.

Made blueprints and sketches of original designs of motor cylinders for cars, trucks and tractors. Investigated and corrected design imperfections in cylinders already in operation in motor vehicles, for more efficient functioning.

EDUCATION

B.S. in Automotive Engineering, 1957 – Pace Polytechnic Institute

PUBLICATIONS

Series of five articles on investigative research into the causes of malfunction and correction of defective auto parts, published in *Automotive America*, January–May issues, 1985.

REFERENCES

References on request.

GREGORY L. CHARLESTON

78 OAKTREE DRIVE
PHILADELPHIA, PENNSYLVANIA 19012
(215) 547-9834

PROFESSIONAL EXPERIENCE

LENOX CHINA/CRYSTAL	Trenton, N.J.
Coordinator of Advertising and Promotion	8-85 to present

- ➤ Hold responsibility for production and printing of all 4-color sales promotional materials, including catalogs.
- ➤ Write original copy, supervise others in copy writing, artwork, layouts and production.
- ➤ Supervise production of dealer newspaper portfolio.
- ➤ Work on designs for p.o.p. materials and displays.
- ➤ P.R. release preparation and agency coordination.
- ➤ Supervise copy, preparation and production of retail store envelope enclosure program.
- ➤ Budget work, have submitted several substantial cost reduction items.
- ➤ Trade show supervision and participation.
- ➤ Arrange and coordinate national press show.
- ➤ Sales meeting preparation and assistance.

BUSINESS NEWS, INC.	Philadelphia, Pa.
Associate Advertising Sales Manager	1-84 to 7-85

- ➤ Account supervisor, sold and serviced over 500 accounts.
- ➤ Supervised in-house agency services for clients, including copy, ad design, production and media planning.
- ➤ Wrote P.R. releases for clients.
- ➤ Did publication expansion research.
- ➤ Increased commission rate from $10 K/yr. to $17 K/yr. in 18-month period.

DUN & BRADSTREET, INC.	Philadelphia, Pa.
Credit Services Salesman	8-83 to 1-84

MASSACHUSETTS MUTUAL LIFE INSURANCE COMPANY	Honolulu, Hawaii
Life and Health Sales	Allentown, Pa.
	1-81 to 7-83

EDUCATION

Muhlenberg College, Allentown, Pa., B.A. in Psychology
U.S. Air Force Telecommunications – Electronics Management School
Charles Morris Price School of Advertising
Sales and Marketing Schools

GEORGE MYLES

10 Main Street
Louisville, Kentucky 40211
(502) 623-4120

EXPERIENCE:

1994–Present   INFINITE COUPONS, INC., Louisville, Kentucky

Director of Merchandising/Sales Promotion

Infinite Coupons, Inc. is a new company formed to develop and exploit the concept of automatic coupon delivery within the supermarket.

Responsible for development of key account target list with appropriate individuals to be contacted within the food, H&BA, and package goods industry. Developed presentations, sales letters, direct mail, advertising, and brochures necessary to present and sell the programs, including making the actual sales calls.

1993–1994   JAMES DALEY ASSOCIATES (Sales Promotion Agency), Cincinnati, Ohio

Director of Account Services

Was responsible for servicing and sales to accounts such as American Home Foods, Bristol-Myers, Life Savers, Nabisco, St. Regis Paper, and Trailways. Responsibilities included submitting written proposals to clients, issuing contact reports, and selecting sources for supply of items and services required by agency.

1991–1993   GARNER PRODUCTS, INC., Cincinnati, Ohio

Director of Sales Promotion

Directed and administered merchandising programs for all Garner Products including Arrid, Pearl Drops, Answer, Sea & Ski, and Rise, with an annual promotion budget in the millions. Defined promotional objectives for all brands and developed event schedules in conjunction with Marketing, Sales, and Division Management. Controlled operating budget and analyzed and evaluated the effectiveness of promotional programs. Contacted and supervised the services of outside sales promotion suppliers and reviewed all promotional programs for potential use.

Recommended and implemented cost saving programs, resulting in an annual savings of $100,000. Examples of these are—changing coupon redemption services, instituting centralized purchasing and placement of Trade Advertising and Free-Standing Insert services. Directed a staff of four, including both administrative and creative aspects of all in-house merchandising.

1979–1991   BRISTOL-MYERS PRODUCTS, INC., New York, New York

Manager of Sales Promotion

Developed and implemented Sales Promotion programs for all Bristol-Myers products, such as Woolite, Pam, Easy-Off, Old English, Wizard Air Freshener and Charcoal Lighter, Black Flag, Aero Shave, Griffin Shoe Polish, Sani-Flush, Easy-On Speed Starch, Woolite Rug Cleaners, and all new products. Developed and implemented sales promotion programs in support of individual brand marketing objectives. Total coordination of marketing and sales department objectives was accomplished through extensive communications and travel. Purchased all promotional requirements such as P.O.P. Displays (recipient of POPAI Award), Artwork, Photography, Couponing, Coupon Redemption, Premiums, Sales Incentive Programs, and outside Promotion House Services.

Cost-saving program resulted in the development of in-house distribution and mailing service to sales force resulting in annual savings of over $100,000. Supervised staff of eight including Artist, Production Manager, and administrative assistants. Sales meeting responsibilities included site selection, planning and coordinating agenda, preparing necessary promotional materials, and audiovisual presentations.

1977–1979 BARBIZON, INC., New York, New York

Advertising and Sales Promotion Production Manager

Responsible for production and purchasing of all Graphic Arts including type, art, displays, printing, and photography. Scheduled projects from concept through completion. Performed vendor contact and estimate evaluation.

1973–1977 DANBURY FIBERS, Hartford, Connecticut

Graphic Arts Purchasing Agent

Responsible for purchasing all Graphic Arts including type, art design, mechanicals and printing for direct mail pieces, statement enclosures, broadside, hang tags, labels, packaging, color cards, premiums, from concept through completion. Scheduled and established volume control for Production Department. Handled vendor contact and estimate evaluation.

1971–1973 ROGERS & JIMES, INC., New Haven, Connecticut

Resident Manager

Complete responsibility for contact, sales and servicing of all accounts (Advertising Agencies). Coordinated orders to three manufacturing plants of plastic plates, mats, electrotypes, typography. Managed an office staff and established procedures.

EDUCATION: UNIVERSITY OF CONNECTICUT
1971, B.S.

REFERENCES: Submitted on request.

ELIZABETH R. JONAS

3450 Downer Road
Seattle, Washington 98116

Telephone: (206) 576-8934
(206) 570-1200

PROFESSIONAL EXPERIENCE

Benton & Bowles, Inc.   *June 1990–Present*
Seattle, Washington

Vice President—Advertising/Sales Promotion
Responsible for the management supervision of advertising, sales promotion, and specialty promotional development for clients in the financial services industry. Additionally responsible for new business development.

Linen, Inc.   *May 1989–June 1990*
San Diego, California

Advertising Manager
Responsible for budget development and execution, development, along with firm's advertising agency, of network and major market television commercials, consumer and trade advertisements, and sales promotional activities for this fiber marketing company of America's Cotton Producers. Budget level exceeded $6 million.

Martin & Jacobs, Inc.   *July 1986–May 1989*
San Diego, California

Senior Account Executive
Responsible for the supervision of The Home Insurance Company account, which included the supervision of internal creative activities for network television, consumer and trade advertising, and public relations activity for this $3 million client.

Emerson Electronics   *July 1983–July 1986*
San Diego, California

Assistant Advertising Manager, Creative Group Head
Product line responsibility: Home appliances, personal care products, radios, portable tape recorders. Developed planning and selection of media and promotional outlets. Directed copywriting and art direction for trade advertising, merchandising, and sales promotional support to national advertising efforts.

G & S Records   *March 1982–July 1983*
Los Angeles, California

Advertising and Sales Promotion Manager
Directed advertising and promotional activities for the Special Products/Marketing Division. Developed markets and strategy for employing entertainment as a catalyst in merchandising and promotional programs for major distribution outlets such as: mass merchandisers, retail outlets, fast food chains.

EDUCATION   George Washington University – BS-Marketing, 1982

REFERENCES   Supplied upon request. Please do not contact former emloyers until a mutual interest has been established.

David R. Krauss

987 Chicago Street
St. Louis, Missouri 63101
(314) 548-4375

EXPERIENCE:

Kenyon and Eckhardt, Inc. *April 1989–June 1996*

Hired as Account Coordinator for Air France, Helena Rubinstein, and Foreign Vintage accounts. In addition to the regular duties, other responsibilities as coordinator were to check the monthly production invoices prior to their submission to the client and to ensure that an ad was released to a publication for every insertion placed on a media estimate. The Anaconda, French West Indies Tourist Board, Royal Air Maroc, and Alfred Dunner accounts were added to the coordinating assignments.

In March 1992, promoted to *Account Executive* on Air France account. During past three years gained experience in supervising all facets of the account. In detail, this included initiating and approving overall campaigns, writing copy, planning media, and complete supervision of print, radio, and TV production.

Doyle Dane Bernbach, Inc. *June 1988–April 1989*

Hired as *Account Assistant* specifically to traffic portions of the Monsanto account in TV and print. Handled these portions until February, 1989, then was transferred to the tire and corporate divisions of Uniroyal (TV and print). During this time, also assisted with traffic on Sony, portions of Burlington Industries, and other house accounts. Subsequently, the shoe and golfball divisions of Uniroyal and American Tourister Luggage were added.

McCall Corporation *December 1983–June 1988*

In January 1988, promoted to the position of *Advertising Traffic Manager*. In this capacity had complete charge over the responsibilities listed below, in addition to supervising a small staff.

Assistant Advertising Quality and Control Manager for production department of McCall's Magazine. Channeled flow of plates from various advertising agencies throughout the United States to our printing plant in time for each closing date of McCall's and Redbook magazines. Gained experience in control of color quality as well as in the ordering of safety shells and electros.

Kaiser, Sedlow & Temple *December 1982–December 1983*

Started with Burke, Charles and Guignon Advertising as *Traffic Manager*. Was *Traffic Manager and Media Director* on Twentieth Century Fox, Columbia Pictures, Embassy Pictures, and Arco Lighting.

Compton Advertising Agency *August 1980–October 1982*

Started as messenger in traffic department and gradually assisted *Traffic Manager* with accounts such as Kelly-Springfield and some Proctor & Gamble products.

EDUCATION: Queens and City Colleges, NYC, B.A., 1980
New York University, M.B.A., 1988

Sandra Martin

800 Arroyo Drive • Phoenix, Arizona 85661 • (602) 296-6227

Bernard Guss, Inc., Phoenix, Arizona
1993 to Present
Account Executive, INFO-PAC Publicity Services Division

Initiate and develop new clients as well as provide full client services for this company that distributes product publicity to 4000+ newspapers in the US and Canada. Sensitive to marketing strategies; Have redesigned several of their current vehicles, authored innumerable pitch-letters as well as client publicity. Clients are most of the PR firms in the US as well as manufacturers' in-house PR personnel.

Prior to this, served as Executive Assistant to the President of the corporation as well as to the Marketing Vice President. Varied and interesting duties included management of luncheon seminars, corporate parties, organization of fund-raising drives, media planning and buying, research and report writing, direct mail list management.

The Rabin Services Co., Phoenix, Arizona
1992 to 1993
Marketing Communications Coordinator

Helped plan and implement the market launch for a new auto-related product, negotiating package and collateral design, media liaison. Organized focus groups, trade show participation, worked with our PR house, Hill & Knowlton, supervising their involvement.

Owner/Sandra Martin Associates, Garden City, N.Y.
1981 to 1992

Production Assistant and Researcher for the Metro Corporation of America's packaging of children's TV series (Silly George), now sold to Melody Tunes, licensed to SONY, Atlas Toys, others.

Founder, Vice President for PR, Greater Nassau Arts Council. Completely responsible for program development, budgeting, fund raising. Special events planning and implementation attracted national as well as local media attention.

Media Rep for the first campaign of State Senator James Dunne. Over a 5-month period, designed and placed advertising (print and broadcast) that helped him win by a 20,000 vote landslide.

Special Projects Director for the Nassau Public Library System. Created and implemented special displays, exhibits, printed matter, events and programs. Gained intense local media coverage for the Library throughout 7 years in this capacity.

Data gathering and research assignments for the Marketing Committee, Youngston, Pennsylvania and for Carlton-Doyle, Bridgeport, Connecticut. Arranged medical conferences for the latter as well.

Other accounts in which writing and research were major components: Pepsico Youth Marketing Division, North Shore Dinner Theater, Harrison Conference Center, Denny's Restaurant, Sunrise Communications, the Bessinger Agency, Reuben Donnelly Marketing.

Prior to 1981
Editor/Writer, WMGM Radio, 1980.
Research/reference assistant, TIME/LIFE Publications, 1979.

EDUCATION   New York University   Scholarship
                                          BS 1979

MEMBERSHIPS   The Publicity Club of Phoenix
                  The Advertising Club of Arizona
                  Pueblo Preservation Association
                  TIME/LIFE Alumni Association

PORTFOLIO AND REFERENCES AT YOUR REQUEST

STACY HALL

42 Knot Road
Tenafly, NJ 07670
(201) 567-6987

SUMMARY:

Ten years' experience in advertising with direct client contact throughout, three years in account management. Demonstrated expertise in budget management. Creative copywriter on variety of industrial, consumer and corporate campaigns including print ads, direct mail, and collateral material. Proven ability to supervise production, assist in new business development, and maintain excellent client relations with all levels of management.

Clients included Conrac Corporation, Maserati Automobiles, McGraw-Hill Publications Company, North American Philips Corporation, Thomas J. Lipton Company, "21" Brands, U.S. Industries, Xerox Corporation, and Zeiss-Ikon.

EXPERIENCE:

1987–1996

DOBBS ADVERTISING COMPANY, INC., New York, NY
Account Executive (1989–1996)

◆ Successfully planned and administrated advertising and promotion for several clients, in many cases maximizing limited funds through knowledge of media and production (utilizing free media publicity to support insertions, negotiating most advantageous rate structures, and getting the most efficiency from production expenditures)
◆ Conceived, developed, and directed advertising and promotion programs for numerous industrial and consumer accounts
◆ Planned and supervised selection and purchase of print and broadcast media
◆ Wrote or directed copy on all accounts handled

Copy Director (1987–1989)
◆ Created concepts and wrote copy for print and broadcast media as well as collateral, sales material, direct mail literature, and publicity releases
◆ Supervised all in-house and freelance copywriting
◆ Served as client contact on several accounts
◆ Recommended media schedules

Highlights
◆ During tenure as account supervisor and head writer, one account experienced twenty percent sales increases on numerous products
◆ Developed print ad for leading surveying equipment manufacturer that completely repositioned client in the market, increased sales, and influenced the "look" of future advertising in publication in which it appeared
◆ Created and directed a campaign which reaffirmed client, the Bank of Toms River, as the number one bank based in Ocean County, NJ

1982–1987　　MULLER JORDAN HERRICK/N.J., Inc., Fort Lee, NJ and New York, NY
(Formerly Richard James Associates)
Copywriter and Assistant Account Executive

◆ Conceived and wrote advertising and promotion copy for print ads and collateral material for industrial and consumer accounts
◆ Served as account executive for numerous clients
◆ Planned and purchased media

Highlights
◆ Created a coupon-response newspaper campaign for retail tire dealer; as a result, client had to restaff and reorganize to handle increased business
◆ Produced print ad for new account that generated more inquiries from the first insertion than had been achieved by former agency's year-long campaign

1980–1982　　KALMAR ADVERTISING, INC., Englewood Cliffs, NJ
Copywriter

◆ Wrote advertising and promotional copy for consumer and industrial accounts
◆ Served as copy contact
◆ Recommended and purchased print and broadcast media
◆ Developed numerous public relations programs for clients

1969–1980　　PRENTICE-HALL, INC., Englewood Cliffs, NJ
Assistant Production Editor

◆ Planned and coordinated book production from manuscript to completed bound book
◆ Copyedited and supervised same
◆ Acted as liaison with authors, suppliers and internal personnel
◆ Checked galleys, page proofs, blueprints
◆ Generated advertising copy for book jackets

EDUCATION:　　Fairleigh Dickinson University, Teaneck, NJ
1979 – Bachelor of Science

LANGUAGE:　　French

Paul R. Joseph

2803 Chesapeake St., NW
Washington, DC 20008
(202) 345-9876
(202) 433-3134

EXPERIENCE:
1984–Present

BANK OF MARYLAND, Bethesda, Maryland
Vice President and Regional Marketing Coordinator

Responsible for all aspects of the marketing effort for 30 branches, including advertising, liaison with the media, public relations, internal and external promotions, business development and product knowledge training in addition to writing a regular newsletter. Report directly to the Regional President. Member of the Regional "Steering" Committee consisting of the 5 senior department heads and the president. This group is responsible for determining all regional policies.

Joined Bank of Maryland as a Branch Manager. Later served on task force responsible for developing "Checkinvest," a unique service linking business checking and money market accounts. Leading member of the sales team that introduced the product to the Washington, D.C. market. Subsequently organized and headed the Mid-Atlantic Sales Team, the most successful of the Bank's 8 regional teams. Obtained $25,000,000 in new business the first year. Assumed responsibility for the Regional Marketing Department and developed programs resulting in a 110% increase in ATM usage, and an 80% increase in total business obtained. Administered the regional effort that won first prize in our bank-wide sales contest.

1974–1984

WASHINGTON NATIONAL BANK, Washington, D.C.
Branch Manager

Joined the bank as a trainee, progressing through various positions including teller, head teller, assistant manager and finally branch manger. Instrumental in establishing the bank's MasterCard program.

EDUCATION:

American University. A.A.S. degree in Business Management.
Currently attending in pursuit of a Bachelor's degree in Marketing.

ACTIVITIES & ACHIEVEMENTS:

Past President, A & W Banker's Club. Served 4 years as bulletin editor, winning competition for best club publication 3 times.

Publicity Chairman, A & W Banker's Club

Past Treasurer, Spartan's Athletic Club.

REFERENCES:

Available upon request.

Marketing Management

JAMES WINTERS

14 West Brook Drive
Cambridge, Mass. 02157

(617) 462-1964 *home*   (617) 961-4405

EXPERIENCE

January, 1985–
present

INJUNCTION SYSTEMS, Cambridge, Mass.
Telemarketing Representative – Responsible for generating leads for various software and hardware products. Duties include initial contact, dispensing product information, qualifying prospective clients, and arranging appointments.

Summer, 1984

SECURITY SAVINGS & LOAN ASSOCIATION, Boston, Mass.
Product Analyst – Under the supervision of the Product Manager, responsible for recommending product modifications. Work included preparing marketing plans, research objectives, advertising/promotional programs, pricing strategies, competitive studies, and coordinating programming changes with data processing department.

September, 1983–
January, 1984

Exchange Flea Market, Boston, Mass.
Partnership in business selling children's garments.

Summer, 1982

GRACE MANUFACTURING CORPORATION, New York, NY
Assistant to National Sales Manager – Assisted in selling children's sleepwear to major retail outlets, formulating sales analysis reports, handling buyer complaints and inquiries, and making transportation arrangements.

Summers of
1980 and 1981

JACOBSON'S INDUSTRIES, INC., New York, NY
Clerk – Duties included light bookkeeping, processing checks, reconciliations, and general office work.

EDUCATION

Boston College
B.S. June, 1985
Dual Major: Management Science – *Marketing*
              Computer Science – *Data Processing*
Grade Point Average: 3.94 (A=4.0)

HONORS

Received the following academic scholarships in college:
Student Organization Scholarship (1982–83 and 1984–85)
Presidential Trust Fund Scholarship (1984–85)
Isadore and Frieda Holtz Foundation Scholarship (1983–84)

Have been inducted into the following honor societies:
Phi Kappa Phi, Omicron Delta Epsilon, and Lambda Alpha Sigma.

Have made Dean's List every semester in college.

**PERTINENT
BACKGROUND**

Member of: American Marketing Association
              Association for Computing Machinery

Valid Massachusetts Real Estate Salesperson License

REFERENCES FURNISHED UPON REQUEST

JOANNE FIELDS
Ten Dreyfus Circle
Montgomery, New York 10984
(914) 444-3313

COSMETICS/IMAGE/MAKE-UP SPECIALIST

QUALIFICATIONS:
- Comprehensive experience in all aspects of make-up and cosmetics design and application.
- Communicate effectively with all levels of management, staff, and clients.
- Work well under pressure and time constraints.

PROFESSIONAL EXPERIENCE:

RODEL IMAGES, Thiells, NY   1991–Present

Image Consultant

Provide professional marketing consultation to major cosmetics companies—Chanel Inc., and Rose Chandal Cosmetics (an Italian cosmetics company)—on new product development and launches, coloring etc. Also provide image consultation and services to individuals, bridal parties, and photographers, e.g., *Fred Marcus, Ron Breland, John Fortunato,* and *Michael Ian,* for photo shoots. Work has been featured in *Connoisseur* (Cover, February 1986), *Savvy* (July 1985 & 1989 Article), *Cosmopolitan* (April 1990), and *Glamour* (December 1990).

TERME DI SATURNIA (USA), INC., New York, NY   1989–1991

Executive Vice President

Maintained bottom-line responsibility for new business development, marketing, and merchandising for this exclusive European skin care line. Developed new marketing programs, to reposition the corporation as necessary to increase profitability. Refocused efforts to train and motivate personnel, particularly in the upscale specialty store market, e.g., Saks Fifth Avenue.

SHISEIDO COSMETICS (AMERICA), New York, NY   1982–1989

Northeast Regional Promotional Training Director (213-door territory)

Created and launched promotional events utilizing state-of-the-art diagnostic equipment for all the major department and specialty store accounts. Directed account executives and monitored growth, profitability, sell-in, and sell-through of merchandise. Trained and motivated promotional coordinators and beauty consultants. Conducted in-store meetings/seminars, and semi-annual regional seminars for top retail managers. Programs included Replica Skin Diagnosis System, Shiseido Eyes, The Body Clinic, and Facial Aerobics.

- Region maintained #1 sales position in the United States.
- Held U.S. record for special promotional sales figures.

STAGELIGHT COSMETICS, New York, NY   1980–1982
Account Executive

Supervised sales, staffing, training, location, and design in the department and chain store division for a tri-state region. Served as liaison between store-line merchants and headquarters.

PRIOR EMPLOYMENT EXPERIENCE

ALLIED STORES MARKETING CORP., New York, NY   1979–1980
Associate Marketing Representative

MARK VII, LTD., New York, NY   1977–1979
Showroom Sales Representative

GIMBEL'S INC., New York, NY   1976–1977
Assistant Market Representative

SAKS FIFTH AVENUE, New York, NY   1975–1976
Department Manager/Selling Head

EDUCATION:

SUNY Fashion Institute of Technology, New York, NY
BS Fashion Buying and Merchandising...May 1976

Rockland Community College, Suffern, NY
AAS English...Graduated May 1974

REFERENCES:

Professional and personal references provided upon request.

ROY CHURNUTT

40 Maple Road
Princeton, New Jersey 08540
(609) 921-2329 – home
(609) 975-6443 – work

GENERAL SUMMARY

Over 10 years' experience with emphasis on MAIL ORDER MARKETING, CATALOG MERCHANDISING, DIRECT MAIL PROGRAMS, Space Advertising, Retail Operations, New Product Investment, New Product Planning, Foreign Operations, Product Pricing and Marketing Strategies.

BUSINESS EXPERIENCE

January 1984 to Present:

REEVE'S MARKETING, INC., Princeton, N.J.

President

Responsible for the full P&L, business, and marketing management at this manufacturer, distributor, and mail order operation. Major activities center on directing 26 employees; innovating systems for all phases of the business, purchasing and negotiation; supervising all copy composition, artwork and layout of catalogs, advertising literature and P.O.P. displays. Major accomplishments: DOUBLED SALES IN ONE YEAR; initiated overseas production to drastically lower cost of goods; increasing profitability.

June 1977 to December 1983:

HOCOS POCOS MAGIC SHOP, Trenton, N.J.

Manager

Responsibility included all purchasing, and full P&L, business and marketing planning of this retail store and mail order supplier to amateur and professional magicians. Activities centered on creating direct mail catalogs and media advertising, managing retail store, and supervising 8 employees (18 at seasonal period). Major accomplishment: Initiated policies that provided company with over 1000% GROWTH FROM 1977 to 1983.

EDUCATION

Bachelor's Degree in Business Administration and Marketing

New Jersey State College 1977

HONORS

Who's Who in America

REFERENCES

Available upon request.

Renée Johnson

210 W. 95TH STREET • NEW YORK, NY 10023 • H 212-555-1441

BUSINESS ACHIEVEMENTS

➤ A proven record of originating financial strategies to optimize ROA/E.
➤ Broad, successful experience in direct selling and management of personnel.
➤ Presently, collaborate with design, packaging, purchasing and production in generating promotions, creative and media support for product lines.

WORK EXPERIENCE

Marketing Manager, Coty, Inc., New York, NY, 1993–present. Develop product line marketing and promotion programs for 200 International/Domestic Military Exchanges and 250 Fashion Stores.

Asst. Marketing Manager, Coty, Inc., New York, NY, 1991–1993. Oversee the effective and timely presentation of creative product. Assess market trends and recommend marketing/promotion support levels for U.S. Department Stores.

Supervisor, Resource Management, U.S. Postal Service, Kalamazoo, MI, 1985–1989. Concurrent with M.B.A. studies. Full-time management of new mail processing unit, including staffing, performance evaluation and union negotiation.

Account Auditor, General Motors Financial Group, Lansing, MI, 1983–1985. Responsible for reconciliation of inventory, invoices and accounts payable.

Merchandising and Retail Sales, Dayton Hudson Dept. Store, Battle Creek, MI, 1981–1982. Direct selling including design and format of merchandise displays. Exceeded unit sales targets.

Advertising Sales Representative, The State News, E. Lansing, MI, 1978–1980. Direct selling of ad space and development of art and copy.

EDUCATION

M.B.A. Marketing, Western Michigan University, Kalamazoo, MI, 1989.
B.S. Communications, Michigan State University, E. Lansing, MI, 1980.

COMMUNITY ACTIVITIES

➤ Treasurer, Frederick Fund for Neurologic Education, New York.
➤ Member: Explorers Club; New York Cycle Club.
➤ Personal/Charitable Interests: Calvary Baptist Church, W. 43rd St., New York; Film Society of Lincoln Center; New York Philharmonic.

PATRICK KELLEY

400 Main Street
Newark, N.J. 07169
(201) 555-6142

EXPERIENCE

1995 to 1996

DELTA MARKETING SERVICES, INC., Newark, N.J.

Marketing Manager, Australia-New Zealand

Overall responsibility for the daily operations of a $12 million liner service. Job functions were in the areas of marketing, pricing, and operations. Major responsibilities were:
- All port/port and intermodal pricing—both domestic and international.
- Developed marketing planning and pricing strategies with all U.S. and overseas sales offices to increase market share.
- Handled key account development, sales, and supervision.
- Identified account shortfalls and developed plans to improve liftings against competition.
- Negotiated all inland rail and truck rates used in independent and conference intermodal tariff
- Published non-conference intermodal tariff and routing guide.
- Australia-New Zealand conference representative encompassing conference meetings, negotiating with U.S. shippers on tariff rates, structuring of conference tariff—both port/port and intermodal.

1994 to 1995

THE NEWARK HERALD, Newark, N.J.

Customer Service Representative
- Performed customer service work in the PIERS Department, which was responsible for all computerized import/export shipping statistics.
- Assisted subscribers to the PIERS data base in writing programs and trained new customers on the system.
- Assisted in the development of end-user's training manual.

1986 to 1994

GRACE LINES, INC., New York, N.Y.

Manager, Sales Administration (1993 to 1994)
- Established corporate sales plan and District Sales Office Expense budgets.
- Developed marketing sales management program.
- Coordinated the development, upgrading, and implementation of all marketing reports with the data processing department.
- Designed and implemented sales incentive program.

Product Marketing Analyst, Australia/New Zealand (1992 to 1993)
- Established overall marketing plan for service (total sales $250M), which resulted in a 6% increase in market share between 1992 and 1993.
- Conducted all statistical marketing analysis for service.
- Developed all computer programs with outside vendor for in-house statistical analysis to increase market share.

Prior positions with Grace Lines:
- **Manager, Booking** (1990 to 1992)
- **Administrative Manager, Documentation** (1989 to 1990)
- **Assistant Manager, Documentation** (1987 to 1989)
- **Sales Trainee** (1986 to 1987)

1984 to 1986   **AKRON INSTRUMENT CO.,** Akron, Ohio

Plant Personnel Administrator

Responsible for the placement of all skilled and unskilled personnel within the plant.

Corporate Recruiter
- Recruited sales reps through college campuses, technical schools, military bases and advertising.

1980 to 1984   **HONEYWELL, INC.,** Columbus, Ohio

Corporate Branch Manager
- Provided personnel and business services to various in-house divisions, which encompassed all non-exempt professional and technical recruiting; wage, benefit, and salary administration; and EEO Coordinator.
- Administered all accounting and purchasing functions, office facilities, and car/truck fleet leasing.

1978 to 1980   **Social Studies Teacher,**
UNION CATHOLIC BOYS HIGH SCHOOL

EDUCATION

Rutgers University
30 Credits toward Master's Degree – 1991 to Present

Fairleigh Dickinson University
B.A. Degree in Political Science – 1977

REFERENCES

Available upon request.

BERT GUENTHER

225 Hollywood Blvd. • Miami, Florida 33180 • (305) 679-2175

CAREER SUMMARY: Wide, diversified upper-management experience in recruiting, training and supervising high-performance teams in the Hospitality Industry; in directing 500 + line managers and support personnel; in designing and implementing highly effective incentive programs; in analyzing product/service environments, and initiating appropriate quality-control mechanisms; in planning and managing operating budgets based on annual revenues of $30 + MM. Excellent communication, leadership skills.

Illustrating my ability to contribute significantly to the sound administration, efficient management and increased profitability of an organization:

- As *Director, Division of Food and Beverages*, Holiday Inn Corporation, January 1993–Present. Conducted a series of internal marketing/training seminars to counter negative consumer trend and increase product awareness; introduced new lines, updated mature products, deleted marginal items. Over nine-month period, gross sales increased by 27%.

  Initiated four action-teams to devise and implement more cost effective handling/storage procedures and promote closer cooperation between line supervisors and union personnel. Over nine-month period, operational changes were introduced, which resulted in savings of $250 + K.

  Planned and directed new employee incentive programs, which produced, annually, an increase in Service-Sales of over $2MM. Transformed marginally utilized space into lucrative business area, generating additional monthly revenues of $30 + K.

  Redesigned a product-service line to reflect the needs of a highly defined market, whose increased consumer activity generated an additional $436K in annualized revenues. Devised a new amenities-services line for V.I.P. guests that, during the first operational year, produced a revenue increase of $480K.

- *As Executive Steward*, Florida Corporation Convention Center, May 1989–November 1992. Created new logistical plans—equipment, personnel, formal areas, work preparation space, storage and warehousing, etc.—for a 6,000 banquet guest facility. Coordinated all purchasing, operational, and marketing functions. Increase in operating profits over preceding year exceeded $1.9MM.

EDUCATION: M.B.A., Marketing and Management, Miami University Graduate School of Business, 1995.

Computer Experience:
- – ECCO – Hotel Computer System
- – Apple Software/Graphics
- – Microsoft Word, Lotus 1-2-3
- – Four years, Financial/Statistical MIS (Basic) Systems

Member: American Marketing Association; American Institute of Food and Wine; American Management Association; Miami GBA Marketing Club.

Military service: Captain, U.S. Army, Frankfurt, Germany, 1984–1989; Major, Active Reserve, 1989–Present.

REFERENCES: On request.

BERNARD FEINSTEIN
135-31 112TH STREET
JAMAICA ESTATES, NY 11420
(718) 529-8203

EMPLOYMENT HISTORY:

September, 1993–
Present

WAVERLEY, INC.: — ($3 Million Annual Sales). Nation's leading company in the oil reclamation market with capabilities that encompass both the manufacture and sale of oil reclamation equipment and an on-site reclamation service.

DIRECTOR OF MARKETING & SALES: Reporting directly to President, managed and coordinated many aspects of company including strategic market planning, marketing and sales functions. Directed advertising agency, direct sales force (5 regional and marketing sales managers) and independent sales representatives (6). In addition, managed day-to-day sales operations for on-site service subsidiary (AQUATECH) and responsible for generation of annual marketing plan.

January, 1991–
September, 1993

ARTSMITH CORPORATION: — ($1 Billion Annual Sales). World's leading manufacturer and distributor of commercial art and design materials. Other principal divisions comprised business systems (office supplies and stationery), computer applications, printing and packaging, publishing, and book retailing.

VICE-PRESIDENT—BUSINESS PLANNING MANAGER: Deeply involved in the identification and satisfaction of both corporate and divisional marketing goals. Key responsibilities included directing and writing corporate strategic plan, seeking out and developing new business opportunities, and managing specific market development projects for both existing and new products. In addition, acted as Divisional New Ventures/Acquisitions Manager in terms of identifying profitable companies/opportunities for existing and/or associated markets.

September, 1987–
January, 1991

WALLACE & BYOIR, INC.: — ($800 Million Gross Billings). One of world's top ten advertising agencies.

MARKETING ANALYST: Involved in evaluation and solution of current and future marketing problems, as seen by client and agency.

EDUCATION:

City College, BS, 1987

REFERENCES:

Submitted on request.

HAROLD P. MONTGOMERY
5653 Pacific Boulevard
Boca Raton, Florida 33433
407-455-8666

SALES/MARKETING • MANAGEMENT • CUSTOMER SERVICE

Sales and Marketing Professional with more than six years of broad-based background developing and exploiting markets for major U.S. Corporations. Skill and expertise in developing territory, expanding market share and providing "total quality customer service."

Proven sales ability demonstrated by steady promotions up the corporate ladder.

SUMMARY OF QUALIFICATIONS:

- Successful track record of introducing product in new territory and building accounts.
- Planned and developed marketing strategies and implemented total sales campaigns.
- Strong aptitude in direct client contact and closing sales.
- Strong communication, public speaking and interpersonal skills.
- Broad exposure and capabilities in a variety of related areas, including time management, needs assessment, client profile evaluation, negotiations and commitment strategies.

EXPERIENCE:

CABLE & WIRELESS, INC., BOCA RATON, FL   **AUGUST 1993 TO PRESENT**

Major Account Manager – Specialized Calling Division   *March 1995 to Present*
- Prospect manor national accounts for this new division, developing the emerging technology of prepaid calling services.
- Plan and develop cost-effective customized programs for customers based upon needs assessment.
- Negotiate contracts conforming to all Federal and State Regulations.
- Conduct informational and motivational public speaking presentations to large audiences.
- Prepare financial reports and credit checks to qualify prospective clients.

Senior Sales Representative – General Business Division   *June 1994 to March 1995*
- Developed new business and maintained existing accounts within territory for long distance services.
- Performed as consultant to business clients to assess and design effective solutions to their communication needs.
- Achieved 123% of expected annual quota and recognized as Top Performer in 1995.
- Planned and developed customized packages and made sales presentations.
- Organized sales territory to maximize coverage, including time management and planning.
- Employed latest marketing techniques, including SPIN, involving investigative questioning to uncover business challenges.
- Established strong working relationships with clients to ensure high standards of customer service.

Sales Representative – General Business Division   *August 1993 to June 1994*
- Initially employed as Sales Rep and chosen as MVP in training class.
- Recipient of five "Sales Rep of the Month" awards.

Regional Sales Automation Advisory Board Member   October 1994 to March 1995
- Selected as Regional Representative to participate on Advisory Board responsible for coordinating and implementing sales automation efforts for 6 sales districts.
- Participants based upon merit and company's recognition of outstanding job performance.

PITNEY BOWES, INC. MIAMI LAKES, FL   SEPTEMBER 1991 TO JULY 1993
Sales Associate – Copier System Division
- Complete responsibility for acquiring new business and managing existing accounts within the territory.
- Contacted qualified leads in person to make sales presentations of product line and corporate capabilities.
- Conducted telephone campaigns to develop new leads, as well as targeted direct mail.
- Consistently met or surpassed all established sales goals and quotas; qualified for annual Sales Achievement Conference in 1993.
- Achieved a national sales ranking of 13 out of 303 sales associates in 1993.
- Achieved a national sales ranking of 47 out of 352 sales associates in 1992.
- Attended the 1992 Annual Freshman Achievement Conference.
- Selected as District Representative for the Council of Personnel Relations.

Full and Part-time employment throughout the school year and summers to assist with college expenses.

CONTINENTAL POOLS, INC. LAUREL, MD   FEBRUARY 1989 TO NOVEMBER 1990
Marketing Director
- Developed successful marketing program targeting government HUD properties, for the management and renovation of pools.
- Created a new construction and renovation division to service customers.

CONGRESSWOMAN HELEN D. BENTLEY, Washington, D.C.   JANUARY 1990 TO JUNE 1990
Congressional Intern and Legislative Assistant
- Performed various duties, including constituent relations, attendance at committee hearings and research on specific legislative issues.

EDUCATION:

UNIVERSITY OF MARYLAND, COLLEGE PARK, MD
Bachelor of Arts Degree

Major: Political Science Minor: Economics
Activities:
- Member: Delta Tau Delta National Fraternity
- Pledge Educator • Interfraternity Council Representative • Greek Leadership Council
- Maryland Lacrosse Club

COMPUTER PROFICIENCY:

IBM PC • DOS • Microsoft Word • Excel • Powerpoint • On Track

REFERENCES:

Furnished upon request

Edward Smith

159-01 Brooks Place • Citadel, California 90010 • Telephone: (714) 539-8486

EXPERIENCE

12/93 to Present   NORCROSS INDUSTRIES, INC., Los Angeles, California
Energy Management Products Division

Marketing Manager

Fully responsible for $4.7 million line of products, options and accessories. Duties include managing advertising/promotion/publicity, product enhancement and new product development, target segment definition and market penetration, pricing strategy, sales force selection and training, market research.

- Introduced product line to new market segments, resulting in multiple purchases and a $218,000 increase in sales.
- Planned and conducted sales training of sales representatives and Regional Sales Managers, leading to a $472,000 improvement in sales.
- Formulated new product designs in current product that were adopted by management, the effect of which was a $184,000 sales increase.
- Instituted telemarketing into the company to qualify sales leads, leading to a $124,000 gain in sales.
- Developed co-op advertising/promotion program with rental company customers, producing an additional $96,000 in sales from this target group.
- Provided guidelines and specific direction for the adoption of additional channels of distribution, yielding further sales growth of $142,000.
- Organized and conducted first company-run product seminars for customers and prospects. Result was a gain in awareness, commendations by these groups, and a $103,000 sales increase.

6/92 to 12/93   WOLF & CLARK ADVERTISING, INC., Santa Monica, California

Director, Market Research

Major clients: Allied Corporation, Almay, Apple & Eve, Associated Biscuits (Peek Freans, U.S. & Canada), Foster Grant, Wm. Grant & Sons, Guinness, INA, CIGNA, LIFE magazine, Mercedes Benz (Canada), Norelco.

- Established and directed all facilities of agency's marketing research department. Successfully developed the marketing research function into a profit center, an unprecedented accomplishment for the agency.
- Improved the quality of client and agency management decision making and new business presentations through interpretation of marketing research and recommendations. Helped agency attract two new client accounts through presentation of marketing recommendations derived from marketing research.

5/91 to 6/92   CARL S. PAUL ASSOCIATES, San Diego, California
New Products Development and Marketing Consulting

Director of Marketing Services

Major clients: Proctor & Gamble, Plough, Hoffmann-La Roche, BankAmerica.

- Formulated the conceptual process for Fortune 500 companies to plan and position new products in the $15 million to $50 million sales range.
- Developed, via proprietary research, a meaningful approach to reporting and interpreting consumer change for management.

9/88 to 5/91	THE CREATIVE GROUP, INC., Advertising, San Diego, California

Vice President, Director of Marketing Services

Major clients: Paddington Corporation (J&B Scotch), Wearever, Loft's Candy, Asahi Beer, Parent's and Dun's Review magazines.

- Established and directed all facilities of agency's marketing research and services department.
- Hired and trained a research assistant and set up research library.
- Recommended, produced, interpreted and presented all marketing research information, improving the quality of client and agency management decision making.

7/85 to 9/88	PROCTOR & GAMBLE, INC., Long Beach, California
	New Products, Household Products Division

Marketing Research Services Manager (8/87 to 9/88)

Marketing Research Brand Manager (7/85 to 8/87)

- Planned and conducted all marketing research for new consumer household products from idea conception through test market.
- Initiated new products team approach by successfully collaborating with members of virtually every corporate group while conducting several new product projects at various stages of development.

EDUCATION **M.B.A.**, Marketing, Columbia University, 1985 (New York State Scholar Incentive Award)

B.S., Electrical Engineering, Brooklyn Polytechnic Institute, 1980 (New York State Regent Scholarship)

Dale Carnegie Course in Effective Speaking and Human Relations (Received Human Relations Award)

Communispond Executive Communications Program

MARLA KENNEDY

16 Hill Road
San Diego, California 92177
Home: (714) 621-9876 • *Office:* (714) 640-4000

CAREER SUMMARY

Over 9 years experience in marketing and operations management in the retail financial services industry with expertise in electronic banking, product management, advertising, direct response marketing, and merchandising. Strengths include creativity, effective communications skills, and "can-do" spirit.

WORK HISTORY AND ACCOMPLISHMENTS

WESTERN NATIONAL BANK, San Diego, California, May 1991–Jan. 1996
SENIOR MARKETING MANAGER, ASSISTANT VICE-PRESIDENT
Consumer Marketing Services – Branch Marketing

- ◆ Developed Retail Merchandising Portfolio which allows District and Regional Marketing Managers to effect de-centralized advertising and promotional programs.
  - – Ensures a consistent message in state-wide advertising.
  - – Reduces the bank's exposure to lawsuits and fines. Savings are estimated at $350,000.
  - – Coordinated production with Marketing Managers, Product Managers, Advertising Agency, Legal Department, and Senior Management.
- ◆ Developed and implemented use of premiums as in-house training incentives. Increased response of sales staff by 35%.

SENIOR MARKETING MANAGER, ASSISTANT VICE-PRESIDENT
Consumer Marketing Services – Direct Marketing

- ◆ Developed, repriced, and repackaged Grouplan program which provides employees of qualified corporate clients with comprehensive, discounted packages of retail banking services.
  - – Portfolio consists of 70,000 accounts.
  - – Total funds managed exceeds $250 million.
  - – Increased portfolio profitability by $800,000 by increasing fee income and expanding cross-sale of asset products with 1995 incremental sales of $5.8 million.
- ◆ Developed bank's telemarketing strategy to increase sales efficiently and effectively using telephone direct marketing personnel.
  - – Identified first-year potential of $800 million in sales versus an incremental $800,000 in expense.
  - – In-house portion of proposal in effect, with 1984 sales of $90 million.
- ◆ Coordinated bank's direct response programs with advertising agency, market research, product management, and market information departments to maximize efficiency using existing customer base for cross-sales of additional bank products.
- ◆ Developed multi-media presentation to motivate bank's calling officers to support Direct Marketing Department's sales goals.
  - – Developed over 150 leads for Grouplan and Western Financial Centers.

SENIOR PRODUCT MANAGER, RETAIL BANKING OFFICER
Electronic Banking – Special Projects
- ◆ Developed the Western Financial Center Concept, an electronic banking program that provides qualified sponsoring corporate clients with dedicated ATMs at their workplaces.
  - – Increased business from resident workplace population by 22%.
  - – Developed over 50 corporate relationships for the retail bank through calls on Fortune 200 companies.
- ◆ Developed ATM promotions using customer incentives, which increased usage by 15%.
  - – Responsible for the research, development, testing, and marketing of increased ATM withdrawal limits, ATM access by "savings-only" customers, and expanded use of lobby ATMs, drive-up ATMs, and self-service statement printers.
  - – Contributed to overall in-branch staff reduction of 28%.
- ◆ Developed model to measure customer value as a function of time as customer, product usage, and account balances.
  - – Demonstrated the utility of the matched funding concept to evaluate product profitability and the residual value of a customer's relationship with the bank over time.

PRODUCT MANAGER
Personal Financial Center Administration
- ◆ Generated 23% of new loan dollars from 3% of bank's offices.
  - – Responsible for administration of 33 Personal Financial Centers and staff of 120 throughout California.

SECURITY BANK, Long Beach, California, Oct. 1988–Mar. 1991
VICE-PRESIDENT – MARKETING AND BRANCH OPERATIONS
- ◆ Responsible for operation of 12 branch offices and management of over 100 departmental personnel, data processing, and advertising budget of $500,000. Increased mortgage loan portfolio by 500%. Increased deposits by 200%.

FEDERAL SAVINGS BANK, Los Angeles, California, Jan. 1986–Aug. 1988
- ◆ Responsible for site selection, staffing, and operation of 20 branch offices and over 200 personnel.

EDUCATION

M.B.A. Emphasis in Marketing and Finance, 1988. San Francisco State University
B.S. Emphasis in Business, 1980. United States Naval Academy

REFERENCES

Submitted on request.

ROBERT WARNER

215 STATE STREET • ALBANY, N.Y. 12257
(518) 126-4153 (HOME) • (518) 622-8000 (OFFICE)

SUMMARY

Results-oriented executive combining problem-solving analytical skills with a strong creative flair. Outstanding track record of marketing accomplishments with several blue-chip companies. Top references.

CAREER HISTORY

TROY CABLE COMMUNICATIONS, INC.   *1995–Present*

Director of Marketing

Responsible for corporate marketing direction and support for over 100 Troy Cable Systems throughout the United States, representing annual sales in excess of $300 million.

➤ Created and produced a company-wide marketing and sales plan that was used by individual cable systems as a model for implementing proven acquisition and retention programs.

➤ Developed and directed a new subscriber sales acquisition campaign for the Troy Chicago system that generated over 1,800 new customers during an 8-week period. This record-setting sales program added a minimum value of $500,000 to the system's selling price.

GROUP W – HOME CABLE CORP., INC.   *1989–1995*

Executive Director/Marketing and Creative Services

Responsible for planning and execution of marketing and advertising activities for Group W's 140 cable systems across the country. Directed the design and production of collateral and promotional material for local system use.

➤ Designed and implemented Group W Cable's first major research study identifying the main reasons for customer disconnects. Based on research results, developed marketing program that has reduced disconnect rate by an average of 26%.

➤ Responsible for signing the Tom and Jerry radio advertising team to an exclusive contract within the cable industry. The radio campaign increased company awareness and purchase intent dramatically, and received several major creative awards.

➤ Developed annual national marketing plans which tripled revenues in 5 years.

➤ Introduced a national television campaign in 1994 (using the "W W Wonderful" theme), becoming the first cable operator to utilize its own medium in a major way.

THE AVIS CORPORATION   *1984–1989*

Director of Marketing

Directed national print and broadcast advertising for the Avis Rent-A-Car Division. Responsibilities included market planning, budget control, development and production of promotional and collateral material directed to the customer.

➤ Conceived and implemented the award-winning Pete Wilson "Superstar in Rent-A-Car" advertising campaign.

➤ Created a unified "family look" for all external and internal Avis communications to help increase corporate awareness.

➤ Conceived and designed a combination #1 Club Credit Card that more than doubled customer usage of the card.

➤ With a budget in excess of $9 million, developed advertising and direct mail promotions that significantly increased Avis's market share and strengthened its number one position in the industry.

MARSHALL & PRATT ADVERTISING, INC.   *1973–1984*

Vice President and Account Supervisor – Avon Products, Inc.

Managed a $12 million annual budget of print and broadcast advertising for Avon's product lines. Also served as *Research Director* for other agency clients, including Benjamin Moore Paints, Stroehmann Bread, and VIASA Airlines.

- ➤ Responsible for a $12 million advertising budget that increased Avon's market share in the industry to more than 50%
- ➤ Developed a unique and economical method of pre-testing television commercials to determine their effectiveness.
- ➤ Created the strategy of combining Avon product and service advertising for optimum sales results.

PROCTOR & GAMBLE COMPANY   *1972–1973*

Traffic Manager

After completion of P&G Management Training Program, was promoted to Traffic Manager. Primary responsibility was the supervision of products ordered and shipped to overseas military installations. Training in all phases of management was an integral part of the P&G program.

EDUCATION

Cornell University – B.S. in Marketing, minor in Management 1971

REFERENCES

On request.

WILLIAM CUNNINGHAM

18 BROOK COURT
ST. PAUL, MINNESOTA 55147
(612) 775-7261

SUMMARY:

Entire career has been devoted to marketing and general management, reporting to chief executive officer for major corporations in various industries. Emphasis has been in product development, new market penetration, and marketing/sales management. Widely experienced in market research, advertising and sales promotion, public relations, training/supervision, P&L responsibility, public speaking-seminar leadership, telemarketing, direct mail, trade show exhibit administration, and strong entrepreneurial, interpersonal and leadership skills.

EXPERIENCE:

1992–present   BRANDON CORPORATION, St. Paul, Minnesota

Vice President, Marketing and Sales **for specialty printing consumer products division (sales $19M). Responsible for all marketing/sales management and new product and market development.**

Major Accomplishments:
– After only 16 months, increased profitability by implementing a plan to streamline sales organization, develop strong relationships with customer base, and upgrade both quality and range of products offered.
– Received industry awards for innovative new product introductions and creativity in design.

1990–1991   KODAK CORP., St. Paul, Minnesota

Vice President and General Manager **(sales $12M). Had P&L responsibility for advertising, promotion, public and press relations, merchandising, packaging design, and new product development.**

Major Accomplishments:
– Implemented a new video merchandising concept.
– Increased retail impulse sales by 32%.
– Developed strategy for new product range introduction realizing $530k in new sales volume for first year.

1987–1990   MARKETING ASSOCIATES, St. Paul, Minnesota

Director of Marketing **(sales $60M)**

Major Accomplishments:
– Initiated a new product planning and development program which contributed $1.3M in new product sales during first year.
– Attained diversification for company into 3 new high profit/growth segments, significantly changing prior cyclical nature of corporation's business.
– Introduced and structured formal market/sales planning programs.

1982–1986   UNITED PULP & PAPER CO., Minneapolis, Minnesota

U.S. Director of Marketing and Sales for U.K.-based, leading manufacturer of graphic arts products. Responsible for North American sales and marketing, budgeting, sales forecasts, trade show exhibits, formulation and implementation of marketing objectives and strategies.

Major Accomplishments:
- Increased U.S. operation from $1.2M to $8.3M in sales with pre-tax profit realization of 22% annually.
- Organized national sales force of 16 to sell via retail channels that resulted in expanding key dealer network from 116 to 630 dealers.
- Developed extensive end user seminar program for U.S. market that successfully created consumer demand for products at retail level.

1980–1982   AMERICAN LITHOGRAPH, INC., St. Paul, Minnesota

National Sales and Marketing Manager (sales $30M). Organized and launched new venture division comprising 7 distinct product categories.

Major Accomplishments:
- Each product group was successfully introduced into market.
- Publicity and product literature prepared, advertising initiated, distribution channels identified and sales organization established.
- Sales exceeded projected goals by 41%.

1974–1980   PINETIME WOOD AND PAPER COMPANY, Seattle, Washington

Midwestern Regional Sales Manager

Major Accomplishments:
- Initiated and implemented warehouse distribution centers in key market areas, providing stimulus for increasing business activity in Midwestern market.
- Increased specialty product sales from $62k (1974) to $3.5M (1980).
- Based on successful program, warehouse distribution concept became model for further expansion nationwide.

EDUCATION:

B.B.A. Marketing, University of Minnesota 1974

AFFILIATIONS:

American Management Association

REFERENCES:

Available on request

BART CONWAY

45 Corner Road • Troy, New York 14051
716-676-4994

MARKETING/SALES PROFESSIONAL with a strong background in the Health Care Services environment. Proficient in establishing and implementing strategic plans for business development and sales growth. Skilled in developing market plans and launching new products to market. Management expertise includes direction and supervision of product managers, sales/service representatives, and interaction with a diversified clientele.

NATIONAL TRAFFIC SERVICE   1992–Present
Amherst, NY

Vice President, Sales and Marketing

Responsible for all sales and marketing activities for this auditing and information services company, whose clients include many Fortune 500 companies. Duties include market plan development market research; advertising and promotion, public relations and management of five-person sales force.

- Expanded market area from regional to national coverage.
- Increased total sales volume 45% in first year.

MDS LABORATORIES   1991–1992
Buffalo, NY
Division of MDS Health Group, Inc.

Vice President, Marketing

Responsible for development and implementation of all marketing programs for clinical laboratory and toxicology services to physicians, nursing homes and industry. Also responsible for corporate strategic direction including new business development and integration of company acquisitions. Duties included all advertising, promotion and public relations for this $50 million company.

- Established new corporate positioning and implemented image building program.
- Increased new sales by 105% throughout year.
- Established joint ventures and working relationships with prestigious reference laboratory, information systems company, advertising agency and public relations firm.
- Developed new program for toxicology and nursing home segments.

WESTWOOD PHARMACEUTICALS   1986–1991
Buffalo, NY
Division of Bristol-Myers/Squibb

Group Product Director

Responsible for marketing of ethical OTC and prescription dermatological products. Duties included market plan development, full profit and loss responsibilities, all advertising and promotion, market research and new product development for major product lines. Total sales of managed brands exceeded $50 million with a $6 million promotional budget. Worked closely with sales, production, finance and research and development to achieve sales and profit objectives.

- Introduced three major prescription products. New steroid product had greatest first-year sales in company's history and was 100% on budget.
- Integrated product lines from Squibb Derm into existing business following merger.
- Trained and supervised three product managers.

REICHERT SCIENTIFIC INSTRUMENTS   1981–1986
Buffalo, NY

Senior Product Planner (1984–1986)

Responsible for marketing of clinical, educational and research microscopes and scientific testing equipment. Worked closely with research and development, production and sales departments to introduce new products and attain sales and profit objectives.

- Introduced new clinical microscope line to replace older existing product.
- Introduced new research microscope for pathology/university use.
- Developed new educational microscope line in conjunction with overseas manufacturer.

Sales Representative (1981–1984)

Responsible for sales of microscopes and scientific equipment to hospitals, physicians, universities and industries. Also worked closely with dealer representatives in demonstrating equipment at local shows and exhibits. Sales for the territory were $1 million per year. Was sales leader for division in 1982.

CONSOLIDATED BIOMEDICAL LABORATORIES   1978–1981
Columbus, OH

Sales Representative

Responsible for gaining accounts for this national clinical testing laboratory from hospitals, group clinics, private medical laboratories, physicians, research organizations, and industries. Was responsible for setting up logistics systems for the transport of specimens and reports between the laboratory and individual accounts. Sales for territory was $1 million per year. Was national sales leader in 1980.

EDUCATION

Masters in Business Administration – Canisius College, 1987
Masters in Medical Technology – SUNY at Buffalo, 1977
Bachelors in Biology – SUNY at Fredonia, 1973

EDITH ROBERTS

125 E. 96th St., N.Y.C. 10416
(212) 821-6399

Sales/Marketing Management in the Building Products Industries

---

Top-level managerial skills based on 25 years' solid experience in every facet of the American contract and residential building products industry, in association with major national and international building products manufacturers.

MANAGEMENT POSITIONS

R.D. & S. IMPORTERS, INC., New York, N.Y.   6/95–present

Vice President/Sales and Marketing. Responsibilities include establishing marketing programs, developing distribution, promoting commercial and residential product lines manufactured in the Asian countries, home centers/distributor/architectural/designer specifications in the Northeast.

PYRAMID, INC., New York, N.Y.   1/93–6/95

Vice President/Sales and Marketing. Total P. & L. and operational responsibility. Directed and implemented every aspect of the start-up: Market/analysis, product direction, sales/marketing strategy, location and layout of company headquarters, development of sales (distributors, sales staff and independent sales representatives), direction of advertising and public relations campaigns to both consumer and trade nationwide and local level, liaison with headquarters in the Netherlands.

APEX PRODUCTS, INC., New York, N.Y.   4/91–1/93

Marketing Consultant. Special consulting assignment for commercial/institutional product manufacturer. Developed specifications, cultivated major market areas that resulted in significant contribution to company's bottom line. Opened specialty areas in the mass transit, commercial, and institutional markets, such as hospitals, health care centers, and government properties. Liaison with distributors dealers/contractors and trade associations to promote company's products.

Organized regional and national product seminars for distributor/sales personnel/trade associations.

ANDERSON'S FABRICS, INC., New York, N.Y.   1/89–4/91

General Manager. Initiated a series of programs designed to strengthen the company's position in the U.S. marketplace. Responsible for advertising/incentive program, established network of independent manufacturers representatives to work with company sales personnel.

Responsible for sales/marketing goals, for daily business administration, and sales force. Developed sales tools, including unique product and technical manual, extensive sampling/display program, advertising and public relations campaign. Coordinated U.S. activities with headquarters in Italy.

BASIC TILES, INC., New York, N.Y.   5/87–1/89

Held key management positions, starting as *Creative Sales Rep* and moving up through various levels with $50 million manufacturer. As *Marketing Services Director*, responsible for national and distributor promotion, trade shows, and showrooms in New York, Chicago, and Dallas.

Coordinated activities with advertising and public relations programs, sampling displays, supportive budget, and staff responsibilities. Daily administration duties. Managed project timetables. Produced all of company's literature, catalogs, brochures. Managed distributor/dealer/consumer Yellow Page Director program.

LEHMAN PRODUCTS INC., Newark, N.J. 1/73–1/87

Special Representative. Created mass-merchandising accounts (e.g., J.C. Penney). Developed specifications for residential and commercial markets: architects, interior designers, and specifiers. Coordinated public relations program with major national publications, such as HOUSE BEAUTIFUL, HOUSE & GARDEN. Represented company at trade shows for target markets. Planned and hosted press and trade receptions for new product introductions.

EDUCATION

Fairleigh Dickinson University/Business Management – B.S. Degree
Katherine Gibbs/Management Program/One-year night program

PROFESSIONAL AFFILIATIONS

American Society of Interior Designers (ASID)
Construction Specifications Institute (CSI) (Meritorious Services Award)
National Home Fashions League (NHFL)
Ceramic Tile Distributors of America (CTDA)
Association of Tile, Terrazzo, Marble Contractors and Affiliates (ATMCA)

PERSONAL INFORMATION

References on request.

ALLEN CARROTHERS

16 Point View Drive
New Rochelle, N.Y. 10822
(914) 661-4426
(914) 663-9696

QUALIFICATIONS SUMMARY

Excellent background in marketing, public relations, advertising, promotions, direct sales, and the successful sales motivation and management of people.

Proven abilities in developing an advertising/public relations/promotional campaign, as well as reorienting a sales force for a major international airline, with a resulting 50% sales increase within 12 months.

In addition to professional expertise, highly self-motivated and can establish and meet own objectives even when none are provided. Considered by others a problem solver, trouble shooter, and decision maker.

PROFESSIONAL HISTORY

1993–Present CARROTHERS & KLEIN, INC.

Vice President
Co-founded a resort timesharing and travel marketing company.
- Developed and operated travel-agent familiarization trips for airlines, tourist bureaus, and hotel associations.
- Negotiated the sale of a 56-unit timesharing resort in Puerto Vallarta, Mexico.

1984–1992 PANCANADA AIRLINES, INC.

(1990–1992) **Passenger Sales & Service Manager, USA/Canada**
Responsible for the Passenger Sales product in the USA/Canada with revenues in excess of $100 million. Designed, implemented, and integrated with headquarters a coordinated marketing plan to achieve passenger sales objectives. Established reporting procedures to monitor and achieve goals.
- Managed $5 million advertising/public relations budget with final signature authorization.
- Responsible for the development of the company's USA/Canada advertising program. Selected themes and media.
- Selected promotional material company distributed in USA/Canada.
- With public relations agency, coordinated publicity activities that developed image of company. Responsible for the preparation and distribution of press releases and promotion of press activities.
- Responsible for the development of company's direct mail programs. Selected trade shows/seminars to ensure maximum company exposure to trade and consumer.

(1988–1990) **Regional Manager, Western USA/Canada**
Responsible for the development of passenger and cargo sales in a 13-state area encompassing 6,000 travel/cargo agents with total revenues of $40 million. Directly supervised a management staff of 12.

(1984–1988) **Agency & Tour Sales Manager, USA/Canada**
Responsible for developing travel agency and package tour sales plans and policies to meet company and individual city marketing objectives.

1983–1984 HOLIDAY TOURS, INC.
Regional Marketing Representative
Specialized in the development of tour programs and travel agents' revenues in the assigned territory.

1982–1983 MEXICAN AIRLINES, INC.
District Sales Representative
Responsible for the solicitation of travel agency accounts in the assigned sales territory.

EDUCATION

St. Joseph's College, Philadelphia, Pennsylvania
Temple University, Philadelphia, Pennsylvania
Valley Forge Military Academy and Junior College, Wayne, Pennsylvania

PROFESSIONAL ACTIVITIES

Institute of Certified Travel Agents (Fellow)
American Society of Travel Agents
Association of Travel Marketing Executives

REFERENCES

Available upon request.

Reference Lists

SALES BOOKS AND PERIODICALS SALES AND MARKETING MANAGEMENT

1. Bolles, Richard N., *What Color Is Your Parachute?*, 25th ed. Berkeley, CA: Ten Speed Press, 1995.
2. Carnegie, Dale, *How to Win Friends and Influence People*. New York: Simon & Schuster, Rev. 1981.
3. Covey, Stephen, *Seven Habits of Highly Effective People*. New York: Simon & Schuster, 1989.
4. Gitomer, Jeffrey, *The Sales Bible*. New York: William Morrow, 1994.
5. Goldner, Paul S., *Red-Hot Cold Call Selling*. New York: Amacon, Div. of American Management Association, 1995.
6. Hill, Napoleon, *Think & Grow Rich*. N. Hollywood, CA: Wilshire, 1966.
7. Hirsch, Robert, P.h.D., and Jackson, Ralph, P.h.D. *Selling & Sales Management*. Hauppauge, NY: Barron's Educational Series, 1993.
8. Johnson, Spencer, M.D., and Wilson, Larry, M.D. *One-Minute Salesman*. New York: Avon, 1984.
9. Joy, Nicki with Kane, Susan, *Selling Is a Woman's Game*. New York: Avon, 1994.
10. Kotler, Philip, *Marketing Management*, 8th ed. Englewood Cliffs, NJ: Prentice-Hall, 1994.
11. McKay, Harvey, *Swim with the Sharks*. New York: Ballantine Books, 1989.
12. Ziglar, Zig, *Over the Top*. Nashville, TN: Thomas Nelson, 1994.
13. Ziglar, Zig, *Ziglar on Selling*. New York: Ballantine, 1991.
14. Ziglar, Zig, *Secrets of Closing the Sale*. New York: Berkeley, 1984.

MARKETING BOOKS AND PERIODICALS

1. *Advertising Age*, New York.
2. Baker, Sunny, and Baker, Kim, *Desktop Direct Marketing*. New York: McGraw-Hill, 1995.
3. Hiam, Alexander, and Scheive, Charles D., *The Portable MBA in Marketing*. New York: John Wiley, 1992.
4. Kremer, John, *The Complete Direct Marketing Sourcebook*. New York: John Wiley, 1992.
5. Levinson, Jay, and Godin, Seth, *The Guerrilla Marketing Handbook*. Boston: Houghton Mifflin, 1994.
6. Linneman, P.h.D., and Stanton, John L., Jr., P.h.D., *Making Niche Marketing Work*. New York: McGraw-Hill, 1991.

DIRECTORIES

1. *The Greenbook, International Directory of Marketing Research Houses & Services*. New York: American Marketing Association.

2. *International Directory of Market Research Organizations*. London: Market Research Society.

3. *Marketing Service Organization & Membership Roster*. Chicago: American Marketing Association, 1981

4. *Standard & Poors Register of Corporations, Directors and Executives*. New York: Standard & Poors.

5. *Standard Directory of Advertising Agencies* (The "Red Book"). Skokie, IL: National Register Publishing Co.

6. *Ward's Business Directory of U.S. Private and Public Companies*. Petaluma, CA: Ward Publications.

ASSOCIATIONS & ORGANIZATIONS

American Association of Advertising Agencies
666 Third Avenue
New York, NY 10017
(212) 682-2500

American Marketing Association
250 South Wacker Drive
Chicago, IL 60606
(312) 648-3288

Association of National Advertisers
155 East 44th Street
New York, NY 10017
(212) 697-5950

Direct Marketing Association
1100 Avenue of the Americas
New York, NY 10036
(212) 768-7277

Marketing Research Association
2189 Silas Deare Highway, Suite 5
Rocky Hill, CT 06067
(860) 257-4008

National Association of Business and Industrial Saleswomen
90 Corona, Suite 1407
Denver, CO 80218
(303) 777-7257

Notes

Notes

Notes

◇◇◇◇◇◇◇◇

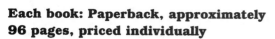

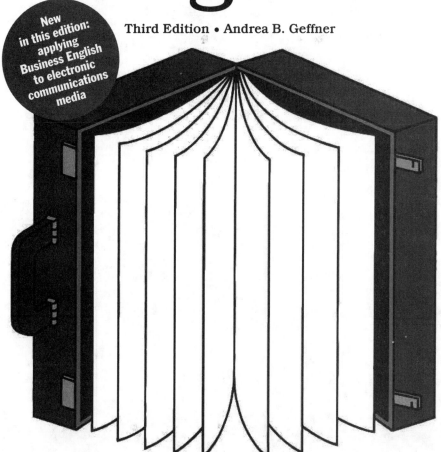